Game
Changer

This fly showcases the Game Changer style of tying in a "full-dress" version that blends a wide range of natural and synthetic materials seamlessly and with purpose. The back three sections are clear Finesse Body Chenille and white hen saddle, and the rest of the fly is white schlappen with Translucy Fly Brush (1" and 2") followed by schlappen and a white fox fur head. Gold mallard flank feathers add contrast and shape.

Game
Changer

Tying Flies that Look & Swim Like the Real Thing

Blane Chocklett

Photography by Jay Nichols

HeadWater
Books

To Kristi, for bringing me back.

Published by

HEADWATER
BOOKS

Headwater Books
PO Box 202
Boiling Springs, PA 17007
www.headwaterbooks.com

All inquiries should be addressed to Headwater Books, PO Box 202, Boiling Springs, Pennsylvania 17007.

Printed in United States of America

First edition

Library of Congress Control Number (LCCN) available

ISBN: 978-1-934753-47-7

Cover design by Gavin Robinson; interior design by Wendy Reynolds. Front cover photo by Jay Nichols.

10 9 8 7 6 5 4 3

Contents

Acknowledgments

Good friend Mike Schultz holds a winter muskie that took a natural Bucktail Changer tied to imitate a hog sucker. Developing these flies has been a team effort, and I am immensely appreciative of all the support from and good times on the water with some of the top talents and best humans in the fly fishing industry.

Thank you to my Lord and Savior Jesus Christ. To my loving wife, Kristi, for making me a better person and for being my rock. My daughter, Erin, for inspiring me every day to keep moving forward and striving to excel in life. To my son, Tyler, you have changed my life for the better. To my stepson, Ryan, his wife, Rebecca, and my grandsons, Elliot and Johna, your love and support is always felt. Thanks to my Mom and Dad, Brenda, and Bev for always being there and supporting me in everything I do. Thanks

to my brother, Keith, for your love and support. To my Granddad Luther for taking the time to take me fishing, and also to my grandmothers, Madeline and Helen, for your love and support.

I want to give a heartfelt thank you to my mentors that have helped shape my career in fly fishing. Lefty Kreh, for being my friend, teacher, guide, and coach in the fly-fishing industry and in life. To my brother in tying, Bob Popovics, thank you for your inspiration and for being a sounding board. To Bob Clouser, for your friendship and support over the years. Larry Dahlberg, for your knowledge of everything fishing and your friendship—thanks for showing me at a young age that there are no boundaries on fly. Rick Pope, for taking a chance on me and adding me to your family. Henry Cowen, for your guidance, support, and friendship—I could never repay you for all your help. Flip Pallot, your show inspired me at a young age to chase my dream of making fly fishing my career. Harrison Steeves, for getting me started at an early age and showing me the possibilities in career tying—your creativity and guidance helped shape my career.

I could write a book on all the people in my life that I am thankful for. To my buddy Cory Sodikoff, thanks for your support and always having my back. To Jake Grove for taking a chance on me—your support and friendship helped get me back. My boy Schultzy for your friendship and support, and you just getting it. My good buddy Rob Kinkoph, thank you for all you do for me and my family, you're the man. To my good friend and editor Jay Nichols, thank you for your patience, knowledge, guidance, and most of all your friendship. Look at it this way—it may have been your longest book project ever but you gained a lifelong friend in me. To all my friends in the fly fishing industry that I've shared my life with and who have helped me in so many ways—there are way too many to acknowledge but you know who you are—words can't express the gratitude and appreciation I have for you.

To all my client friends that I've shared a boat with, your support over the years can never be repaid. Over the years many of you transitioned from client to family, and for that I am blessed. For your continued support I am forever grateful. Without you I wouldn't be able to pursue my passion. I look forward to sharing more memories on the water with you all.

A special thanks to Martin Bawden and Flymen Fishing Company for having the shared vision to see my vision come through. Here's to the future and many more products.

A special thank you to all my sponsors: Temple Fork Outfitters, Yeti Coolers, Costa Del Mar sunglasses, Scientific Anglers, Patagonia, Flymen Fishing Company, Renzetti, Traeger Grills, Hyde Drift Boats, Adipose Boatworks, Sightline Provisions, Fish Pond USA, Hareline Dubbin, Umpqua Feather Merchants, Towee Boats, Hog Island Boatworks, and Just En Case. Your support and belief in me means more to my family and I than you can ever know. For that we are truly blessed and forever grateful.

Finally, thank you to some of the talented tiers and friends that contributed patterns to showcase different variations of the Game Changer platform: Greg Senyo, Justin Pribanic, Jason Taylor, Chris Willen, and Mike Schultz. An entire book could be devoted to their patterns, but I am pleased to be able to show some samples of their work in these pages. Greg Senyo, a designer of flies and materials, is one of the top innovators. His use and blends of fibers and materials to produce great fly designs is a blessing to our sport. Justin Pribanic's eye for how flies should be tied and designed are outstanding, and he's one of the best tiers I've seen. I've relied on Justin to tie flies for me and my guiding. Jason Taylor is one of the best tiers I've ever seen. His creativity and use of natural and synthetic materials is top notch. I love his style and always look forward to what he will come up with next. Chris Willen has dedicated his life to the sport of chasing muskie, and that dedication shows through in his skills as an angler and at the vise. Mike Schultz's passion for our sport and dedication is contagious. He brings that passion to his guiding and development of flies for smallmouth bass. His innovations have helped him become one of the top smallmouth experts in our industry.

Foreword

Larry Dahlberg

Learning all you can about the fish you target can pay big dividends. I've learned a lot about muskies through time on the water, observation, and trial and error.

A great angler, in my opinion, is one that can adapt, find, and catch virtually any species in its own environment. "Reading" is the single most important ability of all really great anglers. It may disappoint you to know that reading words about fishing is not what I am talking about. Articles and books can certainly be informative, but when and where it's valid, or whether it's valid at all, is often questionable. The reading I'm talking about is a twofold deal: first, reading the water and second, reading the fish.

The first "reading" I'm referring to is vital for step one—strategy—in my very basic three-step approach to any angling situation. Basically, it involves reading the water to determine what environmental options are available to the creatures for which I am searching. Depending on species or season, it might be food shelves at various levels, overall structure, types of cover, depth, water temperature, water speed, or in some situations, natural barriers. It also involves determining which of the options are most viable for me as an angler to effectively cover with the equipment and time I have available. When using fly-fishing gear those options are much more limited than they would be with other types of equipment due to limitations in the depths I can effectively fish, the speeds I can move my offerings, the distances I can cast them, and the size range I can effectively manage and deliver with a fly rod. With that information I go to step two, tactics. In fly fishing that involves deciding which fly to use where, which line, which angle to cast, and how fast or slow I plan to fish each area.

The third element is mechanics. This covers how you go about actually executing steps one and two and includes your ability to cast in terms of accuracy and distance, your skill at knots and rigging, controlling your boat, and how you work a fly, set a hook, and fight a fish. Mechanics can be taught in theory from a book, but in most cases require practice to develop the muscle memory and correct reflexive response to actually maximize the performance of the equipment you are using. Mechanics are one of the few constants in angling that can be practiced and honed both on and off the water. Mastering them is a critical part of becoming the best angler you can be.

In many, if not most, environments, using a fly rod as a fishing tool to execute any strategy that involves anything other than delivering an almost weightless insect imitation and dead-drifting it to a fish is akin to fighting with one hand tied behind your back. If I am hunting or trying to scratch the silver off of a very large lottery card, fly fishing doesn't allow me the range or the speed to cover the water effectively and find out where the fish really are. However, once I have found them, there are many times where I can catch more of them on a fly than with a lure—such as when the fish are real spooky or when they are focusing on a particular food that requires an imitation that I can't deliver with a bait-casting outfit. I can also put a fly in places that even a very good tournament angler skilled with a bait caster or spinning rod would have difficulty getting in, and if I am fishing an area with multiple prime targets five feet apart, and I don't have to worry about it after the lure is ten feet from the bank, I can ring ten doorbells in the time it takes him to ring two. Flies are able to drill down into some of the nuances of how fish and insects behave, sometimes more effectively than lures. But the delivery system has inherent limitations.

When we get into the category of large flies designed to catch large fish, either because they prefer large things or to "keep the rats off"—increase your chances of hooking a larger fish by keeping the smaller fish from biting first—the limitations are inherent in

Larry Dahlberg (left) and the author rigged and ready for a James River muskie float.

the system. When fishing with a fly rod, and a system where the fly line carries the fly (instead of the weight of the lure pulling out the line), the weight and wind resistance of the fly can be deal breakers when it comes to actually getting the fly to the fish. Most people have limited amounts of physical strength and have a hard time casting rods in the 10- to 12-weight range without an extreme amount of physical exertion.

If you pick up a typical fly that casts easily with a fly rod and throw it with your hand, like a baseball, it will probably only carry a couple of feet. The stronger and more powerful you are, the farther it will go, but it will also decay quickly as it encounters wind resistance. However, if you glued a piece of lead that weighs 100 grains to it, the fly would go a little farther; add some more and it would go even farther. Eventually you would get to a point where the weight you've added overcomes that wind resistance, and you can throw the fly across the room. That's probably close to the amount of weight that is going to be needed in the head of your fly line in order to propel the fly to the target.

Obviously at a certain point a fly can get so wind resistant that the weight required to overcome its wind resistance is so great a normal human can't deal with

it due to physical strength limitations. That's when it's time to rethink your design!

Making Flies Move

There are fish that eat bugs, and there are fish that eat each other. To catch those that eat bugs, what a fly looks like often matters more than what it does. It must match the hatch so to speak, in size, shape, and color. Ironically, often what it does *not* do (drag) is the most important single factor. In many, if not most, cases it's most effective when it acts as though it is not connected to the line at all. I call these "static" designs. Conversely, most often when it comes to fish that eat each other, what a fly does when you *move it* is more important than what it looks like. I call these dynamic designs. Humans, it seems to me, put too much emphasis on what a fly looks like when they are holding it in their hands. In the development of a fly often adding stuff to make it more realistic looking is detrimental to the way it moves. Static perfection, so to speak, may lead to complete dynamic catastrophe.

The way fish react to a dynamic fly depends on how you manipulate it when it enters a fish's zone of

Casting large flies for a sustained period of time can be difficult for many anglers, but with proper equipment and technique—plus well-designed flies—it becomes much easier. Pinning the rod against your forearm on the backcast helps keep line speed and reduces injury and fatigue. Think of moving your elbow on a shelf to prevent casting in an arc, reducing unwanted slack and unnecessary movements that rob your cast of energy.

After the cast, manipulating the fly in the water with strips and rod action can play a crucial role in triggering a predatory fish to eat. Believe in the retrieve. Even if you haven't had a strike in hours, you have to constantly be in the game. Cory Sodikoff takes his T-Bone into a higher gear with a two-hand retrieve as a muskie follows it in.

awareness. And often most important of all, when you have visual contact with the fish, how you vary your retrieve based on the way the fish reacts or doesn't react to your manipulations is usually what make the difference between a bite and no bite. In other words, once you've got them on your radar, your ability to "read" and judge their attitude changes based on your presentation variations is often the difference between catching and not catching.

Matching the hatch is never a bad idea and is one of fishing's basic tenants. However, appealing to the predator's built-in role of Darwinian natural selection is often a better angle than looking for a hatch to match. The fish on the top of the pyramid often act more like cats who need to be teased by a string being taken away than a guppy sipping fish flakes off the surface of your aquarium.

A control surface is a surface that causes what is behind it to deflect left or right, up or down. On a rocket, the nose cone or fin is designed to reduce turbulence, but on a lure it might be designed to create it. On conventional lures, these control surfaces take the form of lips, propellers, or various body shapes that in conjunction with correct connection, eye placement, and adding lead to control the center of gravity can create

powerful control surfaces capable of driving a floating lure 20 feet deep or more. Moving the connection point as little as $1/64$ inch can sometimes change a stable lure into one that spins out of control on the retrieve, like a misadjusted bridle on a kite flown in a strong wind. The line connection location dictates which control surface is the boss, and it is very touchy indeed.

If a fly is going to move very much, it is going to move because control surfaces impact the water in a way that create vortices that make it shift right, left, up, down, or (god forbid) even spin in circles. These vortices also create the currents that cause soft fibers and feathers to undulate and move in ways that fish like. Fibers and feathers, depending on the angle they are positioned and their relative stiffness and length, can also create control surfaces, but because they are flexible the control surfaces are actually variable control surfaces. Variable because when they are accelerated the fibers will collapse and offer less resistance in the water and in the air. As they decelerate the fibers will begin reorienting to their original angle and create more turbulence. Minor changes in speed can create super sexy fly action as these surfaces change and the fibers dance to the tune the laws of fluid dynamics dictate. The designs that cast and fish the best are those

Guide Chris Willen swims a Bucktail Game Changer through muskie-infested waters up in Wisconsin. Notice the flow and serpentine movement displayed even in photographer Nick Kelly's still shot.

To be successful, you must adapt to the fishing conditions and what fish want. We caught this muskie while filming for Larry's show, *The Hunt for Big Fish*. We had falling water temperatures, snow, and sluggish fish. Larry caught this fish by fishing a Mr. Wiggly with an egg sinker to get it down in the zone longer—adapting was key.

that maximize the illusion of bulk using a minimum amount of material.

With flies, control surfaces are also very touchy, and because of the inherent wind resistance limitations of the fly-casting system, fly designers are limited to the types of control surfaces that can be put on a fly to make it do things. If you go too overboard with a control surface, the fly is going to spin or be nearly impossible to cast. If it's too squirrely, it will hit you in the head when you try to cast it, or it won't go at all.

Unfortunately, most of the control surfaces used on lures do not translate very well to flies. So, half the problem is creating control surfaces that are friendly in the air as well as doing what you want them to do when they are in the water. Weight is always an issue as well. That's why it is important to use materials that shed water quickly when they are in the air so that they don't weigh as much and become a problem to cast. Blane is pushing the envelope and right on the cutting edge in terms of incorporating the best elements in both categories—flies that look realistic and move convincingly. And, like all of us, stumbling along trying to find the best compromises in terms of designing flies that will get the job done better than the ones we are already using.

There haven't been all that many fly guys that have chased muskie. Blane is dancing on that delicate edge of what you can actually throw without killing you, and maximizing your odds of getting a fish to bite. I still believe the challenges of getting the fly to the fish for the average caster, and also a poor (at least compared to gear) hook-up ratio are still there, but we are making some progress. By continually using lighter materials he is making progress on the delivery system as well.

Return to Reading

I'd like to circle back to reading, and what this book is about—flies.

First, you want to read your fly. The different styles of flies behave differently in the water (and in the air) based both on their shape/fuselage and the materials used to make them. Rather than categorize by color, it makes more sense to categorize them by how they behave in the water. Do they jig up and down? Pop? Dive? Wiggle? Hang? Turn? What do they do fast, what do they do slow? And while I'm thinking of it, if you read somewhere about never moving your tip during the retrieve and just stripping, I strongly disagree. I've found if I do whatever it takes to get them to bite, including moving and continually bouncing my tip or even ripping it back to 1 o'clock and hauling if needed to generate crazy fast speed, I catch a substantial number of fish that would not have bit otherwise.

The other, and last part, is reading the fish. It's where you can see the fish and you know the fish sees the fly and does one of three things—either reacts positively and eats it, ignores it, or begins to follow. Now it's a game of cat and string. You have to read the cat's reaction to your movement of the string and do whatever move you think will make it pounce. If you are ignored or refused, it's time to decide whether to change offerings or fling the same one again.

The challenge in fly selection is similar in many ways to lure selection, but decidedly more limited. The

This fish took quite a bit of teasing, but by choosing a more realistic color Yeti's Jake Drees and guide Blane Chocklett (holding fish) were finally able to clinch the deal. When fishing with others, every muskie brought to the boat becomes a team effort. BEN SATTERLEE PHOTO

similarities are in regards to their having both attracting qualities and triggering qualities. Large size, flash, and bright color could be considered attracting qualities and might sometimes be the opposite of what is required to actually trigger a bite rather than a follow, whereas change of speed, change of direction, or bottom contact might be triggers.

I am quick to admit catching large fish on fly rods is great fun and often requires extra-large flies. I've also found that at times (especially on fish that have been pounded with conventional lures) these large flies have an almost magic effect on fish and get bit when lures get ignored. Whereas with conventional muskie gear anglers handle lures that weigh a pound or more and up to three feet long, the weight and wind-resistance limitations on flies presents the greatest challenge of all to fly tiers attempting to create flies large enough to attract and trigger the fish they're after, but not so heavy and wind resistant that King Kong couldn't cast with a 16-weight!

As new materials and new designs evolve with the next generation of anglers and fly tiers my most sincere advice is to not be afraid or even hesitate to color out of the lines. In fact, plan on it. Read every environmental detail clue that leads to the combination of attracting and triggering qualities that get the job done.

Fishing Voodoo

What we all have to fear, more than anything else, is voodoo, and falling victim to our own self-fulfilling prophecies when it comes to angling. These are especially reinforced when you don't see what is going on.

In my own experience I have three crescent wrenches that I can apply to a fishing situation when I can read and see the fish, and I am fishing for fish that eat other fish. One, having something at the end of my line that allows me the widest options in terms of speed; in other words, something that works very well from 0 to 100. Two, lures that have the ability to exhibit random, non-mechanical action. Three, ability to create iterations of them that work in sizes ranging from 3 inches to 12, or more. Basically, they are non-threatening, usually articulated objects, that travel in the water as though they are not connected to the line. If you have fish you can see it becomes completely mechanical and tactical. No strategy really—he's right there. For fish you can't see you have to have a strategy to eliminate the unproductive water.

Blane is in a unique situation where not only does he get to fish almost every day, which in my view is a requisite to combatting voodoo (if you do it with your eyes open), but he fishes for muskies, a species that often reveals itself, and one that isn't always there to attack blindly like a jack crevalle might. Because they'll let you fish right through them and not bite, you have an opportunity to read what is happening. What is it? What did I do or didn't do that made him bite or not bite? What was it on this day? And in time, one finds a handful of tactics that seem to work more often than other things. Instead of your own preconceived ideas or unsubstantiated beliefs, you let the fish decide.

Introduction

From time to time I like to return to the waters where I learned to fly fish. To this day, I apply lessons gleaned from my early days of match-the-hatch trout fishing to all species.

I was brought into fly fishing, like many others in this sport, by fishing for trout. In this case, fishing for brook trout in the tumbling streams of the Blue Ridge Mountains. While my fishing tastes have migrated more toward seeking out the apex predators in any given body of water, whether throwing giant streamers for trophy trout or hunting muskies, those early days of trout fishing have heavily influenced my fishing and fly-tying approach to this day.

Blue Ridge Blue Lines

When I was nine years old, my dad and granddad took me trout fishing for the first time. That first Opening Day we rose early and drove the Parkway out of Blue Ridge. Along the way, my father and granddad joked and told me fishing and hunting tales, interspersed with stories about the area's history. Our destination was Jennings Creek. Just as we reached the top of the

I started fishing early with my dad—this image is of my catch from my first outing in 1982. I was nine years old. I hold these childhood memories of fishing with my dad and granddad close to my heart. It also jumpstarted my lifelong passion for fishing. For that I am so thankful they took me.

My grandfather enjoyed the out-of-doors and taught me at an early age to appreciate it as well. He loved turkey hunting. This shot was taken around 1986.

mountain, before descending the road along McFalls Creek, the sun was rising.

Later on, the state of Virginia would abolish the concept of an Opening Day, instead opting for a year-round trout season. Back then, however, the beginning of trout season was always the first Saturday of April, and you couldn't fish until high noon. Because of this shotgun start, it was important to get there early. Though still wild and somewhat remote, Jennings Creek was a popular Opening Day destination because of its size and because it was stocked heavily by the state. I can remember waiting on the bank and staring at all the trout swimming in the pools as the sun kept climbing higher in the sky. It was enough to drive a kid crazy.

My father and grandfather used fly rods, but no flies. They spooled monofilament line onto fly reels and used live bait or corn, and that is how they taught me to fish. I learned very quickly that the difference between catching a trout and not catching one—even a stocked fish—was letting the bait drift naturally in the currents and following it with your rod tip. I learned on that trip how important different colors could be, how important size was, and how deadly live bait and good drag-free presentations were. And though it was fun and exhilarating and we caught our limits, I also learned that I preferred to fish around fewer people. I didn't like the crowds, even from the start, and didn't understand why other anglers would swarm one another when there was so much water to fish.

We returned to fish the area several more times, exploring nearby North, Middle, and McFalls creeks, and I was hooked. A week or so after that Opening Day, I was with my mom in the grocery store and noticed a *Fly Fisherman* magazine on the racks, featuring a man holding a beautiful brown trout. In addition to the fish, the fly line coming off of his rod and reel caught my attention, probably because I hadn't yet seen that part of fly-fishing tackle before. So, I found my mom and talked her into buying it for me.

I poured over that magazine on the way to my grandmother's house that day. My grandfather on my mom's side passed away before I was born, but my grandmother still kept his shop in the basement, and down there was old fishing tackle among other things. I was rummaging around and found this bright colored line on a spool that looked just like the fly line in the magazine. I took it with me, and when I got home, put it on the reel, strung it through the rod guides, and just started whipping it around. When my dad came home from work later that day and saw me in the yard whipping around weedeater line, he started laughing and then told me what I was casting. But my parents saw that I was serious about learning how to fly fish.

For Christmas that year my parents got me my first really good fly rod and reel setup and also my first fly-tying kit, and by early spring I was tying my own flies. Orvis Roanoke had just opened, and I would buy some flies here and there to copy, and mom would help me buy tying materials. (Later on, I would squirrel away my lunch money for fly fishing and tying supplies.) I bought the *Orvis Fly Pattern Index* as a reference, and I devoured the fishing and fly-tying lessons in every new issue of *Fly Fisherman* that would hit the stands.

The following spring, Opening Day was a little different. We fished Jennings Creek with bait in the morning, but after we caught our limit, I talked my grandfather into taking me to the native brook trout water on North Creek, a tributary to Jennings. This mountain freestone had catch-and-release regulations, and it was much tighter than Jennings. Now, instead of the reel spooled with monofilament, I had a proper fly line; instead of bait, flies that I had tied the previous winter. In one of North's long pools, I caught my first brook trout on a #12 Royal Wulff. That five-inch fish sparked a fire in me that has lasted to this day.

Jackson River Lessons

By my early teens, the smaller trout streams that fed the James River also fed my curiosity for larger waters and warmwater species, and I would wade-fish or fish from a canoe on the James and Maury rivers for smallmouth, especially as the trout waters warmed in the heat of summer. Fishing these broad waters with larger flies required that I learn how to cast farther, which was rarely necessary on even the largest of mountain streams.

Information was much harder to come by in this pre-Internet age, though the local fly shop was a hub for tips and tantalizing stories. I had been going to Orvis Roanoke quite a bit for tackle and tying materials and I kept hearing about the good fishing on the Jackson River, which was about an hour north, near Covington, Virginia. It, like the mountain streams that I learned to fly fish on, was a tributary of the James, but it was wider and held larger wild trout than the others. I saw pictures of it, and the fish from it, on the walls of the shop. Because it flowed out of a dam from the bottom of a deep reservoir, it stayed cold, providing excellent trout fishing even in the heat of summer. But winter time provided some of the best fishing.

The winter before I turned 16, my mother took me up there for the first time, as I didn't yet have my driver's license. When I saw the river for the first time, I couldn't help but think it must be what a perfect trout stream looked like. It had tons of fishy water, pockets,

Fishing the Jackson River on a late spring day. I learned so much about fish behavior and fly design on this river. It will always hold a special place in my heart as it has taught me so much. I also guided my first client on this river back in the early 1990s.

I cut my teeth wade fishing, and I often still like to get out of the boat and stalk fish. Unlike when floating, you can make several casts and drifts to the same lie.

riffles, runs, and it was crystal clear. Even at that time, I thought it looked like one of the "western" rivers that always appeared in the magazines.

That day I fished up at the dam, while my mom waited patiently in the car. I was catching a few fish, but two other older guys fishing near me really looked like they knew what they were doing. They weren't dressed like they came from the Orvis store, but they were catching a lot of fish. After a few hours of slow fishing (for me), I got up the gumption to go over and talk to one of them who was sitting on the bank of the river, taking a break. He introduced himself as Steve Hiner, and we talked a bit. He was an aquatic entomologist at Virginia Tech. He gave me encouraging words about my casting and mending, and offered some rigging tips, telling me to downsize my tippet to 5X. He also gave me some strike indicators.

As we were talking, the other gentleman came over and introduced himself as Harry Steeves. He was also a biologist at Virginia Tech. After more talk about the fishing, I asked them both about flies, and they said that they weren't going to tell me what to use. "Figure it out," Steeves said. Hiner added, "Look around, the answer is right in front of you."

They walked back with me, met my mom, and Hiner gave me some vials and alcohol and encouraged me to collect specimens and take them home and match them. He also loaned me a copy of W. Patrick McCafferty's *Aquatic Entomology: The Fisherman's and Ecologist's Illustrated Guide to Insects and Their Relatives.* I was hoping they would just give me some flies—I wanted instant satisfaction just like anybody does—but before my mom took me home, I began collecting.

The river had enormous concentrations of bug life. You could pick up a rock and there would be thousands of bugs on it. I quickly learned that every fly I was using looked nothing like what was on the bottom of the river, on and under the rocks. I could also see that the bottom of the rocks just downstream of the dam were literally crawling with one particular type of insect. So much so that the rocks looked alive with a swarming mass. I took the samples home and began tying patterns that replicated what I had collected. I had materials from Orvis Roanoke, but also yarns and stuff from craft stores.

The book Hiner loaned me was like having the keys to the kingdom, or at least the keys to the Jackson River. The book covered all of the major trout stream insects, and in its pages, I found a match for the bowling-pin-shaped bugs that were so abundant below the dam. They were blackfly larvae.

Once I dialed in the basic bowling-pin shape and color of the naturals I had collected, McCafferty's book filled out a few more pieces of the puzzle. I read how the larvae would suspend on silken threads from rocks and dangle in the currents, so I began to think of a downstream presentation. I also read that when they emerged from their pupal shucks, they released shiny air bubbles. Coincidentally, my mom and I were in a craft store that week and I noticed a wall of tiny glass beads that seemed to come in every color in the rainbow—pearls, silver, pearls with silver in them, pearl with black in them. I lashed the pearlescent beads my mom bought for me to dozens of hooks and also tied some plain thread body patterns as well in anticipation of my next trip to the Jackson.

My mom took me back up to the river the following weekend. Hiner and Steeves were there, but I didn't want to bother them and just started fishing because I was anxious to see how my flies worked. I simply swung my rig downstream, just holding it in the current, and the fish would eat it like crazy. I immediately started catching fish, and I remember thinking how excited I was to have solved that mystery. Hiner and Steeves saw that I was catching a lot of fish, and also breaking off some large fish, and came over. They now wanted to see my box, and when I opened it, they immediately started laughing. When I asked what was so funny, they both pulled their boxes out, opened them up, and showed me the contents—they also had the beads. I do believe I earned their respect, at least a little, that day, and we all became good friends after that.

The Jackson is where I cut my teeth in fly fishing (and would later launch my guiding career). It taught me a lot about fish behavior, daily feeding as well as seasonal movements, as well as casting and presentation, from mending to achieving proper depth control. It also taught me early that I needed to find out more about fly design, because I could see that with the right pattern you could go from two to five fish in a day to fifty. It doesn't matter how good your cast is, it doesn't matter if you have $1,000 rod or $100 rod or the right line or any of that. If you didn't have the right fly you were not going to catch fish.

Hiner and Steeves' way of teaching was a big part of my early learning process—they wouldn't tell me exactly how to do anything, but they would give me hints. I had to learn it on my own, which helped me immensely. I realized that you needed to adapt to what

I was extremely fortunate at a young age to meet Harrison Steeves, who took me under his wing and introduced me to several fly-fishing icons, one of which is Pennsylvania limestone legend Ed Koch. Here Ed and I are fishing a limestone spring creek that is one of the last strongholds of large wild brook trout. On this day, Ed landed one of these giants, which brought him to tears because it reminded him of the Pennsylvania spring creeks of his youth. That was an emotional day for all of us.

The first muskie that I caught on a fly launched an obsession that will last me a lifetime. To this day, I am in awe at this great predator and never take bringing one to the boat for granted.

nature provides for you. You need to look around, take samples, and figure it out at the vise and on the water. I learned that thinking outside of the box was important because the flies that I saw in Harry and Steve's boxes were not in the shop bins or catalogs. I saw how I could recreate something that I saw on the water, and that the best examples of all come straight from the natural world.

Hiner and Steeves were incredible mentors, and though I kept in touch with Steve Hiner, Harry and I developed a special relationship. During those early times on the Jackson, and as we fished more together in the future on different rivers such as the Smith, Harry taught me a lot of things. At times it hurt my feelings a bit that he wouldn't just give up the goods and give me the right flies, but I do believe he was teaching me to figure it out on my own. Ever since then, we started fishing more and more together. Years later, when I opened up my fly shop, we became even better friends and started traveling to shows together. Steeves and I worked together in developing Loco Foam—he showcased its uses in terrestrials, and I focused more on bass and saltwater patterns. He had a few design ideas that

he shared with me that I ended up developing into the Disc Slider, the first fly that Umpqua sold commercially. And later, he and I began working with Loco Skin, which was a precursor to Sili Skin. He taught me so much, and I am forever grateful for those early lessons, not the least of which was to listen to and learn from those who know what they are talking about.

Steeves and Hiner also introduced me to David Garst, who was my age and equally obsessed with fly fishing and fly tying. He became a fast friend and steady fishing companion, and we would travel to the Jackson and Smith rivers for trout. Later on, Garst would go on to study biology, and he got heavily into muskie fishing by his twenties. After guiding all day for smallmouth, I'd meet up with him on the James and we'd hunt muskies together. I knew where they were because I would see them on the river while smallmouth fishing, and he had the tackle and the understanding of the fish. I learned a lot fishing alongside him during those times. At first I, too, fished conventional gear with him, but then tried to fly fish for them. I was immediately humbled by the fact that David would get ten follows to my one.

This giant river smallmouth taken by friend and client Joe Harris from North Carolina on a blue Flymen Double Barrel Popper marks one of the highlights of my fishing and guiding career. During "bug season" in the summer the biggest bass in the river key on surface foods such as cicadas, damsels, and dragonflies. This fish was holding just off a rocky bank in a pocket using the current to its advantage to ambush its prey.

Problem Solving

As Bob Popovics always says, a good fly design comes from solving a problem. It doesn't always come immediately and may take years, but it usually fills a hole in your fly box. The Game Changer was developed through a long process of trial and error as I tried to figure out how to replicate with a fly the erratic swimming motion of a baitfish, which many conventional lures are able to do successfully.

During that time on the Jackson River with Steve and Harry, I was able to learn something that I might not have if they just gave me a bunch of flies and didn't have me go looking for the answer myself. From the very early days, fly fishing and fly tying, at least how I saw and experienced it, were about figuring out problems. Remember, the easy days don't teach you much (unless you have the sheer will to stop doing what works and experiment). The fish you cannot catch teach you the most.

Over the last ten years or so, I have carved out a niche as a muskie and smallmouth guide, and fishing for those two species has had the most impact on my recent developments in fly design. Obsessed by the quest of designing a fly that swims like a real baitfish, for over twenty years now I have experimented endlessly with different materials and designs to find the right action. Even though I think I am getting closer, I continue to tweak designs almost weekly based on feedback from the fish. Muskie can be some of the most difficult fish in the world to catch, and though I am blessed with being able to guide on world-class muskie rivers that give up their fish with still-surprising regularity, the tough days can teach you a lot about flies, approach, and presentation techniques. I feel like failure teaches more than success, especially when you're fishing for muskies like I do for a living. Learning by not catching is very important because what doesn't work usually gets put away and then I try to figure out what will work from there. So, you have to observe by failing, and by failing you end up winning—or you quit. I'm too stupid to quit. ■

Friend and client John Ringenbach with a tremendous muskie caught in clear water.

Matching the Hatch: Minutia to Muskie Baits

Over time, I started fishing for many other species abundant in the area, including smallmouth, stripers, carp, and muskies, but my match-the-hatch lessons on the Jackson stuck with me. These early lessons engrained in me that you must learn as much about the food sources in any given fishery as you can. Always look at the environment in which you are going to be fishing, try to match the food source that is available to those fish, and then try to understand the baits or the prey items that the fish are feeding on.

Tying flies teaches you about fly fishing because it requires that you learn what the fish are eating. It allows you to not only make a fly that's going to catch fish, but it teaches you why and how they're going to eat it. That, to me, is the most important thing about fly fishing and fly tying—knowing what your prey is looking for. The more you understand that prey, the better your chances of catching that predator.

As a first step I will choose the color and profile that most likely represents the bait in that area or have those colors closely related to the baits that these fish are generally feeding upon. Profile is always going to be based on the food source available.

Food source is primary. Fish will adapt their feeding habits based on seasonal abundance of different foods. Those blackflies on the Jackson are a prime example. They were primarily a winter phenomenon, and when they were prevalent, the fish switched gears and focused almost exclusively on them. Same goes with seasonal patterns of baitfish, crayfish, or aquatic insects. In the end, your equipment is important as is your casting and other techniques. But if you don't have the right fly to match what the fish are keying on, you won't do so well that day.

Second, matching the size, shape, and color of your quarry's food is critical for consistent success. If I didn't flip over rocks and capture specimens, I wouldn't have been able to tie replicas. This same practice became important when tying baitfish imitations for other species such as freshwater stripers, which can become far pickier about fly pattern than their salty cousins. Thinking about how to fool these fish led me to eventually develop the Gummy Minnow. These fish required something extra, and at the time ultra-realism was the only trick in my bag.

At 54½ inches, this is a personal best fish for me, but it is special for another reason. I caught it on a Lefty's Deceiver tied by legend Bob Clouser in honor of Lefty Kreh. BOB CLOUSER PHOTO

While sight-fishing for peacocks on sand in shallow water, we noticed they became a little more selective. Yellow and chartreuse were getting more action in the tannin stained waters. PAUL BOURCQ PHOTO

I believe that the more realistic the fly, the more opportunities you are going to have for the fish you are fishing for. Predatory fish have an instinctual reaction to their prey swimming away from them, much like a mountain lion does when it sees its prey fleeing from it. Most often, anglers try appealing to this response. But what happens when this approach doesn't work? I have often had a number of giant fish follow a fly to the boat but not eat it. This could be because I or my client wasn't fishing the fly properly to create the trigger that the fish needed, or maybe the fish ate recently, and simply needed more convincing then we were able to provide. I have found that to catch giant fish—the 10%— consistently you have to have a realistic looking fly.

Third, matching behavioral triggers, which can be anything from a gas bubble on an emerging pupa to a swimming motion of a baitfish is often the first thing that attracts a predator to its prey. In many situations, such as muskie fishing or fishing for large piscivorous trout, I think it is the fly's motion that draws them close and then the realism that seals the deal, especially on

a tough negotiator like an older, wiser fish. Other considerations, such as time it takes to tie and castability, are concerns, but they are not as important as realistic appearance, profile, and movement. Depending on your quarry, one of these might be more important than the other, but some form of realism almost always outfishes a fly that doesn't have any of these attractive qualities to the fish.

On an almost daily basis, I guide my clients in a highly visual game due to the clear water we fish in. I get to fish through my anglers' eyes and watch how they are making the fly work as well as how the fish are reacting to it. These fish are seeing an increasing amount of pressure and see a wide variety of lures and flies. I take pride in the fact that we are still able to catch them as they reach trophy size. When you strip away all of your preconceptions, and are left with what the fish respond to day in and day out, I think that you get closer to understanding what is real—this is what Larry Dahlberg means when he says getting rid of the "voodoo."

1 | The Game Changer Platform

Getting ready to float Idaho's South Fork Snake River. Game Changer-style patterns are extremely versatile and when tied to match local baits, fool everything from trout to tarpon. NICK KELLY PHOTO

I'd like to provide here a broad overview of what I can only describe as a constant evolution. I will cover each of the flies in detail throughout the book and talk about how they came to be, but I think that it is important to trace the lineage of what might be considered a fairly basic idea through my fly design process so far—though sometimes arriving at simplicity involves quite a bit of work. That basic idea, or goal, is trying to get a fly to move like what it is supposed to imitate—in a nutshell, trying to get a fly to swim like a fish or act convincingly crippled, like a wounded or dying fish.

Through all of these years, I have always looked to the conventional tackle world for inspiration. Most of my designs are influenced in some way or the other by conventional lures and fishing techniques. Lures like Rapalas and soft plastics are so effective worldwide it only makes sense to pay attention to them and try to borrow some of their best attributes and integrate them in designs for the fly rod. The Flypala is a fly rod version of the Rapala, the Game Changer my version of a soft plastic fluke, the T-Bone a glide bait.

In many ways I have tried to blend the best of both worlds. I have adopted some of the concepts that lure

This Game Changer shingles hen-pheasant-back fibers to not only create contrast but also to create a V shape on top of the fly, where the top is broader and tapered inward. This matches the profile of some bait with broader backs and allows you to move beyond simple fusiform shapes where a fly is tied in the round.

designers have used to create absolutely deadly soft plastics and lures to enhance some of the advantages of flies (lightweight, motion at rest, and the way that they can hover and breathe without being intrusive). While I respect immensely lure designers like Larry Dahlberg, I am also very steeped in the fly-tying tradition. Despite criticism from some that my designs that rely on building imitative patterns with synthetics such as the Gummy Minnow or Flypala are not proper "flies," I absolutely love working with fur and feathers. While I appreciate and rely on synthetics for many practical reasons, and also think that they can be quite beautiful in a fly, if treated properly, I think that many characteristics of natural materials—both in the water and aesthetically—are unparalleled.

For me though, it doesn't have to be an either/or choice. Some of the best, and most intriguing, fly patterns to me are the ones that are able to seamlessly blend synthetics and natural materials so that they complement one another. Being able to match the hatch with natural and synthetic materials to me is the epitome of our sport, and to be able to do that with baitfish that are sometimes pushing sixteen inches has been something that I have been proud of. And conversely, way on the other end of the spectrum, being able to truly change how we imitate smaller baitfish and insects by tying them on micro spines is exciting and ground breaking. I, along with the help, insight, and inspiration from many terrific tiers and anglers and friends, have accomplished this despite of and because of many failures and dead-ends.

The Game Changer provides a platform for tying flies that can be adapted to any fishing circumstance you might encounter. What do I mean by the word platform? In its very basic sense, the Game Changer platform is the shanks that the flies are tied on. These shanks act like the vertebrae of a baitfish spine and allow the fly to move in a way that we have not really been able to achieve previously, whether that is in a serpentine swimming motion or in a more jackknifing, jerking motion. Any fly that I can think of can be adapted to this platform of shanks, so it really opens up a lot of possibilities, both for future designs as well as bringing life to older patterns. The shanks themselves continue to be refined, and even during the writing of this book I was working with Flymen Fishing Company to fine tune the tooling of micro shanks to be able to extend the platform to smaller baitfish and aquatic insects.

In these brown- and rainbow-trout versions of the Feather Game Changer you can see the inner Filler Flash that adds bulk and supports the feathers veiled over it. When choosing a filler material, I want it to be stiffer and springy so that it supports the veiling materials, yet be lightweight enough and not absorb water so that it doesn't add much weight to the fly.

The platform is only part of the story, much like the chassis to a vehicle is far from what determines its performance. The shanks enable certain design features to translate into particular movements; they enable motion that is engineered by shapes and tapers and different materials. Arriving at how to best maximize the movement that the shanks facilitate has been a journey in and of itself and I can honestly say that I am still learning about it. However, I have learned quite a bit, and I will share these observations in this book. Some of the key design concepts that have become part and parcel with the shanks to get them to perform their best are combining a denser bulkier head with a lighter rear for maximum movement and using softer, flatter fibers as a veil for a smoother flow. Other key things that I have learned along the way have been to use stiffer materials on the insides of flies, whether that is Filler Flash or brushes, to prop up fibers that veil over them, which not only helps in the profile and taper of the fly but also helps a fly *maintain* that lift and profile over time.

A critical concept in the Game Changer platform is not just the shanks and the movement of the flies, but also the way in which they are built. For years I've called what I do fly "construction" more than fly "tying" because of my approach to design. When I tie, I like to think of framing flies, building them up in layers almost as you would build a house. The most obvious example of this is the Flypala where there is a Body Tubing frame covered by Sili Skin. However, this idea of creating an underlying framework over which you can lay other materials extends into almost all of my fly designs.

Another way of looking at this concept is to consider a tree. It has an underlying structure of branches that provide support but a covering of leaves. I like to use a core material that acts like the branches of a tree or the frame of a house, over which I tie in veiling fibers that act like leaves or, to use the house analogy, siding. Put another way, the core is very much like a brushpile—it has a certain volume but it doesn't have a lot of density. You can push down on the branches in the pile, but they spring back up. Filler Flash, different brushes, or other materials can act as the support system for the fly (framing, branches, however you like to think of it) over which you can veil softer, straighter fibers to create the illusion of mass without having the materials collapse. I have found that straight fibers flow best in the water and provide optimal swim.

The Hybrid Changer takes the basic concept of a Feather Changer and uses all synthetics for a larger, lighter fly. Flash Blend Baitfish Brush provides a stiffer core over which I wrap a veil of Polar Fibre, which has softer fibers.

After the framing concept, tapers become critical to understand and implement. The fly should have the profile of the fish it is imitating. While movement gets the fish to the fly, profile and silhouette seal the deal. The overall flow of the fly is important, and it should look like one continuous body, despite the many sections. The fly should flow in the water, but also the entire creation from the front to back should flow together. I discuss the proportions for this in later chapters.

As my thoughts about framing flies and taper evolved, and I came to understand how to use inner materials to provide support, I have been able to get closer to designing flies that are large, easy to cast, and maintain their shape (in the water and also throughout the rigors of fishing them for weeks on end). To be able to take the Game Changer platform and build very large flies on it that can be cast easily with a fly rod is

a huge breakthrough for me, and I am excited to share the journey with you in these pages.

I have tried to order the flies in this book in such a way that makes some sense and shows a progression, but in truth so many of these ideas came at the same time and meld with one another that it would be inaccurate to say that they all developed in an orderly and deliberate fashion. I tend to have more ideas than the

It is very gratifying for me to have refined these flies to the point where Flymen Fishing Company and I could start to produce them commercially, so that they are available in fly shops. Learning to tie these flies yourself will allow you to modify them to your local waters and baits.

Flymen Fishing Co. X *Blane Chocklett*

CHOCKLETT'S FINESSE CHANGE

The Blane Chocklett Signature Fly Collection

Matching the hatch is important not just in trout fishing but also when hunting many predatory fish, which can get locked into specific size and color of baitfish. Here, Finesse Game Changers and Gummy Minnows sit beside North Carolina bay anchovies. Although both patterns worked very well, on this particular trip the Game Changer was the winner for finicky albies.

time to tie, so while I may have thought out a particular pattern in my mind, it could be many years before I actually sit down and bring it to life at the vise. And more than once I've had the idea for a fly in my mind but have been without the materials to make it a reality. When the materials come along, whether found or invented for the purpose, then that idea becomes real. And this is why it is logical for me to start the book with the Gummy Minnow because it was the beginning of my search for the ultimate fly pattern, and though it is not built on the Game Changer platform, many of the principles that it embodies—framing a fly, precise imitation, taper—are important concepts to me today and, combined with the shanks, are what make the flies work so well.

Getting to that point has been a very long journey for me, involving a lot of trial and error. I do know that the flies that I am tying now, which are doing a pretty good job of fooling some very difficult fish, can very well look different down the road, because if my journey has taught me anything, it is that one idea invariably leads to another, and then another. And as we continue to develop new materials and new techniques, and come to a greater understanding about the mechanics of lure design, our fly designs continue to evolve as well. Even as I was wrapping up this book, we were writing and photographing new chapters. On a regular basis, new ideas are coming to me for how to create new patterns, or breathe newfound life into older ideas.

The potential for this concept is far from being exhausted and that is why I also feature a few flies from other tiers in this book as a way to showcase what some other creative minds are producing. As these fundamental concepts travel from vise to vise of so many talented tiers, so too the flies are traveling the world and proving themselves in different fisheries and for so many species. It is incredibly gratifying for me to see the flies work in so many places. That the design concept travels well and can be dressed in local colors and fool predators around the globe is the greatest compliment I could receive.

Frontiers
Far and Near

The number of different species caught on the Game Changer blows my mind. It has all the triggers that fish that eat other fish like, you can tie it in a variety of sizes to match different baits, and it is extremely durable. I'll be the first to tell you that these flies can take a long time to tie (though certain materials and techniques are making them faster) and taking this time on a fly isn't always necessary. Many times, a simpler pattern to tie such as a Clouser Minnow, Half and Half, or Deceiver works just fine; however, it's for those moments where extra realism is required that I have kept refining the Game Changer style of tying. There are a lot of times when a Game Changer is not necessary and some of the older standbys still have a place in my kit—especially when the fish aren't fussy or I know I am going to lose a lot of flies. But I almost always reach for one of these newer designs because I know that every time I pitch one into the water, there is a possibility of catching *that one fish* of a lifetime. ∎

1) Jacks are one of my favorite fish to target. Sometimes they can be hard to catch, and other times they'd eat a beer can. This Louisiana giant fell for a Feather Game Changer. PAUL PSONNEN PHOTO **2)** I'm not aware of any bass species—whether peacock bass (above), stripers, or smallmouth—that will turn down a properly presented Game Changer. MATT HARRIS PHOTO **3)** The much-maligned alligator gar is an amazing fish to sight-cast to. The vicious eats and ensuing cartwheeling jumps with gaping jaws are something to behold. This one ate a Feather Game Changer tied on a jig hook. **4)** I caught this snakehead while sight-fishing in a Virginia tidal creek with Grant Alvis. It ate a Feather Game Changer slowly teased in front of it. GRANT ALVIS PHOTO **5)** Big bull red doubles in Louisiana while fishing with guide Greg Dini and Mike Schultz. We found that they couldn't refuse Feather Game Changers. GREG DINI PHOTO **6)** This surprise freshwater drum took a Crafty Game Changer on the swing while spring striper fishing. These fish are fantastic fighters. **7)** Bowfin are not only breathtakingly beautiful in my mind, but they take flies aggressively and are incredibly strong. I caught this giant with Jeff Pierce in Michigan while sight-fishing in less than two feet of crystal-clear water. JEFF PIERCE PHOTO **8)** Matt Harris caught this redtail catfish on a Game Changer in the remote jungles of South America. MATT HARRIS PHOTO **9)** Black drum are an underrated fly-rod species. They can require delicate presentations, stealth, and patience to catch them consistently on fly. This one fell for a black jigged-out Feather Game Changer tied by Justin Pribanic.

Live Scale
Gummy Minnow

Flypala
(hybrid, early version)

Flypala

T-Bone

Gummy Minnow

To me the Holy Grail of fly tying was to come up with something that looked, felt, and moved like the real thing. I created the Gummy Minnow (Live Scale version pictured above) in an attempt to replicate conventional soft plastics. Conventional lures such as Senkos, Bass Assassins, Zoom Flukes, and Sebile Magic Swimmers all have a realistic swimming action, but we hadn't really cracked the code on the fly-tying bench.

Though a commercial success, the Gummy was a failure in my search for motion. But it was an early step in the progression and showcased the concept of framing a fly that I would build on with the Flypala. Even though it may be hard to see the connection, the Gummy Minnow is the first link in the chain of evolution of my fly designs and still showcases two concepts that are critical to me: realistic shape and appearance.

Flypala

When I stretched Sili Skin over the Body Tubing core and saw impressions that looked like scales show through the skin, I knew I had to keep experimenting.

Inspired by other tiers using a tubing core, and the versatility of the new Sili Skin material, I continued on with the framing concept, this time focusing on increasing movement. I tried to create movement by introducing a lip, which is common on many great lures, and this got me thinking more about the play of water on the head of a fly and how that influences the overall action of a pattern.

The hybrid version with the tail (above, a white CK Baitfish Tail) was designed to get more of the swimbait look in the water and was a transition from the Flypala with a lip to the Game Changer style. I saw how the solid head diverted water and caused the Ultra Suede to move enticingly in the water.

T-Bone

As I became more and more obsessed with catching muskies, and continued to see how my flies were not doing the trick, I knew I needed to design a large fly that would swim like a jerkbait in the water and show lots of profile. This fly was the first to incorporate shanks (at first handmade) that allowed me to build a fly that would either swim or jackknife depending on the number of shanks and how it was retrieved. I used the same Body Tubing that I had been using for the Flypala body and started to think about using that material in other ways, especially on larger flies. Body Tubing dams inside the fly not only add lift and bulk to the hair but they also help control taper. This, and the use of shanks, was a huge breakthrough for me, and I continue to use this basic concept today in my Game Changers. Experimenting with different head designs and styles showed me how much of an effect you had on swim action by changing the head of the fly, but this concept was still a little vague and unrefined before the Game Changer. Later, I would return to the T-Bone and apply some of the lessons that I have learned in the process to improve it. What I have loved about this journey is that all of the ideas seem to feed one another.

Game Changer

The Game Changer was, for me, the result of years of experimentation trying to figure out how to make a fly swim. I have explored, and developed, different chenilles and brushes to make tying this fly as efficient as possible, and with many different variations and sizes. Pictured below is a very early Game Changer tied by stacking Bestway Neer Hair, a variation tied with Sili Skin, and a later model tied with Finesse Body Chenille. No matter the material—and there are many that you can use—the goal with these flies is to achieve a natural taper while building a dense head that interrupts

the flow of water and creates, along with the spines, an enticing swimming action.

When I first tied the original Game Changers, I could see that the shape of the front of the fly, combined with the number of spines, was critical in getting it to swim right. Later I learned much more about how the head impacts the fly. You need to create a ramp for the water to pass around. A diversion up front creates vortices behind the head that cause the more flexible materials to move enticingly. The denser the body the better it's going to swim.

I am not an engineer, but I have talked to some very gifted ones that are also excellent fly fishermen, such as good friend Kirk Klingensmith. Klingensmith is a true student of fly tying and fly fishing and has offered the excellent visual analogy that the dense head on a Game Changer fly is like strapping a piece of plywood to the front of a sports car. "Sportscars and airplanes are examples of shapes that are streamlined to minimize drag. A sleek sportscar cuts through wind easily, because its streamlined shape maintains laminar flow over its surface. If we were to fasten a large sheet of plywood vertically on its front, the flow would be chaotic and turbulent. Turbulence eddies cause our car to weave or jerk sideways unpredictably and almost uncontrollably. If we were to try to drive with the hood of the car open into the wind, the turbulent conditions will be even more dramatic."

"In addition to turbulence, unstable resistance is another source to induce sideways motion. To illustrate

Game Changer, Stacked
(Brown Trout)

Gummy Style
Changer

Finesse Changer
(Silverside)

this, consider again our car with a vertical plywood wall on the front. In this case, however, half the plywood is less stiff than the other. As speed increases, the weak side of the wall collapses—causing the car to kick sideways. When the car veers, the plywood springs back flat as the flow pressure reduces. The resistance on the front of the car rebalances allowing the car to straighten. And the cycle will begin again.

This phenomenon of unstable resistance is important in fly motion. Most fly materials have some inherent stiffness. The stiffness is never perfectly uniform or symmetrical. This sets up the conditions for the springing/collapsing mechanism and its potential to impart sideways motion. Further, the instability can couple with turbulent effects and further amplify motion."

As materials changed and evolved, I was able to later on create Game Changers that were even more realistic and more effective for fussy fish. These are lightweight, sparser, and less flashy versions of Game Changers that represent the epitome of stealth and accurate imitation for finicky fish, especially in clear water. These flies not only swim, but they die out and stall in the water extremely well, just like a crippled bait. They are meant to be finessed and fished very subtly, drifting them without strips at times, and the fish suck them in.

As I became to better understand this concept of turbulence and laminar flow—thanks to guys like Kirk and Larry Dahlberg, as well as tons of time tying and trying flies in the water—I could see that how a fly swims is directly related to not only the distribution of density throughout it (bulking up the forward portion of the fly, for instance) but also the characteristics of the fibers themselves.

The biggest breakthrough to date for me has come in understanding how combining fibers with different characteristics—some springy, some smooth—can create flies that swim even more realistically and also have a taper and overall three-dimensional look to them. Using smoother, flatter fibers, whether those are hen feathers, mallard flank feathers, or flat synthetic fibers in a Translucy Brush, seems to result in a smoother, more sinuous swim than using crinkly fibers. However, these softer, flatter, smoother fibers require something underneath them for support. The Feather Game Changer opened the door to understanding all of that.

Feather Game Changer

My first departures from synthetics with the Game Changer came with deer hair and bucktail, primarily because these materials are such staples in all of fly tying, readily available, and the longer fibers could help me tie larger flies. These types of flies still have a

Crafty Changer

Feather Game Changer

valuable place in my box, but they are buoyant, and it was in an attempt to find a natural material that would sink quickly—and a tip from Bob Popovics—that I came to use feathers. At first I simply wrapped feathers on the shanks, but a major breakthrough that would forever influence my designs moving forward would be to wrap a Filler Flash core and veil the natural feathers over that. As I was experimenting with magnum hen and schlappen, I also played with other feathers (inspired by tiers such as Bob Popovics and Jason Taylor, to name only a few). The strength of the Game Changer platform is that it allows you to move fluidly from synthetics to naturals to blending the two, as in the Mallard Changer where the smooth veiling of mallard flank feathers makes the fly swim and the inner core supports the feathers and provides shape.

The lessons that I learned with this fly cannot be understated. Feathers are certainly nature's super material, but you are limited in size. So when I went searching for synthetics and found Craft Fur and then shortly after Polar Fibre, I was able to lean on the techniques that I was refining with the feather flies but leverage the characteristics of each of those synthetics. As I tied Game Changers with different materials, I could see how the characteristics of the fibers, in coordination with the taper, would influence the swim of the fly. Using Polar Fibre brushes showed me how quickly you can make this process by using brushes. And then it was a natural leap to start creating my own brushes from a wide variety of materials, which eventually led to using Big Fly Fiber brushes for Synthetic T-Bones and brushes for Hybrid Changers.

Extreme Changers

The Game Changer platform accommodates all creatures great and small. The first breakthrough I had was using store-bought brushes to tie very large Game Changers, which I called Mega Changers. These flies were fast to tie, very light, and shed water immediately, making them very easy to cast. I could now very efficiently imitate large baits with a Game Changer-style fly.

Hybrid Changers push this concept even farther forward. They combine the brushes used with the Mega

Redhorse Mega Changer

Hybrid Changer

Changer and the concept of veiling highlighted in flies such as the Feather Game Changer or Synthetic T-Bones to create a very large fly that is easy to cast and also swims like no other. An inner core provides the support system and smooth outer veiling fibers create an enticing swimming action. To date it is my most effective design for large predators, from muskies to tarpon.

The Game Changer platform will continue to evolve and can be used to tie many other patterns including large nymphs, crayfish, and shrimp. Micro shanks allow tying miniscule patterns while still retaining the swimming action of many aquatic insects. And you are not just relegated to subsurface flies with these micro shanks. I've been experimenting with a series of surface flies for trout and bass that imitate common insects and other foods. These small shanks have opened up not just another chapter in Game Changer fly design, but perhaps an entire book.

For me, a large part of writing this book is to inspire and challenge readers to adapt or improve on what I have created. In this day and age, there are thousands of videos online for you to watch and learn how to tie specific flies. I am not encouraging you to tie these flies exactly how I do. I would like you to understand the design choices that I make and why I do them, so that you can take what you have learned and apply it to your own designs for your own fisheries and fishing circumstances.

The sky is really the limit at this point, and that is very exciting to me as a fly tier and angler. You can use a wide range of materials and apply them to the shanks in different ways to achieve different profiles, sink rates, and behaviors in the water. Natural materials, synthetics, and combinations of the two are fair game, and the applications for these materials, existing and ones being developed, are almost limitless. No matter the material being used, I know other tiers will continue to build on this platform and explore its potential for not only the fish species that they are targeting but the unique characteristics of their watersheds.

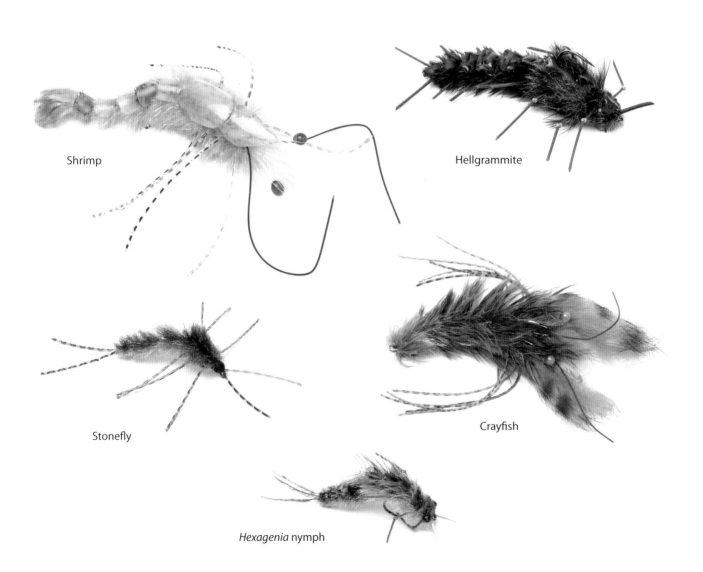

Shrimp

Hellgrammite

Stonefly

Crayfish

Hexagenia nymph

Senyo's Chromatic Changer, Goby
(Black and Purple)

Change Ur Leech

Pribanic Jig

Sodikoff's Wacky
Worm Changer

Four examples of a thousand different ways to modify the Game Changer platform for any fish species or specific needs, in this case trout, smallmouth bass, and steelhead. The articulated Change Ur Leech tied by Chris Willen is more or less the popular Mike's Red Eye Leech adapted to the Game Changer platform. Lots of materials—including rabbit in a dubbing loop, shown here—can be used in Game Changer-style flies and the platform can be used with many existing flies to show the fish something different, which might give you an edge on tougher days. Greg Senyo puts his own spin on the Feather Changer by integrating 1½" Midnight Senyo Chromatic Brush as filler and for the head. An interesting addition is the #12 Micro Treble in the rear of the fly, hidden by the materials, for nippy trout and steelhead. Justin Pribanic's jig variation with an Australian opossum head, spun in a loop, is influenced by Kevin Feenstra. This pattern combines the Game Changer wiggle with a vertical jigging presentation. Cory Sodikoff developed his wacky-style worm tied on shanks with mop tails for his home river, the Shenandoah. Mop tails can be added to many Game Changers for a little bit of a different action in the water.

2 | Materials

Just as with fishing gear, having the right tying tools and materials can make things a lot easier, whether that is choosing the right size Filler Flash, proper part of a bucktail, or sourcing a great magnum hen saddle for Feather Game Changers. One of my biggest challenges as a fly designer is finding the right materials to make the fly do what I want it to do. And then once you have found the right material for the job, you still have to be able to source good quality, especially with natural materials.

The materials that you select and integrate into your fly not only affect how the fly looks to you, but they also dictate the shape/profile of the finished fly as it swims in the water, how well the fly fishes—including how well it casts—and how well it holds up both to extended time in the water and after being run through the jaws of toothy critters. It's one thing for a fly to look good in the vise or the bin, but ultimately it has to perform on the water. And when you take the time that some of these flies require to tie, you want them to last for many fish.

Just as I develop flies to solve problems, I also choose materials to help solve design challenges in any given fly such as weight, imitation (whether I am going for realistic or impressionistic), and more subtle considerations such as flow and overall spring, or recovery, of material. Then you also need to consider how the materials in the fly interact with one another. In many flies that move well, soft materials interplay with stiff ones. For example, the Feather Game Changer and Crafty Changers use the softer veiling material like hen saddle and Craft Fur as well as Polar Fibre over a stiffer filler like Finesse Body Chenille or Filler Flash. The Hybrid Changer uses Flash Blend Baitfish Brush as a core with a veil of Translucy Fly Brush or Polar Fibre Streamer Brush. The stiffer core acts like branches; the veiling materials the leaves.

In this chapter, I am going to focus on some core components of many of the flies in this book that I think require a little more elaboration. I can't cover all of the materials that I use. So many books have covered the common materials; I want to focus on some newer or less explored items such as chenilles and shanks.

An important note about fly pattern recipes and materials: I constantly refer to these materials throughout the book, though may only do so generally in some instances where several products may suffice. For instance, I may refer to a particular hook that I use as a short-shank wide-gap, but if you would like more details on hook models, for instance, please refer back to this chapter. Also, one of the points that I want to make sure to drive home is that you can often substitute materials as long as you understand the fundamental fly design concepts of taper, veiling, and what makes a fly move. That is why I'd like to emphasize these design concepts in the book more than the actual materials, though no doubt the materials themselves play a large role in the effectiveness of the designs.

For many of the flies in the book, I provide a list of materials. This list looks a little different than the typical fly pattern "recipes" you see in tying books for several reasons. Listing them in a running format instead of in a vertical list saves precious space. Second, while I realize that readers will want to know what the specific materials are, for the most part many things like thread, eyes, hooks, UV resins, and flash are all interchangeable and depend on your preference. Same with the number of shanks and hook and shank configurations. Though I will provide some guidelines, you can mix and match depending on your needs and the length and profile of your bait.

Colors of material are definitely interchangeable depending on the baits that you are trying to imitate for your local waters. Because of my art background, it's natural for me to reach for a set of markers to get the exact shade I am looking for. I will use different colored markers for realism or to help blend Filler Flash, for instance, into a fly by matching or adding complementary colors. With a good set of markers you can really work wonders with lighter colors of chenilles, brushes, or Sili Skin, especially white and pearl.

You do not always need to follow the strict recipe if you have different needs. Be resourceful. Many times it may make sense to use good materials that you have

Matching the hatch is not just for trout and bugs. This Mega Changer matches fallfish very well. Shanks have allowed me to create a wide range of baitfish patterns with realistic swimming motion. Combining that with lightweight materials that shed water makes it possible to create larger flies that fish very well.

on hand and come up with a way to use them, rather than try and force using poor materials just to follow a recipe. A few times over the years I have had to create a material because it wasn't available for what I had in my mind. Sili Skin is a prime example of that. No matter what course you take, consider the deliberate application of materials—make every one count. Many tiers simply put materials in the wrong spot, or place a hodge podge of different materials on the shank with no or little thought to function and flow. Less is almost always better, and taking out anything not essential from a fly can often make it perform better.

One of the most important lessons I learned early on the Jackson was that the best flies weren't the ones found in the shop bins or the catalogs and that you needed to innovate to imitate. In this book I want to share what I have done, but I want you to take that and apply it to something you want to do. And don't be afraid to fail. Over the last thirty-some years, I have tied a lot of terrible flies.

Shanks

A shank is a piece of stainless-steel wire with a rear connecting loop and a front eye. If you are looking at a profile of a shank, the rear loop goes up and down (vertical) and the front eye goes side to side (horizontal). You can slide a rear loop through an eye of a hook or to another shank. By closing off the rear loop with tying thread, you create a durable, fail-safe system for articulated flies. Shanks have revolutionized articulated flies and are the backbone of the T-Bone and Game Changer series.

Tying sections of a fly on shanks allows for built-in movement and action that you would otherwise not be able to achieve by tying on a single hook. While previously tiers would connect multiple hooks with braid or wire, sometimes just using hooks with the bend and point clipped off to create a makeshift shank, a dedicated shank system makes this job more efficient and results in more durable flies because the shanks interlock.

The first fly that I designed that really benefited from shanks was the T-Bone, a fly that replicates a jerk bait, which has a jackknifing, kicking action in the water that shows the profile of the fly to the fish. This style of fly is effective fished on an intermediate or sinking line while drifting. The angler makes a hard strip and long pause, allowing the fly to jackknife in the water once the fly stops. It will suspend for a few seconds and then another hard strip will jackknife it the other way. You can enhance the action by adding more shanks, but usually two to four are only all that are needed to get the kicking motion that makes this fly style so effective when fish are looking for this type of presentation.

I recommend that new tiers consider designing the fly ahead of time. Even now, I will often lay the

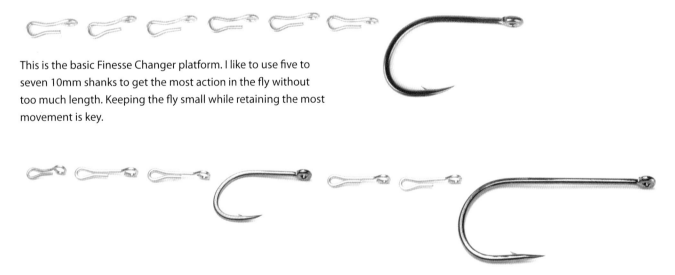

This is the basic Finesse Changer platform. I like to use five to seven 10mm shanks to get the most action in the fly without too much length. Keeping the fly small while retaining the most movement is key.

The Game Changer represents a fluid design concept that can be changed and rearranged depending on your imagination and what you are trying to achieve. But I often use this configuration for a two-hook fly: 10mm, 15mm, 15mm, 1/0 Big Game Hunter, two 15mm, 2/0 Big Game Carnivore. The actual shanks and hooks here are not nearly as important as the overall layout. I like six to seven articulations, I generally use the same size shanks through a fly (there are notable exceptions), and choose a rear hook that has a similar shank length to the shanks.

shanks out on a white piece of paper, along with the hooks that I am going to use to guide my choices for shanks moving forward. A lot of times I use the same sizes if I can because I want to generally keep the length at a minimum. But if I know I am getting a bigger fly, sometimes I will have smaller ones to get more movement and then gradually increase as I move forward. For example, on my Finesse Changers I like to use five to seven 10mm Fish-Spines to achieve maximum movement but keep the overall size small. For a 6- to 7-inch fly, I might use three 15mms to the hook and then two 20mms in front of that. To keep the hook and shanks integrated and maintain the flow of the fly, I try to match the overall hook length to a 20mm shank. By matching the hook length to the shank length, you maintain the flow as it is easier to achieve proper taper and profile, and you get a better uniform swim.

Weight is another important consideration, especially with larger flies. As you increase the size of the fly, you want to minimize weight, and one way you can do this is to use lighter shanks. For instance, on the Mega Changers, I use the larger Flymen Fish-Skull Articulated Shanks rather than the thicker wire Big Game Shanks that I designed for the T-Bone. The wire gauge is much smaller and lighter than the Big Game Shanks.

For smooth, seamless bodies, I try to attach materials all the way up to the halfway point on the rear loop that you pass through the eye of the previous shank, so that when I tie in the material it closes off any gaps to the rear. Other times I stop my thread wraps lower, just at the beginning of the rear loop, to allow more motion. Along these lines, consider that the coated wire that you use to connect the shanks to the hook also plays a role in alignment and flow of the fly. After I tie in the wire, I wrap down the hook bend a bit before looping it through shank eye. Then I take a few thread wraps over the doubled-over wire and pull the wire tight so that it is only slightly bigger than the diameter of the shank eye behind it. This helps with movement but it also keeps everything in line. After you tie down the coated wire you want the rear shanks even with the hook shank for the best swim. Just as if our spine gets out of whack we don't walk or run as well, the fly swims at its best when everything lines up.

In the early days, I made my own shanks by bending wire, but now commercial availability of a wide range of lengths and sizes makes it easier than ever to create flies with tantalizing action. I have worked with Flymen Fishing Company to develop three series of shanks specifically for T-Bones and Game Changer-style flies, including one series of micro shanks for trout nymphs and other critters.

Rick Kustich lifts a monster of a muskie hooked on a T-Bone. Big Game Shanks are not only strong enough for fish this large but they also provide enough of a base for all the materials in a large fly.

Fish-Skull Articulated Fish-Spine

Flymen Fishing Company (10mm, 15mm, 20mm, 25mm)

Fish-Spines are my go-to shank for Game Changers in the 3- to 7-inch range. The size, diameter, and length have been designed to achieve maximum movement with minimal weight. Depending on the length of your overall fly, you can stair-step these shanks or use all the same size. A Tail Shank is also available that makes tying the tail portion of your Changers a little easier. Rather than having to tie around the rear loop of a shank or having to modify the shank by cutting part of it off, you simply insert the tag into the vise.

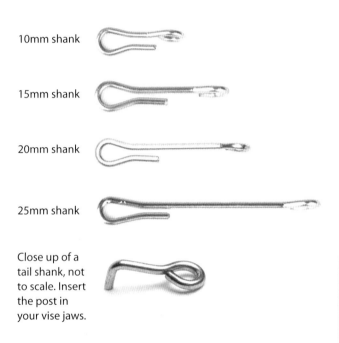

10mm shank

15mm shank

20mm shank

25mm shank

Close up of a tail shank, not to scale. Insert the post in your vise jaws.

Fish-Skull Chocklett's Articulated Big Game Shank

Flymen Fishing Company (28mm, 40mm, and 80mm)

I use the Big Game Shanks on my T-Bone patterns as well as for larger popper faces. The beefier shanks provide a better base for more bulky materials. These shanks are made from a heavier gauge wire and come in longer lengths. Oversized loops give the eye of the fly enough room to use a heavy-duty bite tippet and creates space for bigger hooks (6/0 or 7/0) to move freely on the back loop. The extended loop length allows you to tie them down farther along the shank, which adds strength and helps prevent bigger fish pulling out the loop during an extended fight.

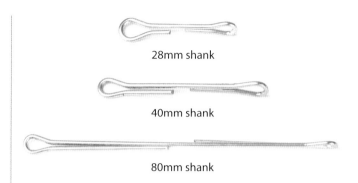

28mm shank

40mm shank

80mm shank

Fish-Skull Articulated Shank

Flymen Fishing Company (20mm, 35mm, and 55mm)

The original shanks from Flymen (not pictured) are a good midsized shank system not only for Game Changers and smaller T-Bones but also for many types of articulated streamer patterns. I used the 20mm shanks on some earlier versions of the Game Changers, and that's where my relationship with Martin Bawden from Flymen Fishing Company really got started. These shanks work well for smaller T-Bones from 6 to 10 inches and larger Game Changers from 8 to 12 inches. I also use these shanks on the Mega Changer tied in this book.

Fish-Skull Chocklett's Articulated Micro-Spine

Flymen Fishing Company (6mm, 8mm, and 6mm Tail Shank)

These minute spines allow you to imitate insects, small baitfish, crustaceans, and other aquatic critters. The new triangular back-loop design reduces the gap between segments, provides for more movement, and makes each spine easier to fit in your vise jaws. These, like the original Fish-Spines, are available in separate sizes as well as a starter pack that includes both sizes

Micro Changer

Micro-Spines are available in three sizes. The close up of the Micro-Spine (not to scale) shows the triangular rear portion.

Sculpin Micro Changer

and tail shanks. In the Micro Changer pictured above, tied with pearl Light Brite dubbing colored with Copic marker, I use five 6mm and one 8mm Micro-Spines and a Gamakatsu C14S hook. The 2-inch-long Sculpin Micro Changer next to it is tied almost entirely out of Ice Dub, however any long-fibered dubbing such as Senyo Laser Dub is also a great choice. I trim it to the shape of a real sculpin at the end, not as I tie each section as with the standard Game Changer.

Hooks

The hook serves several critical roles in both fly design and fly performance. I cover here the hooks that I like to use, but I'll first offer a few thoughts on important characteristics that I often get questions about: hook gap, length, gauge, and number and placement of hooks in the fly.

First, gap. Gap, the distance between the business end of the hook and the hook shank, is important because you want to make sure there is enough of it after you lash a bunch of materials to the shank. One of my basic design tenets for T-Bones and Game Changers is to build bulk in the front of the fly for movement (not always, but often) so you need a wide gap to accommodate all the materials without sacrificing hooking ability. If you have a fly with a gap that is too narrow, the material on your fly can prevent the hook from doing its job. A wide gap is also critical with large popper heads that are firm and don't compress when the fish eats the fly. As an added benefit, a wider gap also provides more area to the bend of the hook for keeling, which I'll discuss in a bit.

Hook length is also an important consideration. I like short shanks for Game Changers for a couple of

A wide-gap, short-shank hook helps keep the fly small in its overall appearance, often necessary when finesse fishing, and the wide gap helps with hook-ups. Mike Schultz holds a trophy smallmouth I caught with him while sight-fishing with a Finesse Changer in low, clear water.

reasons. First, I think they hold fish better than long-shank hooks. Second, the short shank on the hook aligns best with the shorter shanks that I like to use on most of my Game Changers. I don't like to increase size too quickly between shanks or between shanks and hooks so that I can keep a nice, smooth transition. With shorter shanks you not only get a nice swimming action, but you can also control the transition of materials much better. In this regard, the biggest takeaway is to consider the shank length of the hook that you are using in the overall design of the fly, especially when you are incorporating shanks.

One of the biggest considerations for me when designing larger flies is the ability to cast them, so being able to trim weight where you can is essential. I generally want to go with the lightest wire gauge that I can use without sacrificing strength for the species of fish I am targeting. Choosing the lightest wire gauge does a few things. First, the lighter wire means a lighter hook, overall, and that makes the fly easier to cast. Also, a light-wire hook penetrates better. Some fish such as muskies have a lot of bone in their mouth and you can set all you want to but if it finds bone it is going to be harder to get it in there. In general, I think finer wire

hooks are easier on the fish as well. With that said, I was reminded recently on a trip to South America that there is no free lunch. If you are fishing for large fish or strong fish such as arapaima or peacock bass you have to sacrifice castability for durability—you do not want your hooks to open up on the fish of a lifetime, so that means using a heavier hook.

The number of hooks that I use in each fly is frequently dictated by the primary species that I am fishing for. For fish that suck in their prey, such as big striped bass, a largemouth bass, or tarpon, one hook will suffice. These fish tend to suck in the fly and hooking up is rarely a problem, though you could always fish a fly with multiple hooks for insurance.

For fish that grab, or fishing for any species in turbid water where I feel like they might miss the fly, I use multiple hooks, either adding one in the middle of the fly for fish such as trout, pike, and muskie that often hit a fly from the side, or adding a rear stinger hook for smaller, or nippier fish. A lot of times with smaller fish—for instance, trout and smallmouth under 18 inches—you can get a lot of nips on the tail end of the fly. When guiding an angler that wants to connect with a lot of fish, I'll use a fly with a trailing hook for

This wild brown grabbed a rainbow-flavored Feather Game Changer on a Jackson River float. Trout often nip their prey from behind, especially smaller trout, and adding a rear stinger hook in the fly can ensure hook-ups that you otherwise might not get.

the 14- to 16-inch-range bass that can light up a client's day. Many of my clients don't get out much and when they do, they want to have lots of action. I can't blame them for that.

My choice of hooks for most of the flies in this book is relatively simple, and there are several manufacturers that have similar hooks that I will cross-reference here. Whenever I reference one hook in the text, chances are good that you can substitute another hook with similar attributes. For the longest time, most of the hooks that I preferred to use came from the conventional world, but more and more manufacturers such as Kona and Ahrex are coming out with models that I like. I use short-shank, wide-gap hook as stinger hooks on larger flies and as the main hook on Finesse Changers. I like longer-shank hooks listed below for the lead hook on most of my larger flies.

Short Shank, Wide Gap

Main Uses: Stinger hooks and front hooks on Finesse Changers

Gamakatsu SL12S 1X Short Big Game Wide Gap Hook, #1-3/0
Gamakatsu SL12 Big Game, #1/0-6/0
Tiemco 600SP, #2-4/0
Kona Big Game Hunter (BGH), #8-6/0
Ahrex NS 172 Nordic Salt Gammerus Hook, #2-8
Gamakatsu B10S, #6-3/0
Trokar Flippen, #3/0-5/0

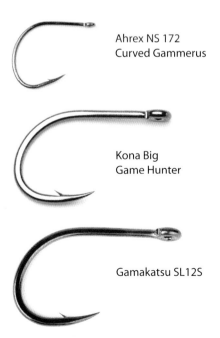

Ahrex NS 172
Curved Gammerus

Kona Big
Game Hunter

Gamakatsu SL12S

Long Shank, Wide Gap

Main Uses: Main hook on muskie flies, larger Game Changers and Mega Changers and T-Bones

Gamakatsu B10S Stinger Hook, #2/0-8
Gamakatsu Heavy Cover Worm Hook, #3/0-5/0
Kona Big Game Carnivore (BGC), #6/0-1/0
Berkley Fusion Heavy Cover Worm, #3/0-6/0

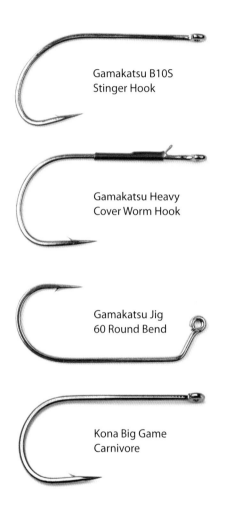

Gamakatsu B10S
Stinger Hook

Gamakatsu Heavy
Cover Worm Hook

Gamakatsu Jig
60 Round Bend

Kona Big Game
Carnivore

Body Materials

A lot of traditional streamer patterns use marabou, bucktail, and synthetics tied in at various points to create the illusion of mass. But for the most part, at least in earlier designs, these flies were only two-dimensional. Bob Popovics revolutionized how flies were tied and conceived by showing us how to create three-dimensional flies by reverse-tying bucktail. His designs not only had height, width, and depth, but they were tied in the round so that this realism showed from all sides. As well, he was able to shape some of his bucktail patterns by pinching the fibers as he tied them in so

Senyo's Laser Hair Changer (Baitfish) showcases how to use a long-strand dubbing to create Game Changers in almost any color configuration. Flies pictured above use polar white, light olive, medium brown, and royal blue Senyo's Laser Hair Dubbing, which is available in over 100 colors.

that they had different shapes other than the standard fusiform shape.

Streamer and baitfish designs have come a long way in recent years. In my own journey, I have focused on expanding concepts introduced by Bob Popovics, but also using materials such as Body Tubing, Sili Skin, various feathers, and chenilles and brushes to not only create a realistic look and profile, but also flies that swim well.

Body materials can be loosely divided into two categories based on how they are used in the fly. Some are better as supporting materials, the core, and others are better for the outer layer, which I also call the skin or veil. Some fibers, such as Finesse Body Chenille or

various brushes, can serve double duty as both a core in a fly or as the sole body material. New materials seem to come on the market every few months—and we are constantly learning how to use old materials in a new way. What is more important than the actual material is a material's properties. Materials that are crinkly and springy are candidates for your inner support system; smoother and softer materials tend to be better choices for the outer veil.

This fly, featured in *Fly Fisherman* magazine, is tied with Chocklett's Body Wrap, which was available before Game Changer Chenille. The techniques of tying with Body Wrap are exactly the same as with Game Changer Chenille. It comes in many colors and takes markers well if you want to simply tie a white one and mark it up on the water or add accents to other colors. When marking chenilles or brush heads, make sure you get down to the core of the fiber and stroke the fibers with the marker. Many people just mark the ends of the fibers or the surface and that doesn't last as long. Consider that you are layering on your colors, so first build your base color, then outer color, and then top color.

Chocklett's Game Changer Chenille and Finesse Body Chenille

The first chenille product that I designed specifically for Game Changers was Chocklett's Body Wrap. I wanted a material that was denser and easier to use than CCT Body Fur, which Chuck Kraft used in his patterns. Body Wrap, which is still available, has a core on both sides so you can cut it in half and even pretaper each section to save material and reduce trimming time. It is best for flies in the 4- to 8-inch range; however, I have now almost exclusively replaced it with brushes on flies that require this length of fibers.

Body Wrap creates a very dense body, which is good for creating movement, but water gets trapped in the fibers (the fibers do not absorb water) and it becomes heavy. I came out with Game Changer Chenille to solve this weight problem as it sheds water very well. The material gives you the bulk and the body that you're looking for without absorbing water, which keeps it lightweight. When you wrap it, the fibers stand up immediately on the braided core and create a lot of body with an attractive sheen (it does have subtle flash built into it), yet it is lightweight. It comes in a variety of colors, but you can also color it with markers to match any baitfish you want, from shad to darters to dace. At this time, it only comes with fibers about ¾- to 1-inch wide, so you are limited to patterns smaller than 4½ inches.

The latest addition to the body material lineup is Chocklett's Finesse Body Chenille, which comes in two sizes: medium (¾") and large (1¼"). It perfect for flies 5 inches and smaller. Unlike Filler Flash and Game Changer Chenille, it has no flash in it, which makes it ideal for when fish are spooky or put off by flash. The fibers themselves are translucent, though they come in a wide range of colors. You can also use it as a filler material, and when you require flies with less flash, it is an excellent alternative to Filler Flash.

The main difference between Game Changer Chenille and Finesse Body Chenille is that the Game Changer Chenille fibers are attached around a core whereas the Finesse Body Chenille fibers are only on one side, which makes it easier to wrap bodies. However, with Game Changer Chenille you can build up nice, full bodies more easily. Hareline sells Finesse Fibers, the same fibers that are used to make the Finesse Body Chenille, in longer hanks, so if you want to tie very large flies with it you can make your own brushes.

With any of these chenilles (Body Wrap, Game Changer Chenille, Finesse Body Chenille, Filler Flash)

you want to pick out any trapped fibers as you wrap the core on the shank or hook. I also periodically use a brush to sweep them back. Paying attention to this detail through the tying process results in much cleaner flies.

Finesse Changers were first tied with my then-new Game Changer Chenille, and that is what we illustrate in the book. The term "Finesse Changer" originally

Game Changer Chenille sheds water quickly and holds shape in the water. Steaming the fibers rejuvenates them and makes the fibers stick straight out. Doing this first gives you a fuller, denser body that not only makes your fly look better but also makes it swim better.

Keeling Flies

To keel something means to stabilize it and keep it upright. If you retrieve some streamers quickly, or fish them in faster currents, they become unstable and will often twist or turn in the water. This in and of itself is not always a bad thing, but if you want to keep your fly tracking upright in the water during a retrieve, you can add some weight to the bottom of it.

Though you can counterbalance a fly in many ways, adding wraps of .010- to .035-inch diameter wire to the hook bend is a fast fix, can be done on the water, and is adjustable. Keeling in this manner also helps sink your fly, and an extra 3 or 4 inches in depth sometimes is the difference in getting the fish to react or not. For a more polished, but more permanent look, you can coat your lead-wire wraps at the bench with UV resin. ■

Sometimes you may need to keel your flies so that they track better under heavy current flows or faster retrieves. Adding weight can also help in casting the fly or make it sink faster or deeper. For these reasons I keep lead wire in different sizes in my boat bag at all times.

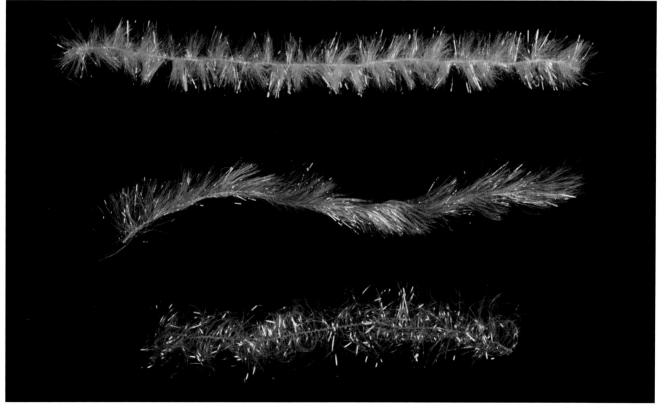

From top to bottom: Game Changer Chenille, Finesse Body Chenille, and Filler Flash.

Finesse Changers are a great choice for clear water and picky fish. The nonthreatening dulled-down fibers and realistic look and profile really help when targeting tough fish.

referred to the small size of the flies, the ease with which they took marker so that you could create highly imitative flies, and the way in which the flies hovered, stalled, and then fell in the water, which proved irresistible to smallmouth. They were excellent for fish that required a little extra finessing to get them to strike. After I developed Finesse Chenille, a fiber very similar to Game Changer Chenille, I almost exclusively use that material for smaller Game Changers. The techniques for building bodies with both of these materials are more or less the same, but with the Finesse Chenille it is important that you stretch it fairly firmly as you wrap it and also wrap the core as close together to the previous wrap as possible. Game Changer Chenille is a little more forgiving for creating nice, dense bodies; however, you have to contend with trapped fibers a little more due to the nature of how the fibers are attached around the core instead of just on one side.

Craft Fur

Craft Fur is a synthetic hair with tapered ends that comes on a fabric "skin." It is available through Hareline and other distributors, as well as, you guessed it, craft stores. It's fairly easy to find Craft Fur in big-box stores, but if you want longer fibers you may need to purchase a product such as Hareline's Extra Select Craft Fur. Though tying a Game Changer with Craft Fur takes longer than one with a brush or chenille, there are a number of benefits to the material including the ability to hand taper the fibers, trim them to length with your fingers, wide availability, and relatively cheap cost. You can also create your own brushes with Craft Fur to speed up the tying process.

The techniques of stacking and reverse tying Craft Fur fibers that we cover in the book translate very well to Polar Fibre and also natural fibers such as marabou,

Crafty Changers swim unbelievably well and are very fishy. I like using them for big brown trout hunting on tailwaters and spring smallmouth and striper fishing. Fibers on them can be stacked to create dark over light color combinations.

Jason Taylor's marabou Game Changer variation.

as demonstrated in Jason Taylor's patterns. In his marabou Game Changers he modifies the profiles with Finesse Body Chenille but substitutes stacked marabou feathers, removing the center tip before tying them in.

Bucktail and Deer Body Hair

Bucktail and deer body hair have always been fly-tying staples for their wide availability, durability, and how the fibers breathe in the water, especially on the pause. For T-Bones and larger Game Changers, I use a lot of bucktail because of the longer fibers and also the distinct action it provides in the water. These fibers are semi buoyant, so pairing them with an intermediate or sinking line can be very effective when you want a fly that swims at a certain depth. The flies are a little heavier than some of the recent synthetic versions that I've developed, but a T-Bone tied with bucktail is still a solid choice when fishing for muskies. Not only does it have a unique action but working with natural materials, and also materials that are traditional to the art of fly tying, is gratifying to me as a fly tier.

Instead of the crinkly fibers at the tips, a common choice for Deceivers and Clousers, I select the hollower fibers at the base of the tail for T-Bones and Game Changers. Not only are the fibers longer if length is required, but the hollow bases flare, providing an internal support system when reverse tied. Also, hollow fibers hold their shape better over time. When tying smaller Game Changers, and by small I mean flies in the 4- to 8-inch range, I prefer body hair. It is much easier to select fibers that are consistent in length, which helps create a better profile in that size range.

Many fly tiers have discouraged stacking bucktail when creating wings on flies because it tends to create an unnatural looking "paintbrush" effect without any taper. However, I have found that with both the bucktail and the deer body hair flies, stacking the hair before tying it in allowed me to even up the tips, trim the uneven butts, and then use the butts to support the

A Bucktail Game Changer rigged and ready for action during a trip to the Amazon for peacock bass.

fibers and add density to the fly. Since the fibers are distributed around the shank 360 degrees, the final flies looked much cleaner than if I didn't stack them, and the overall taper of the fly is created by how you tie in each section relative to the one before it.

Hen Saddle

Webby hen saddle feathers are perfect for tying Feather Game Changers because they are available in a wide range of gorgeous colors and also because they are presized for you as long as you purchase them on the skin. As with a dry-fly neck, feathers at the base of the saddle are smaller and get increasingly larger as you move up.

For average size Game Changers, you need what is marketed as magnum hen saddle so that you can get the sizes that you need. These saddles can be a little hard to obtain, at least those with feathers large enough to tie the forward shoulders of the flies. To overcome this, you can use readily available schlappen feathers, which are larger, to get more length and bulk.

Original Feather Game Changers were tied solely with feathers, and these are still effective, especially for fish that want a subdued fly. However, by taking a few turns of Filler Flash, Finesse Chenille, or another supporting synthetic before you wrap each section of feather, you can really budget out the prime hen saddle feathers, speed up the tying process, and actually improve the action of the fly.

After tying in the feathers by their tips, you can wrap them singularly or all together, it just depends on what you are comfortable with. However, as you wrap, you'll get the best results if you stroke the fibers back after each turn so that they lay nicely. Picking out any trapped fibers with a bodkin also produces the best results. You can combine different colors of feathers for a nice mottling effect that creates depth to the fly, and if you do that it works best to wrap all the feathers at once. Because they are larger feathers, there is no need for hackle pliers.

Other Bird Feathers

The sky is the limit when it comes to combining different materials to create a variety of effects, both visual and functional. Fly tiers have an amazing selection of bird feathers available to them, and these feathers can be used inside, or over, other feathers such as hen saddle to create all sorts of interesting looks and actions. Tiers such as Bob Popovics, David Nelson, Jason Taylor, and many others have been experimenting for a long time with combining different feathers in larger saltwater patterns, and their work has been a source of inspiration for me. Now that we have the ability to tie very small flies on spines, a wide range of smaller feathers that were once not practical or explored for larger flies are now in play. This is a really exciting growth area in my opinion.

The Mallard Changer, though it takes a good deal of time to tie, provides an excellent tutorial of how to use an outer layer of feathers in your fly. In this fly, an inner filler material creates shape, support, and profile. The mallard feathers, tied in reverse and veiled over this core, provide a distinct swimming action and a very realistic look. Using the stem of the feather by tying it in reverse adds spring under pressure while fishing the fly. As the water pushes over the feathers, they flex inward and then rebound, much like shock absorbers.

Another great feather that I've been experimenting with is pheasant. Pheasant feathers have unique markings and they are more readily available on a skin than mallard, which makes it easier to get the right size and quality of feathers. When the fly is swimming, all the mottling blends together and the natural iridescence of

Hen saddles (above) available from Metz, Keough, and other breeders come in many colors and are my go-to body material for Feather Game Changers. Wider and webbier rump feathers (left) are also a great choice, especially for sculpin patterns. Combining these with the hen saddles makes tying Feather Game Changers a breeze.

Mallard feathers are an excellent addition to Game Changers. They can be palmered, used as pectoral fins and tails, or tied in as an outer body to create a three-dimensional profile.

These Pheasant Game Changers tied by Jason Taylor are inspired by a cross between Bob Popovics' Feather Fleye and the Mrs. Simpson trout pattern from New Zealand.

the feathers looks sensational in the water. In the flies above, tied by Jason Taylor, each section is palmered Finesse Body Chenille, then shingled pheasant rump feathers, increasing the amount of chenille and size of the pheasant feathers as you tie each section.

Shingling feathers over hen saddles or other materials results in a color contrast that imitates many baitfish (dark over light) but it also allows you to further refine the body shape. You can not only get fusiform, three-dimensional shapes but create V-shaped bodies or even create different control surfaces that influence action.

Filler Flash

Filler Flash is a pearlescent mylar on a core that is dyed in a wide range of colors. I use it primarily as filler for Feather Changers, Crafty Changers, and Polar Changers to fill out and bridge different sections, though I have tied Game Changers completely out of this material as well. It has a good amount of flash that shines through and accents the materials that you veil over it. As a base it both helps create the illusion of mass and adds lift without adding weight. For less flashier flies, you can use Finesse Body Chenille as a filler.

When I start to approach the front of the fly where I usually want more lift and profile, I often double over the material and twist it with a dubbing loop tool outfitted with an alligator clip (Loon's Gator Grip Dubbing Spinner is one good option) to increase volume and make it stand up on edge, which adds height and extra rigidity and support for the fibers lain over the top of it.

Chocklett's Body Tubing

Chocklett's Body Tubing is a plastic, woven tubing material (think Chinese finger trap) that comes in a wide range of colors and three diameters: ⅛", ¼", and ½". Discovering how to integrate Body Tubing into my flies was one of my first breakthrough concepts in fly design, and I have used it since developing the Flypala on everything from bodies to heads on flies. This material is also great to set tapers throughout flies such as the T-Bone, Crafty Game Changers, Mega Game Changers, and larger Bucktail Changers. With careful positioning of the dam, you have lots of control over

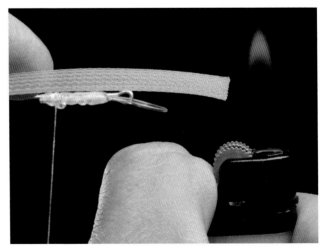

When working with Body Tubing, I singe the ends with a lighter after I trim them to prevent them from unraveling and make the tubing easier to work with. I also almost always cover the thread wraps over the Body Tubing with a cyanoacrylate glue such as Loctite.

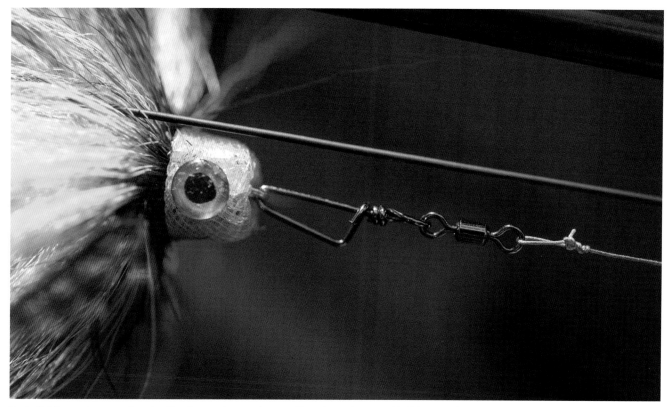

Body Tubing makes excellent bodies, internal spreaders, and heads, such as on this T-Bone. When rigging large flies like T-Bones, I like to use a barrel swivel and clip to prevent line twist.

the taper of the overall fly. You not only controlling the lift of the fibers in front of it but you are also controlling the taper of the fibers behind it. Using dams also supports the fibers permanently whereas other methods eventually tend to fail. For instance, when reverse-tying bucktail, you can create a lot of lift in the fibers, but the fibers will eventually compress over time.

Brushes

Brushes have been around forever, but they are now experiencing a resurgence as more and more anglers are tying larger patterns that are made infinitely easier with premade brushes. A brush is a bunch of fibers (and even other materials such as flash or rubber) trapped and twisted tight between fine wire. As you wrap the brush on the hook or shank, all of the material splays out, just as hackle fibers splay out when you wrap the stem on the hook. A variety of premade brushes are available commercially, or you can make your own with a brush table. Brushes can come in a range of sizes, with fibers from ½ to 6 inches long, giving you the flexibility to create flies from 3 to 14 inches (or longer) with minimal work. Without a brush of some sort, you'd need to create a dubbing loop with thread, insert your fibers, and work through your fly that way, which would take a long time.

By choosing light materials that shed water, you can create enormous flies that cast relatively easily. You can tie an entire fly out of brushes such as the Mega Game Changers and Hybrid Changers, just use brushes to finish off the heads of flies, or use brushes as filler material. Either way, they are an enormous time saver. In this book I tie several flies with home-spun brushes and I will walk you through the steps to make your own, but many manufactures now offer premade brushes that are ideal for the flies that I teach in this book. I will cover some of those below.

Just as I use a core and veil concept when building flies, you can also think of integrating this concept into the construction of actual brushes, if you choose to make your own. For instance, you can create a brush with Baitfish Emulator Flash or Larry Dahlberg's Big Fly Fiber (Hedron, Inc.) and stiffen these longer softer fibers with other stiffer fibers such as Flash Blend, Slinky Fiber, or Super Hair to get more support or lift. Combining these fibers within a brush is an excellent example of the brushpile concept of using stiffer fibers for support. Stiffer fibers add more spring and resilience under pressure for more sustained support over time.

Flash Blend Baitfish Brush. These 11½-inch-long brushes are made from Steve Farrar Flash Blend, which has been a long-time staple of saltwater flies, and come

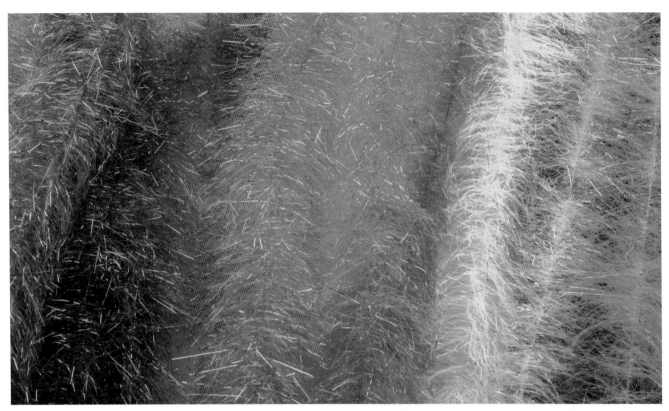

The ability to make homemade brushes opens up many opportunities for controlling taper and profile in fly design. The sky is the limit on combinations of materials. Brushes made from Baitfish Emulator (above) are a great option for Game Changer bodies.

in a variety of sizes, from 1 to 5 inches. The different fiber lengths negate the need for a lot of trimming as you can increase the brush size as you move forward in the fly. You can tie entire Game Changers from these brushes or use this material as a filler on flies such as Game Changers, Polar Changers, and Crafty Game Changers. It is kinky and very springy, which allows the material to hold shape under pressure over time and also act like branches on a bush or tree. The fibers intertwine, creating size without mass, and shed water immediately when taken out of the water for a backcast.

Flash Blend Baitfish Brush (Just Add H2O, distributed by Renzetti)

Translucy Fly Brush. These brushes are made from a combination of fine, translucent fibers that are also flat. This is an important characteristic to me as I have found that the flat, straight fibers allow for a more laminar flow, which translates into more swim with less effort. Just as with air flowing over a sports car, if water travels over a fly with a smooth surface there is less drag and a smoother swimming action. Because of this, I use these brushes frequently as veiling fibers over a stiffer core in Hybrid Changers. The Translucy Changer, tied with a series of Translucy Fly Brushes (it comes in 1", 2", 3", and 5" brushes), swims as well as the Feather Changers and sheds all water immediately after being pulled from the water. It is ideal for fish that demand larger patterns (5 to 8 inches) in clear water. Pictured above

Translucy Changer

(not to scale) is a black Translucy Changer tied with two 10mm, four 15mm, and one 20mm Fish-Spines and a series of Translucy Fly Brushes, each size tied in stages.

Polar Fibre Streamer Brush. These brushes are built with the classic streamer material Polar Fibre and come in ¾", 1½", and 3" lengths. Polar Fibre has long been a favorite with fly tiers because the straight, soft fibers allow a more laminar flow and blocks water from

Translucy Fly Brush (Just Add H2O, distributed by Renzetti)

Polar Fibre Streamer Brush (Just Add H2O, distributed by Renzetti)

Sculpting Flash Brush (Just Add H2O, distributed by Renzetti) comes in fiber lengths of 1", 2", 3", and 5" and can be used as a body material for Game Changers up to 7 inches. However, I like it best for the heads on Game Changers. It is so dense when wrapped that it blocks water flow and causes the fly to swim.

traveling within the fly, all aiding in a better swimming action. Like feathers, the material breathes in the water, even at rest. I like this material for the Polar Express Changer as well as for the veil on my Hybrid Changer, over a bed of Flash Blend Baitfish Brush for support.

Chocklett's Sili Skin and Loco Foam

Sili Skin is a flexible, "gummy" tape that comes in two 2 x 6-inch strips. One side is covered with a peel-off backing. The other side has a foil finish, which comes in a wide array of colors. The fly that popularized this material was the Gummy Minnow, but you can also wrap it around Body Tubing to form entire bodies on flies or just finish off a head on a fly such as on a T-Bone. It's a really versatile material for

which I continue to find new applications in different patterns.

Chocklett's Live Gummy Skin (which used to be called Live Scale Sili Skin) is Sili Skin with one side that has a realistic scale finish. It is a bit easier to use than regular Sili Skin as it doesn't stretch as much; however, it is only available in gold, silver, mother of pearl, and peacock. You can color it easily though.

Sili Skin is self-healing. While you don't want to stretch it too much when you are tying with it, once you have formed the fly, you can stretch it almost twice its length and it will rebound; when it's dry, you can even cut it and then stick it back together, though this

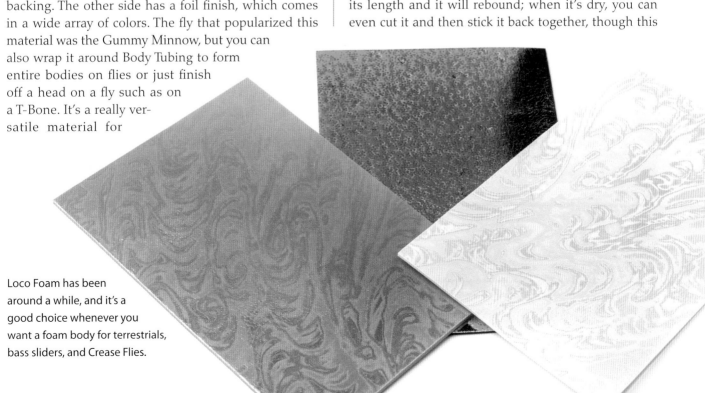

Loco Foam has been around a while, and it's a good choice whenever you want a foam body for terrestrials, bass sliders, and Crease Flies.

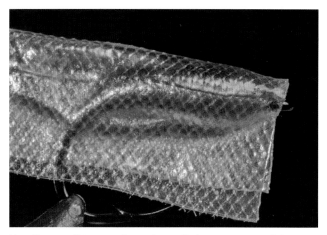

Live Gummy Skin completes the realistic appearance of the Gummy Minnow.

doesn't work when it is wet. This extreme elasticity requires some practice and tips for working with it.

Sili Skin is very sticky. You only need to apply light pressure when touching or holding the material. It will stick to you with light pressure, and the more pressure you apply the more it wants to stick. When working with Sili Skin, adjust your fingers as you are peeling the backing off, a little bit at a time, to minimize stretch and let the material come back to its original shape. Let it adhere to the hook first, and then gradually pat the material down, starting where it is attached to the hook and working back to the end of the fly. Make sure that you are not pulling on or stretching the material as you

do this. If you do, you can end up with a fly that has a pronounced curve in it. Keep in mind that anything oily reduces or takes off the adhesive. Make sure your hands are clean when you are working with it. If the material loses its stickiness and starts separating, a shot of flexible UV resin will take care of it.

Loco Foam, developed with Harrison Steeves many years ago, has endless uses as a tying material. I have used it on everything from terrestrials, mayflies, caddis-flies, and stoneflies to bass bugs and dams on T-Bones. It is a great head material as well as a body material. The prisma and metallic coating gives this foam a unique look that can match real creatures or provide an impressionistic, attractive hot spot.

Heads

The head on a fly can help influence the fly's action and, depending on what it is made of, can determine depth. Some of the premade heads also serve a practical function of finishing off the fly with a polished looking head that is also consistent, which is very important once you dial in the action of a fly and you want it to perform the same way every time. Flymen's Fish-Masks, for instance, provide a quick, efficient, and attractive way to finish your fly and also provide a nice platform on which to set your eyes. Simply prepare a base of che-nille or other material, add UV resin, slip the head over it, and cook the resin through the transparent plastic

Flymen Fishing Company Fish-Masks are a fast, efficient, and effective way to finish off a Game Changer.

for an almost-instant built-up head. Petitjean's Magic Head, seen below on Mike Schultz's Chicken Changer, is another option that some tiers like for durability and consistency, without having to trim a perfect deer hair head every time.

Traditional weights such as cones, beads, and dumbbell eyes still have a place in these designs, and as we continue to tie more and more smaller patterns on shanks they will surely still have a purpose. If I want a weighted head on my pattern, I typically reach for a preformed weighted head such as a Sculpin Helmet from Flymen. These heads already have sockets on them to receive eyes, look great on your fly, and are also extremely heavy. They will help your fly plunge to the bottom for fish that don't want to come up for a fly or if you need to get down in the zone immediately.

Floating heads such as Howitzer Popper Heads or homemade heads made from punched-out discs as in my Disc Slider will help keep your fly on the surface, or float *up* to the surface if you happen to be fishing them with a sinking line. Howitzer Heads are an easy and effective addition to Hybrid and Feather Game Changers for big redfish, jacks, cobia, and pike. I always carry a few heads with me, and if I need to create an instant floating fly, I can slip one on the leader in front of the fly.

Flymen Fishing Company Sculpin Helmets

Flymen Fishing Company Howitzer Popper Heads

Chicken Changer

Swingin' D 2.0

These two Mike Schultz flies were designed for different purposes. The Swingin' D is a tribute to Larry Dahlberg's Diver, from which it gets inspiration for its foam head. It was designed for the pressured fish on his home river, the Huron River. According to Schultz, "Fish this fly on a 45-degree angle downstream so that you can pull the diver head into the current so that the tension makes it swim back and forth." The Chicken Changer is a cross between Mark Sedotti's Kickin Chicken and a Feather Game Changer and is designed for a fairly flat profile that sinks faster for deeper water. Schultz likes to use this fly for bigger rivers when he is covering flats or expansive areas where long casts and long retrieves are required.

Keeping Your Head in the Game

When you fish a floating fly on a sinking line, you can achieve some amazing actions. One trip to the Susquehanna Flats fishing with Bill Dawson was instrumental in helping me develop larger patterns with buoyant heads that moved with enticing action. With these flies, I really started to grasp how head shape affects how the fibers behind it are going to react in the water. Plus, combining a buoyant head with a sinking line results in a wobble and darting side to side action that predatory fish responded to. The early flies that I tied with heads created out of a series of foam discs led the way for the T-Bone. Later, I would integrate this head style into Game Changers, such as the ones pictured.

Much later on, while fishing a local freshwater striper river in Virginia's Piedmont region, I had another a-ha moment around the importance of head design. This particular stream has reddish brown-colored water from the red clay banks, and eroded banks with lots of downed trees in the water. Thousands of stripers migrate into it every spring, and they stage in eddies throughout these "lumber yards" near the banks. Traditionally, I'd lose at least twenty flies a day fishing to them, so I grew accustomed to tying lots of Half & Halfs and Deceivers, which were faster to tie than standard Game Changers—but it still hurt to sacrifice so many flies.

After losing way too many flies it occurred to me to add a foam head to a Game Changer (in this case, a Feather Game Changer) and fish it on a line with a short sinking tip. After a little bit of trial and error, my clients and I cracked the code. We could pitch the fly into one of those eddies, allow the line to sink, and the fly would stay high above the snags. Then I would have my client throw a few stack mends to allow the line to sink and then have him strip the line. The submerged tip would pull the floating fly down into the eddy and then float back up to the surface. As it rose, stripers would boil up to the fly. Stripers like pauses, and while we would always catch them on the fall, now we were catching them on the rise. Whether fishing for stripers or trout, never overlook the possibilities of combining a floating fly (or a sinking fly with a more buoyant head) and a sinking line of some sort. ■

Opposite page: Different combinations that I use for bass species: largemouth, smallmouth, stripers, and hybrids. White is one of my favorite colors in general, but of course you can tie them in different colors for different water conditions or to match different baits. Sometimes you need a pop, sometimes a slide, and sometimes a fly that just hovers, so by using different head designs combined with different floating and sinking lines you can get a diverse range of actions.

Clockwise, from top: Crafty Changer, Polar Changer with medium Flymen Howitzer Popper Head, Feather Changer with medium slider head, Crafty Changer, Pole Dancer Feather Changer with medium pole dancer head, and Feather Changer with a Disc Slider head made from white mother of pearl Loco Foam.

Noise and vibration are a big attractor for muskies and other apex predators. When you strip the Hammerhead T-Bone on a sinking line it's like throwing a knuckle ball in baseball, you don't really know what it's going to do. The thick bubble trail and jackknifing in the water can be the ticket at times, especially fishing over wood for muskies in the spring.

You don't need to buy premade heads to achieve a different action. This head design comes from Tommy Lynch's Drunk and Disorderly, which takes the spun and trimmed deer-hair head to a whole new level to create a fly (in this case a juvenile brown-trout imitation) with a unique action in the water.

A Crease Fly variation tied with Belly Foam. The cupped foam creates a disturbance, yet the sloped face on the bottom doesn't dig into the water and allows you to pick it up out of the water much easier.

The foam heads created to imitate the head design on Larry Dahlberg's Diver are also very effective. Mike Schultz's Swinging D and Swinging D 2.0 use these. Schultz uses the floating head to fish over the top of submerged wood piles common on many of his rivers, such as the Huron River. He'll strip it behind a log and then pause it so that it floats up and over the wood, and then strip it again to fish it a little deeper to prevent snags. I love this kind of fly design where the flies are built to solve particular fishing problems and materials

are incorporated into the patterns with a plan in mind and a purpose.

You can also shape different heads out of deer hair to achieve different swimming actions. The shovel head that Tommy Lynch creates on his Drunken Disorderly is tied on a 60-degree jig hook and acts like a lip on a Rapala. It grabs the water, and pitches and waddles around like someone stumbling around drunk. Combined with the swimming action of the Game Changer the fly is deadly for muskies, bass, and trout and other species.

Eyes

The debate over whether eyes on flies matters will likely go on forever. I've caught plenty of fish without them. However, especially in clearer water I think they help, so I like to include them, even if it is only because I fish flies with eyes with more confidence. Why not give the fish your best effort?

For many of my Feather Game Changers, I like to use jungle cock eyes coated with a flexible UV resin for durability. Though not as imitative as commercially produced eyes, and more expensive, I like the way they look and flow with the feathers. For most of my other flies, I prefer Fish-Skull Living Eyes, which come in four different colors and in eight sizes, from 3mm to 15mm.

Your eyes will tend to look better on the fly if you cut out a little pocket for them to rest in. For weighted versions that jig in the water, you can stamp out discs from tungsten sheets and glue eyes to them or scuff up dumbbell eyes on flies and then glue more realistic eyes to that.

In many of the flies in this book, I use Flymen Living Eyes. I also tied a lot of flies with older Clear Cure Goo Chameleon eyes, which I like a lot. However, the company went out of business. Renzetti Distribution has a similar eye that is a very good substitute, so whenever you see Chameleon eyes in a recipe, you can use Molded Moon Eyes in the Ghost color. You can use what you like; however, I like to tie with translucent eyes because you can cure flexible UV resin behind them with a UV light for maximum durability.

Fire (Red/Orange)
Living Eyes,
8.5mm

Wind (Gold)
Living Eyes,
8.5mm

Ice (Silver)
Living Eyes,
8.5mm

Earth (Green)
Living Eyes,
8.5mm

UV and Blue-Light Cured Resins

Throughout this book, I use the word "resin" to refer to either resins cured with UV or blue light. I do have my preferences currently, which are the UV light cured Solarez products, but I have had good results with the Loon products as well. Some tiers love Tuffleye, a resin cured by blue light (though some other standard UV lights will also cure this). Whatever manufacturer you go with, I recommend one that has a flexible resin—not all do—which I find critical for adhering eyes and forming tails, among other things. Whenever I reference "flexible resin" I am referring to Solarez or Loon Flex formula. Currently Tuffleye also has a Flex resin that is cured by blue light, if you prefer that.

Different lights are available to cure UV resin. I currently use lights from Loon and Solarez, and those are the ones that I would recommend, but there are many good choices on the market including lights from Hareline and a blue light from Tuffleye.

This prespawn smallmouth fell for a Feather Changer. Materials such as feathers and synthetic and real hairs have built-in movement accentuated by the fly construction.

You don't need resins to tie these flies. I made do for years with plain old Zap a Gap or Loctite, but resins make the job a lot easier and also allow you to create shapes, tails for instance, that you wouldn't be able to do otherwise without a lot of fuss. With resins you can also spread out the fibers such as Craft Fur or Polar Fibre for lift and height, similar to what Bob Popovics pioneered many years ago with epoxy and the Spread Fleye.

A few tips when working with your resins. If your resin gets thicker than usual, whether from age or perhaps getting too cold, simply microwave it for 10 seconds or hold the bottle under hot tap water. If you are having trouble applying the resins, you can pour some out on a Post It or something and apply with your bodkin. When curing the resin, use a fully charged light, keep it close to the resin, and take your time. The more powerful the light, the faster the cure time. If you have a little tackiness to your resin, you may not be curing it long enough or the resin itself cures with some tackiness. You can wipe this off with a paper towel and rubbing alcohol.

Some popular UV resins available. I like to have both flexible, thin, and thick viscosities for different purposes.

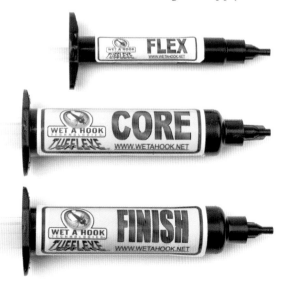

3 | Gummy Minnow and Variations

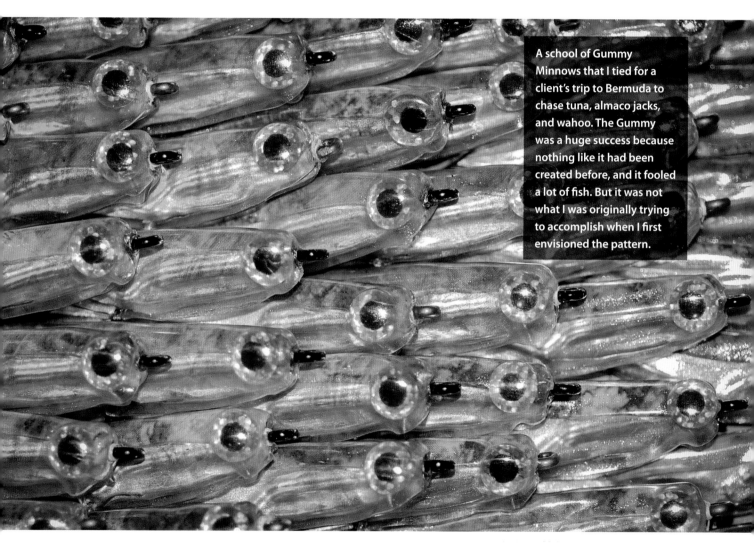

A school of Gummy Minnows that I tied for a client's trip to Bermuda to chase tuna, almaco jacks, and wahoo. The Gummy was a huge success because nothing like it had been created before, and it fooled a lot of fish. But it was not what I was originally trying to accomplish when I first envisioned the pattern.

By the early 1990s I was transitioning from a major diet of trout fishing to guiding for smallmouth, which eventually became the primary focus of my summer guiding business. In the conventional fishing world, the action and three-dimensional look of the soft-plastic baits out on the market such as Sluggos and Bass Assassins was hard to beat for bass, but we didn't have any equivalents in the fly-fishing world. I was consumed with the goal of designing a fly that would look and swim similar to the soft plastics that were coming on to the scene *en masse* and were so deadly.

Around 1997 Harrison Steeves, inspired by Joe Blados' Crease Fly, a popular surface pattern tied with sandwiched foam, designed a material called Loco Foam that added different colors of backing to foam. Through discussions with Harry and after experimenting with this material, I wanted to more or less recreate the "plastic" in the soft plastics that were so effective, but for fly tying I would use a plastic like material that adhered to itself to build different baitfish shapes. With the help of a friend that was a chemist at Johnson and Johnson and also a friend that worked in industrial packaging who helped me source several different products, I applied the basic concept of Loco Foam—a material with an adhesive backing—to an elastic, transparent material that would become Sili Skin. As soon as I had the material in hand, it took me less than five minutes to make the fly I had thought about for so long.

From the start, I tried using the actual physical makeup of the baitfish as inspiration and not just the colors or other cosmetic features. Just like framing a house, I built the Gummy Minnow from the inside out, envisioning the different layers of the body as I went. First, I tied in the belly sac, then an outer skeletal layer, then a muscular layer, so that the fly was three-dimensional. This creates more realism than just a flat baitfish, and this approach to building flies would continue to influence my fly-design process down the road.

By late fall 1998, I had a surplus of these micro baits tied up for Tom Earnhardt's annual party at Cape Lookout, Harker's Island, North Carolina. It was a great opportunity not only for world-class false albacore (albie) fishing, but also to get to hang out and talk with the who's who of the fly-fishing world—everyone, from various owners of fly-fishing companies to legends such as Lefty Kreh, Bob Popovics, and Bob Clouser, would make this annual event in those days.

For this trip, I had well over one hundred Gummy Minnows tied, in all sorts of sizes and colors to imitate silversides and bay anchovies from 1 to 4 inches long. They looked right, but I wasn't yet sure how they would swim, plus I was concerned that people wouldn't think it was a fly because of the materials and the way that it was constructed.

I had about a six-hour drive south, and along the way, I thought about who to show the fly to. I knew I wanted to share it with Brian Horsley and Sarah Gardner and also Bob Popovics, if he was going to be there. At the time I did not know Bob well, but I was hugely influenced by his style of tying. Because of his unconventional use of epoxy and silicone in his patterns, I figured he would be one of those that got what I was trying to achieve.

When I saw Bob at the party, I was elated. I asked him to take a look at the flies, and his initial response was positive. Bob weighed in on the "is this a fly?" conundrum by saying that unless it was pre-molded then it was, at least as far as he was concerned. He said he wanted to show someone the fly, left me for a bit, and then came back. "Follow me," he said, and I did.

He led me through the crowd where I saw a bunch of people in a circle. Then, like the seas parting, people peeled away to give Bob space, and in the middle of the circle was Lefty Kreh. That was the first time that I really got to meet him. He told me that they were innovative, but when asked I confessed that I had not fished them yet and that I didn't know how they would swim. He told me that there was no doubt that if the fish could see it, they would eat it. I gave Lefty, Bob Clouser, Henry Cowen, and Brian Horsley and Sarah Gardner each about twenty of them. Lefty told me that he had to leave so that he wouldn't be able to fish them, but he would definitely give some out and get some feedback for me.

The next day Bill Dawson and I got a late start (maybe the party the night before had something to do with that). On the way out, Brian Horsley came on the radio saying that they were getting into fish and catching them on the "rubber fly," which is what he called the Gummy Minnow. That was on a Sunday morning. That next Monday, while I was still at Cape Lookout, I got a phone call from Umpqua. Lefty, being Lefty and always trying to help people out, told them about the pattern and that they needed to have it. Umpqua wanted it immediately, sight unseen. As soon as I got back from the trip to Harker's, I tied up some samples, and it was in their catalog the following year.

Since then, people have taken Gummies all over the world and the last time I counted, which was years ago, have caught over one hundred species on them. The fly became really popular, not just for albacore but for lots of other species, and was responsible for many line-class world records for yellowfin, wahoo, and almaco jacks, to name a few. The Gummy traveled well and continues to be a go-to fly for many exotic and local destinations.

The fly has proved to be excellent for any sight-feeding fish that tends to be more discerning about precise imitation. Most people don't consider it a bonefish fly, but in certain parts of the world where they are feeding on minnows, it is deadly. Though I have not been there, I am told the Gummy Minnow is the fly to have when you are at Los Roques, for example. The bonefish and tarpon there will eat it every time. In Bermuda, it is very effective for tuna and wahoo that are feeding on hogmouth fry offshore.

I was really happy with the Gummy Minnow and the results from using it, but I was also a little disappointed. It had the realism, which can be super important at times, but it lacked movement. The Gummy was a hugely successful fly that was very good in certain circumstances, but I was searching for something more. I was happy that the fish ate them, but it also motivated me to create something with more movement. The Gummy got the wheels turning more. It taught me things about the material that I was working with and its limitations. I knew I was on to something, and sure enough things started to evolve from there.

The Gummy Minnow has proven to be a great option when fishing for large-eyed sight-feeding fish such as yellowfin tuna. Good friend Bob Cheers (right) caught this beautiful specimen off the banks of Bermuda.

In the late 1990s I got to enjoy many days on the water with Brian Horsley and Sarah Gardner chasing stripers and albies. Between Christmas and New Year's Day, I would host trips to the Outer Banks at Nags Head to fish for large striped bass feeding on big bunker. This nice winter striper fell for a 10-inch Gummy Minnow designed to imitate the big bunker.

Tying the Gummy Minnow

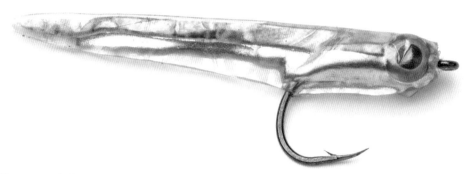

Materials

#2 TMC 600SP | 6/0 chartreuse Veevus and clear monofilament thread | base, belly sac, and underbody of metallic silver Sili Skin | green splash Sili Skin back strap | mother of pearl Sili Skin outer body | Ice Living Eyes

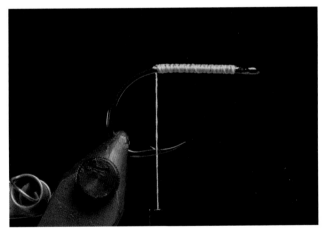

1. Place the hook in the vise, attach the thread, and wrap it down the entire hook shank to provide a textured surface for the Sili Skin. The short-shank, wide-gap hook allows more freedom for the Sili Skin in the middle and rear of the fly and is easier to hide with materials.

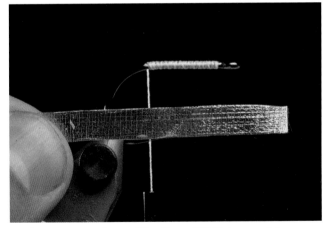

2. Cut a piece of metallic silver Sili Skin roughly ⅛-inch wide by 2-inches long with a pair of straight serrated scissors. If you use the back of the scissors instead of the front you prevent the Sili Skin from rolling and coiling.

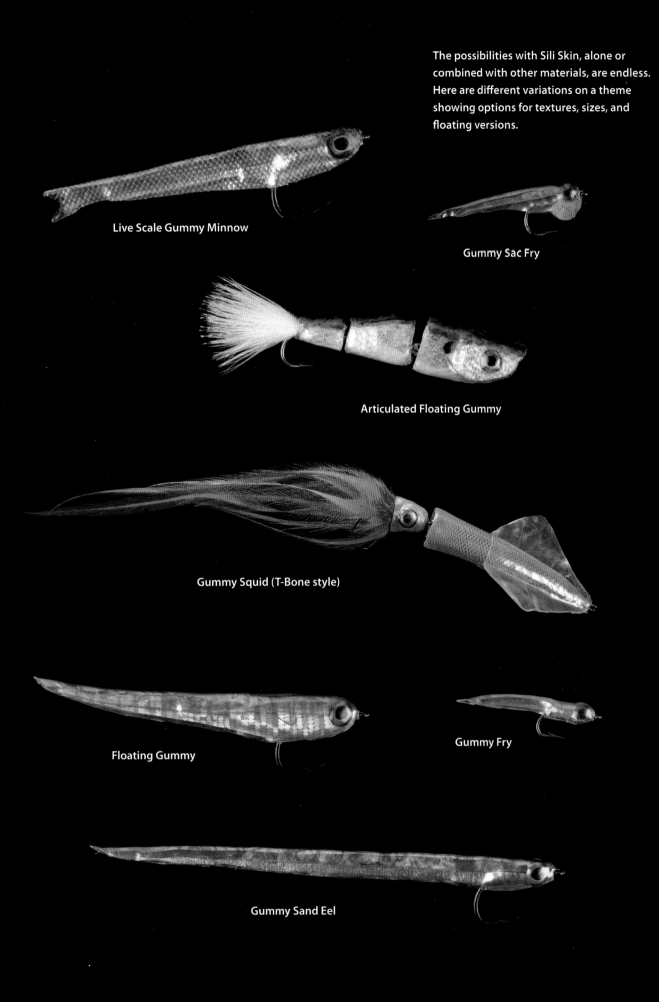

The possibilities with Sili Skin, alone or combined with other materials, are endless. Here are different variations on a theme showing options for textures, sizes, and floating versions.

Live Scale Gummy Minnow

Gummy Sac Fry

Articulated Floating Gummy

Gummy Squid (T-Bone style)

Floating Gummy

Gummy Fry

Gummy Sand Eel

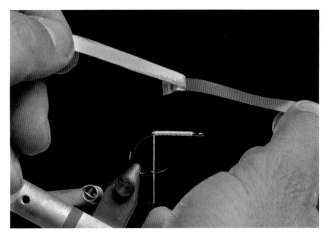

3. Starting from the top corner of the Sili Skin, carefully peel a little backing off at a time, working down toward the back and adjusting your fingers as you do this. Do not stretch the Sili Skin too much to avoid it snapping back when you peel all the backing off. Place one of your fingers in the center of the Sili Skin halfway through the peeling process to help avoid this.

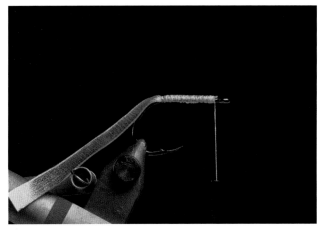

4. Tie in the Sili Skin just behind the hook eye, making sure the sticky side is up. Catch the front right corner of it with the thread and then wrap the thread down the hook shank to the top of the bend, securing the material on top of the shank. Then wrap the thread back to behind the hook eye.

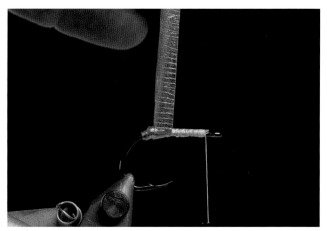

5. Spiral-wrap the Sili Skin forward, slightly overlapping your wraps as you work forward to the hook eye.

6. Once you have wrapped the Sili Skin to just behind the hook eye, tie it off and trim the excess. Then spiral-wrap the thread back to the hook bend and then back to the eye. Whip-finish and trim the thread.

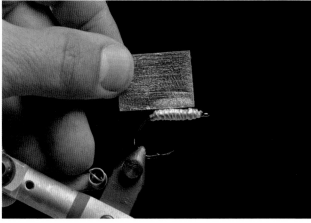

7. Cut a ½-inch-wide strip of another piece of metallic silver Sili Skin. Measure the length of the hook shank from behind the eye to a ¼ inch past the hook bend and cut the Sili Skin to that length.

8. Next cut down the center, two-thirds the length of the Sili Skin. Peel the backing off by starting at the top right-hand corner with your thumb and forefinger.

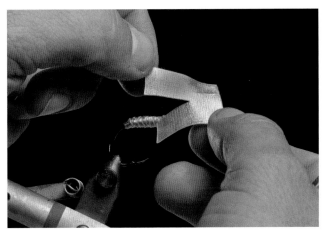

9. Once you peel off the backing, place your right thumb on the front right corner of the Sili Skin, sticky side up. Then take your left thumb and grab the back left corner of the material.

10. Bring the Sili Skin up under the hook shank and position it directly in the middle, one eye length behind the hook eye so the slit that you cut straddles the hook bend. Pull up on the Sili Skin so that it adheres to the bottom of the hook shank. Then release your right thumb, followed by your left.

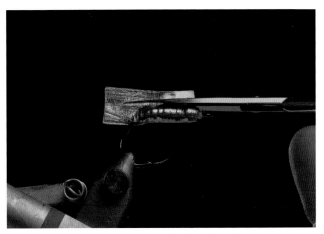

11. Fold the material up on both sides, bringing it together on top of the hook shank. Do not worry if it isn't straight. Cut the Sili Skin straight back just above the underbody.

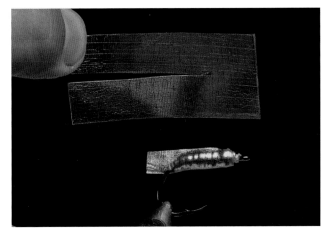

12. Cut another piece of metallic silver Sili Skin 2-inches long by 1-inch wide. Then cut down the center two-thirds of the way.

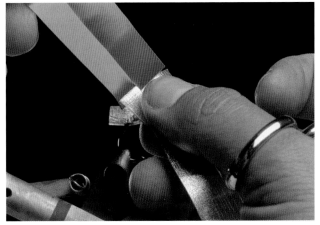

13. Peel the backing off a little at a time, adjusting your fingers as you peel. This is important to prevent the Sili Skin from stretching too much and snapping back on itself.

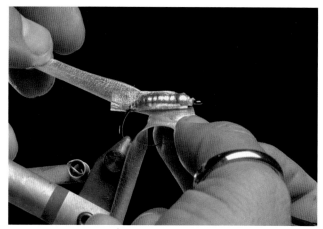

14. Once you've removed the backing, place your right thumb on the right front corner of the Sili Skin, sticky side up. Then place your left thumb on the back-left corner, being careful not to stretch the Sili Skin. Bring the Sili Skin under the hook shank and just behind the hook eye. Line up the middle of the material with the middle of the bottom of the hook shank. Lift up toward the hook shank and allow the Sili Skin to touch the underbody on the hook.

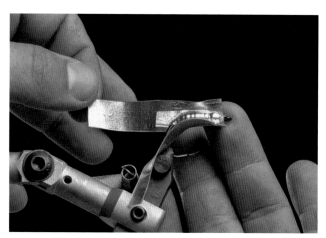

15. Release your thumb in the front right corner. Fold the Sili Skin up on the opposite side of the hook starting behind the eye. Press the Sili Skin on the underbody with your right hand, working toward the back of the shank. Now fold it up on the side nearest you and press it to the underbody.

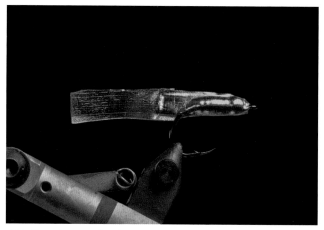

16. Starting at the front, press all the material together, taking care not to stretch the Sili Skin on one side or the other. Make a straight horizontal cut from the top of the underbody all the way back to the end. Then make a sloped cut about a quarter inch back from the hook eye to the hook eye.

17. Cut a 2½-inch long piece of green splash Sili Skin and make a tapered cut as shown above. Then round off the wider front edge.

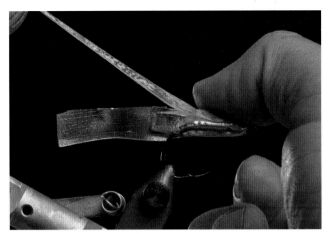

18. Peel the backing from the Sili Skin, starting from the right top corner. As you peel, readjust your fingers to the release point of the Sili Skin and backing. This will minimize stretch and prevent the material from snapping back on itself when it reaches the end. Take the green splash Sili Skin that you just removed from the backing and attach the rounded and wider end just behind the hook eye. Keep the material centered on top of the back.

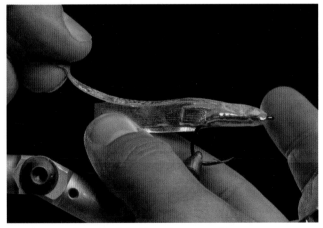

19. As you lay the Sili Skin down make sure not to stretch it as you work toward the back end. Lightly press the material on top and then on the sides so you remove the air bubbles and the material sticks firmly to the underbody. After this you will have roughly a quarter inch of material hanging off the back. Fold that section together and cut it at a slight angle, creating a point to the tail.

20. Trim an eye socket to accommodate the size of the eye you prefer. I usually use eyes that match the bait both in size and color.

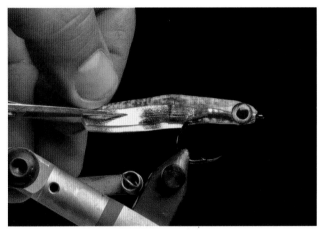

21. Place the eyes in the holes. Then trim a straight line from the back of the Sili Skin ⅛-inch wide to just behind the hook bend. You will be able to see the silver underbody as a guide to stop your cut.

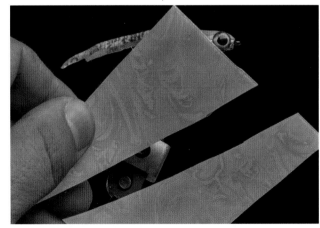

22. Cut a piece of mother of pearl Sili Skin 2-inches wide by 3-inches long. Trim it in half making a triangular cut. This will allow less waste and less trimming at the end.

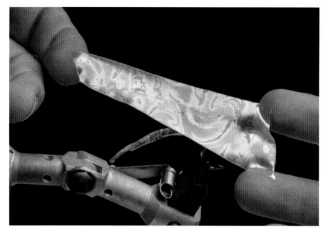

23. Peel the backing off the Sili Skin a little at a time adjusting your fingers as you peel back. Once the backing has been removed adjust your fingers on the Sili Skin so your right middle finger and pointer finger are on each corner of the wider part of the material. The sticky side should be down and your back-left pointer finger should be at the back of the narrower end. Once your fingers are in the correct spot take the wider end and center it over the top of the fly extending over the hook eye. Once it is in place pull down with your right fingers, allowing it to stick to the top of the fly. This will also allow you to release your fingers from the sticky side as well.

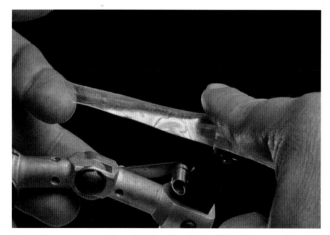

24. Come up under the back of the Sili Skin and hold the back of the tail section of the fly straight. Then, while keeping from stretching the Sili Skin, let your left pointer finger come down onto the back of the tail so that the two materials stick together and release your right hand from under the material. Then slide your pointer finger over the top of the back of the fly, starting at the front working back, to remove the air bubbles and firmly adhere the materials.

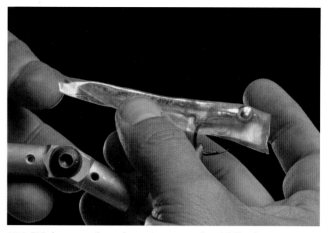

25. With your thumb, pointer, and middle fingers press the materials together on the sides and bottom to ensure the Sili Skin seals together.

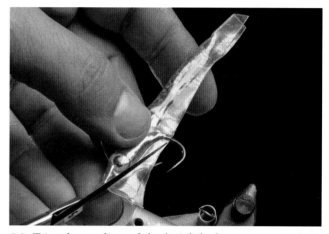

26. Trim the outline of the baitfish that you are trying to match. With this particular pattern I'm trying to match a silverside, but you can change the profile depending on what you're imitating. Be creative and play with shapes to see what profiles work best for you.

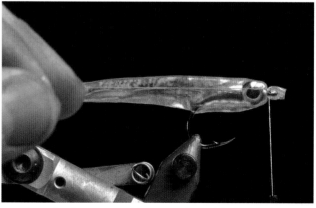

27. Attach clear monofilament thread behind the hook eye. Pull down tight as you wrap it to score the Sili Skin. Then peel off the front of the material that is left over. Whip-finish and you are done.

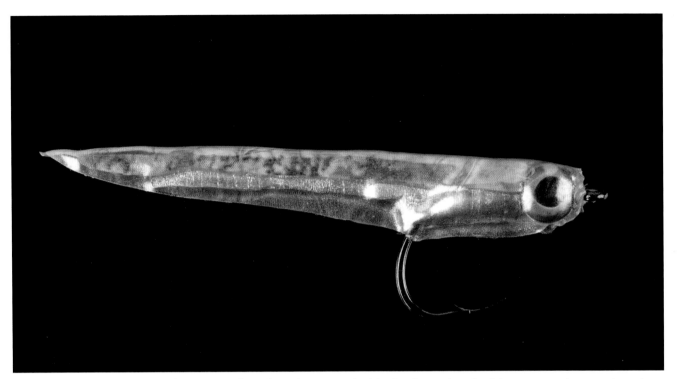

This fly excels for baits from ½ inch to 4 to 5 inches, glass minnows to shad. In sizes larger than that it becomes cumbersome to cast, though it still fishes very well.

Sili Skin opened the door to ultra-realistic imitations that I would almost immediately begin to modify in search of flies with more movement. This striper ate a Floating Gummy prototype designed to replicate a swimbait.

Floating Gummy

Bob Brien, who runs the Bermuda Fly Fishing Invitational, contacted me for a topwater version of the Gummy that would imitate hognose fly that yellowfin, jacks, and wahoo surface feed on. Wrapping Sili Skin around buoyant Body Foam was logical. Belly Foam is a very light foam material I designed that has an adhesive on it. So when you put it together, you have a half of an inch of body that helps gives you that three-dimensional look. The resulting flies turned out to be absolutely deadly when fishing chum slicks or casting into busting stripers or albies. Though it doesn't have any inherent movement, it is an excellent match-the-hatch option for a surface fly that has caught several world records.

Early on, I fooled around with an articulated, segmented version that was a precursor to the Game Changer, the Articulated Gummy. I thought a lot about morphing the Gummy Minnow into a swimming fly and experimented with a variety of designs, with and without lips. Before spines, I used a ribbon of Sili Skin in an attempt to replicate a swimbait lure. Precutting body parts and gluing them to a ribbon of Sili Skin was a novel idea at the time but it was fragile.

On one memorable trip, I was fishing in late winter with Captain Newman Weaver of Kingfisher Charters out of Georgetown, South Carolina. Newman had positioned us upstream of a large school of redfish trapped in an oxbow creek channel. They were waiting for high tide to turn and flood the grass so that they could feed. They wouldn't leave because the main river channel was being patrolled by many porpoises, and our boat was blocking their other way out. I caught fish after fish with this early version of the Game Changer. It swam and darted very similar to a soft plastic, and the reds were all over it in the shallow water. We caught fish every cast for some time until I lost my one prototype to a giant bull red that had no intention of slowing down or stopping. Newman asked me if I wanted to go after it, but I said no, as that would have allowed the entire school to get by our boat. As the big red went around the second corner of the creek channel, we parted ways on an oyster bed.

Even though this fly caught fish, I didn't pursue it for several reasons. Because it was buoyant you needed to fish it on a sinking line. I also wasn't satisfied with the lip at first. I hadn't yet figured out some tricks that I learned from the Flypala. Also, from a visual and artistic standpoint, I didn't like that you could see the segments in the fly. I envisioned something that looked more seamless—but that would have to wait.

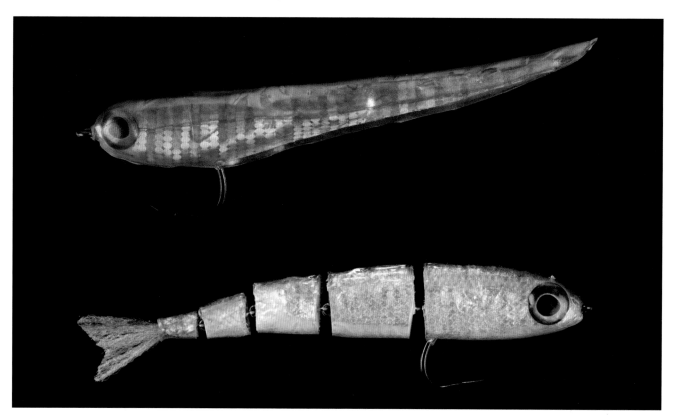

The top fly is a Floating Gummy Minnow and the bottom fly a Gummy Changer. The Floating Gummy Minnow uses Chocklett's Belly Foam covered with prismatic silver scale Sili Skin and mother of pearl Sili Skin, colored with bronze permanent marker. The Gummy Changer uses two 15mm, one 20, and one 25mm shank. The prismatic silver Belly Foam is covered with pearl Live Scale Sili Skin.

Tying the Floating Gummy

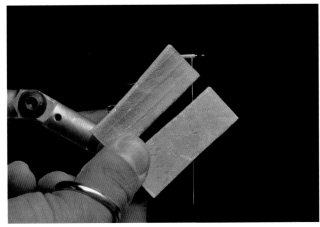

1. Attach the tying thread and wrap a foundation. Select a 2-inch x 2-inch piece of prismatic silver Belly Foam and cut it down the center so that you have two 2-inch x 1-inch pieces. Peel the backing off and attach one piece on each side of the hook shank about one eye length behind the hook eye so that the two pieces adhere to one another.

2. One you have attached both pieces, trim the underbelly to the shape of a baitfish and the underside rear of the foam to an approximately 30-degree angle (straight cut). Choose a bottom shape to mimic the bait that you want to imitate. Trim the top foam in a straight cut so that it is about one quarter inch above the shank. Taper the sides to eliminate the edges (round off the edges) and trim the thread.

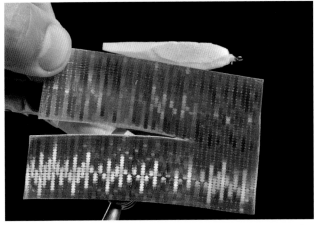

3. Prepare the Sili Skin by precutting the shapes and slits before you peel the backing. This not only makes it easier but keeps the flies cleaner looking.

4. Attach prismatic silver Sili Skin to cover the foam underbelly just as you did with the Gummy Minnow.

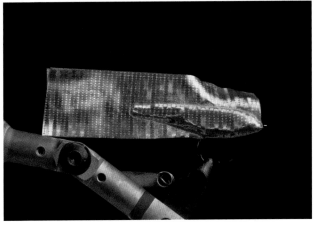

5. Run your fingers along the Sili Skin to remove air bubbles and ensure the material is stuck together. Trim out your shape with scissors.

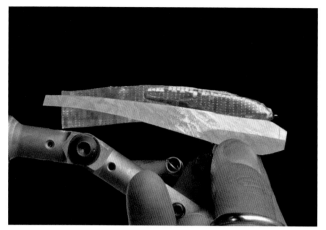

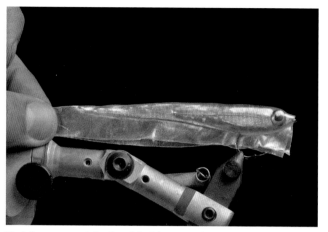

6. Cut the back of the fly from mother of pearl Sili Skin.

7. After you stick the Sili Skin on the fly, color it with a bronze marker or color of your choice and trim the Sili Skin to its final shape.

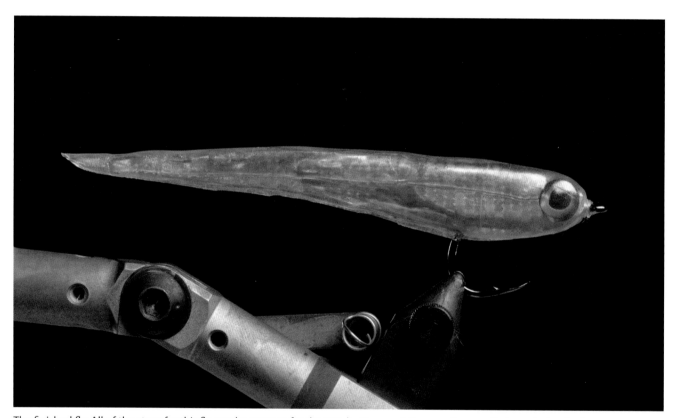

The finished fly. All of the steps for this fly are the same as for the regular Gummy Minnow after you tie in and trim the foam.

Tying the Gummy Changer

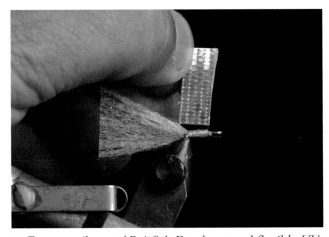

1. Form a tail out of Baitfish Emulator and flexible UV resin on a 10mm shank. Sandwich two 1½-inch-tall pieces of prismatic silver Live Scale Sili Skin together over the shank. Make sure to cut them wide enough to fill out the entire shank.

2. The rest of the shanks in the fly are a stairstep—15mm, 20mm, and 25mm (everything provided in the kit). Apply prismatic silver Live Scale Belly Foam to the remaining shanks. Increase the height of the foam as you increase the size of shank.

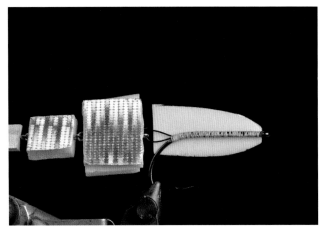

3. Attach the back end to the hook using 26-pound wire. Trim a piece of prismatic silver Belly Foam the shape of the baitfish and then trace that shape onto another piece of foam to match the size.

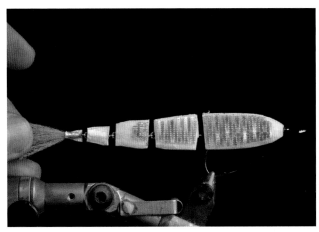

4. After you attach both pieces of foam in the front, trim all of the pieces to a general fish outline. Round off all the edges of the foam.

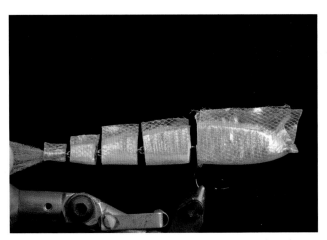

5. Cut five pieces of mother of pearl Live Scale Sili Skin, each piece sized to each section, and attach it from underneath and fold upward.

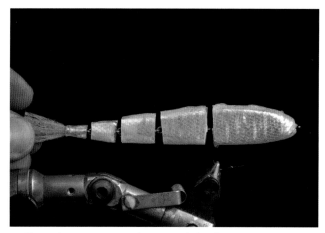

6. Trim the excess on the top of the fly.

7. Cut one long piece of mother of pearl Live Scale Sili Skin for the back. Make it a long, thin triangular shape (from thin to thick) to match the taper of the foam pieces. Cut out the sections. Mark it with your color of choice—here I chose bronze. Attach eyes and coat with flexible UV resin. Trim the tail to shape.

This South Carolina redfish ate a Floating Gummy Changer prototype.

4 | Gummy Spoon Minnow

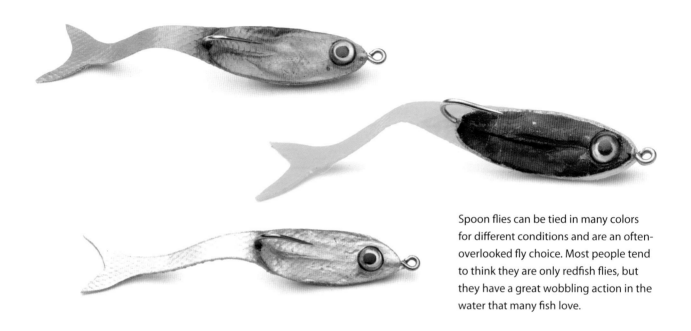

Spoon flies can be tied in many colors for different conditions and are an often-overlooked fly choice. Most people tend to think they are only redfish flies, but they have a great wobbling action in the water that many fish love.

The Gummy Spoon Minnow has a few really good fishing applications and provides an action in the water that is hard to get with any other design that I know of. It offers a couple of key triggers in its design. First it has a minnow shape that can be modified to accurately imitate the baitfish in any given area. Second, it has a wobbling, fluttering action in the water—similar to the action intended by the original spoon flies—that emulate a dying or dead minnow.

A lot of times when stripers, bluefish, false albacore, and tunas are marauding schools of bait, the larger, wiser fish hang underneath the bait, waiting for the scraps to flutter down to them. If you throw this fly into that melee, keeping a tight line as it sinks and having it wobble and fall like a dying bait, you can often hook these fish. I have caught really nice striped bass on this pattern in freshwater lakes, throwing it into busting bait, and I have also caught them in salt water, in shallow and in deep water. The key is letting it fall with a tight line on an intermediate or slow sinking line. Usually you will just feel a tap and the fish is on.

Spoon flies are popular for redfish, and I've caught redfish with this particular fly in South Carolina. Simply let it wobble down and twitch it in front of them and then they will pick it up and eat it pretty readily. I've also had good success with this fly for smallmouth, river stripers, and white bass by dead-drifting it in the currents, adding occasional slight twitches. Cast down and across and the fly will flutter on the swing as the currents move it. Some of my favorite color combinations include chartreuse/purple, copper, and gold for stained or tannic water and prismatic silver to match a lot of silversides and some shad. This is a really good choice for schooling fish feeding during a blitz.

Unlike most conventional spoon flies, which are hard, this one is softer and also incorporates a tail, which I think really helps with the profile. It doesn't get much easier than this fly—just stamp, peel, and stick. The backside view shown below shows the added weight, which, along with how you bend the hook, alters the action as well as the depth at which the fly sinks. Bending the hook in the right place takes some experience, and it will set the tone for how the fly wobbles. You can do it before you tie the fly or in the field. Also, you can add weight for a fly that sinks more or keep it unweighted to have it flutter higher in the currents.

Redfish are notorious for loving spoon flies; however, don't be afraid to try these on other species as well. Gold has produced for me in fresh water for smallmouth bass and stripers and in salt water for redfish.

Tying the Gummy Spoon Minnow

Materials

#1 Mustad 34011, bent | 6/0 chartreuse Veevus | gold Live Scale Sili Skin coated with flexible resin | weight, optional | Ice Living Eyes

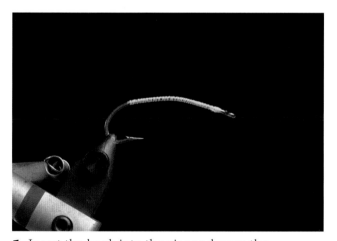

1. Insert the hook into the vise and wrap the shank completely with thread, providing a base for the material and adhesive. Bend the shank at approximately the halfway point to help create the spoon shape and make it wobble in the water. You can bend the hook at the end as well, but I like to do it first.

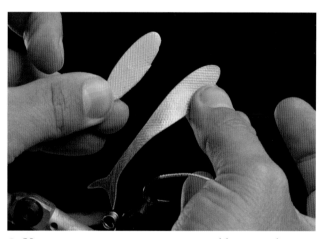

2. Use stamps or cut out your top and bottom shapes. One should be football shaped and the other minnow shaped. I like to use Live Scale Sili Skin because of the textured finish but you can also use regular Sili Skin.

3. Peel the backing from the football-shaped part of the spoon, which is going to be on the underside of the hook. When it flips over, it will be the top. Apply it in the center of the hook, rubbing your fingers against the base of the hook shank over top of the Sili Skin to make sure it adheres evenly from the eye to slightly down the bend.

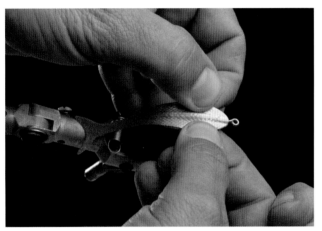

4. Flip the fly over and apply the body part of the Spoon Minnow, which gives you the full silhouette of a baitfish. Squeeze the top and bottom together.

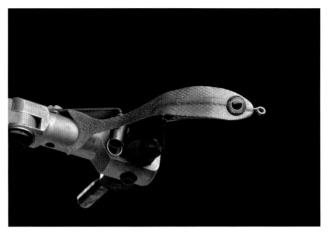

5. Attach an eye to both sides of the fly or just the top side, and then coat with flexible UV resin. This increases the durability of the fly and also enhances its rubbery feel.

The finished fly with the stamps. You can also tie this fly on a shank and then add a trailing hook if you like.

5 | Flypala

The Flypala has stirred up a little controversy, but to me it is more of a fly than a popper because you make everything from scratch. When I demonstrate this fly, people are amazed at how easy it is to create a realistic fly that swims like a Rapala.

The Rapala is a time-tested lure design in the conventional fishing world, and coming up with a fly that achieves the same wobbling action was a big fly-tying goal for me back in the late 1990s and early 2000s. I had flirted with the idea a bit over the years, notably with adding a lip to the early swimbaits I tied with Sili Skin, but I just didn't have the time to refine it. It's not that complicated to build a lip in the front of a fly, but getting it to work with the fly design and also have it able to be cast with a fly rod is a completely different challenge.

It was mid-July 2002, the height of our summer smallmouth season, and I was guiding every day. My wife was nearing the end of her term of pregnancy, and I had a little tying kit packed in case we had a long wait at the hospital. Sure enough, we did. As my wife was in labor, I worked out the initial prototypes of the Flypala by her bedside.

I already had a mental picture of the fly that I wanted to tie. The critical thing for me was just having the time to do it. While guiding, I watch flies swim and watch fish react to them a lot. This gives me a lot of time to think about what works and what doesn't in fly design. I know a lot of tiers that prefer to work out their ideas at the vise, but part of my creative process is to let ideas and concepts marinate for a while and

Kristi Chocklett holds a nice bass that swung for a Flypala. Because of its built-in action, the Flypala is one of my favorite patterns for guiding. The movement in the water from the lip really captures the clients' attention, which means they are actively fishing and focusing on the fly throughout the day.

run through the process in my mind, instead of sitting down at the bench and getting frustrated, just trying to make something happen. I know the ideas will usually come to me in time.

Stretching Sili Skin over a frame of foam opened up a lot of fly-tying possibilities for me, and my mind was racing with different variations on this same theme. For my first attempt, I adhered Belly Foam to both sides of the shank, trimmed out a body shape, and then put Sili Skin over that. I tied the second prototype with Body Tubing. A few years prior, Rich Murphy introduced me to EZ Body, a braided tubing, and I was aware of his method of folding it back over itself to create spreaders and bodies on saltwater striper patterns. Other tiers were using braided tubing coated with epoxy to form bodies. I had experimented with the material a little bit after that but more or less shelved it until this point. The seeds had been sown however, and as soon as I squeezed the Sili Skin against the braided Body Tubing and saw the skin take on the texture of scales, I knew where I wanted to go with this fly.

Body Tubing makes it really easy to create a wide range of shapes with very little cutting. The length of the material combined with the amount of compression dictates the overall body shape. You can easily create bodies to match any bait profile. If you want a broad profile, use a longer piece of tubing; for a narrower profile, use less. The shape of the body, along with the lip, affects how the fly swims in the water. The narrower the profile, the tighter the wiggle on the retrieve. The hollow frame also gives you the flexibility to add things such as beads, rattles, or foam inside.

The lip took a little fine tuning. A hard, solid lip digs into the water when you start your backcast. This creates extra resistance and extra disturbance on the backcast which is not ideal. For the lip on the Flypala, I experimented with several options but finally settled on a hard monofilament such as Mason or fluorocarbon covered with Sili Skin and then coated with UV resin. The result makes the fly swim in the water yet it is flexible enough to fold back on the backcast so that it doesn't dig into the water as much as a solid lip. The lip should not be more than two eye-lengths longer than the hook eye or else the fly will roll. To also combat twisting in the water, I almost always add lead wraps to the hook bend to keel the fly. The longer shank hook that I first tied this fly on still provides the best action. You can add shanks, but a fly tied on them is a little more finicky to keel.

This fly was an important part of my design evolution. The lip provided great movement, and was extremely fun to fish, and I still fish Flypalas today. But I still wanted to try and figure out how to get a swimming action in a fly without a lip by using taper and bulk alone.

This group shot showcases some, but not all, Flypala variations. Note how you can achieve different body shapes very easily and add finishing touches with markers.

Standard long-shank Flypala

Bluegill Flypala

Flypala
with a trailing hook

Brokeback Flypala

Flypala (standard)

Pencil Flypala

Tying the Flypala

Materials

#2 Gamakatsu Octopus | 220-denier white Flymaster | Do-it Corporation shank | three tungsten beads | yellow ¼" Body Tubing | yellow marabou tail with four strands of pearl Flashabou | 60-pound monofilament lip covered with mother of pearl Sili Skin | prismatic gold Sili Skin outer body | mother of pearl Sili Skin back colored olive | Ice Living Eyes

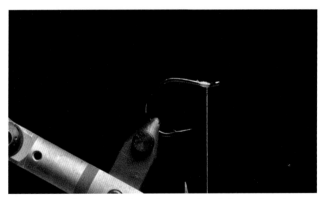

1. Place a short-shank wide-gap hook into the vise and attach the thread just behind the hook eye.

2. Select one marabou plume and measure it so that it is 1½ times the length of the hook shank. Trim the butt ends and place the clump on top of the hook with the fibers extending back approximately half a hook shank's length. Tie it in just behind the hook eye, making sure to keep the wraps directly on top of one another to minimize the amount of marabou that is tied down.

3. Select four to six strands of pearl Flashabou and tie them in on each side of the hook shank just behind the hook eye. Trim the excess Flashabou slightly longer than the marabou. Whip-finish, trim the thread, add UV resin to the head, and cure with a light.

4. Bend one end of a Do-it Corporation shank so you can slide three large tungsten beads onto it. Slide the open end of the shank through the hook eye and insert the bend of the shank into the vise.

5. Attach the thread and wrap it tightly to close the shank. Whip-finish and apply UV resin to the thread.

6. Reattach the thread just behind the eye of the shank, making sure to wrap completely over the front section.

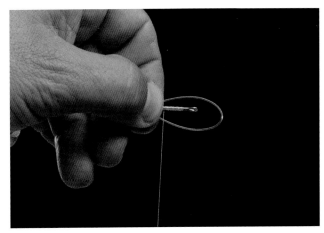

7. Cut a 3-inch piece of 60- to 80-pound stiff monofilament or fluorocarbon. Fold it around the front of the shank so that it extends two to three eye lengths beyond the shank eye. Attach it to each side of the shank, making sure that the mono is square on each side. Make sure the tie-in point is two eye lengths back from the shank eye of the shank.

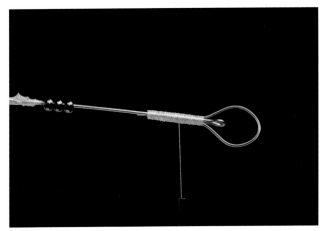

8. Once the loop has been securely tied down round it out with your fingers so that it is symmetrical. Coat the wraps with UV resin.

9. Cut a piece of ¼" Body Tubing 1½ times the length of the shank. The length of the piece can vary depending on the shape of the body you want. Singe each end of the Body Tubing with a lighter to keep it from fraying. If tying a batch of these, cut all the Body Tubing you'll need to save time and for consistency.

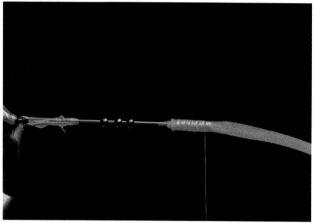

10. Slide the Body Tubing over the eye of the shank and back a quarter inch. Tie it down two eye lengths back from the eye of the shank with firm wraps. I will often add a thin layer of Loctite glue to the shank before sliding the Body Tubing over it. Once the tubing is tied in securely, whip-finish and add UV resin.

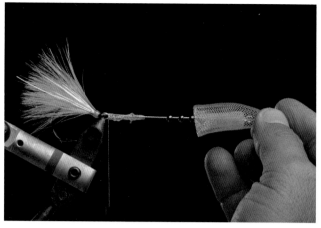

11. Reattach the thread to the very back of the shank. Next push the Body Tubing back, turning it inside out.

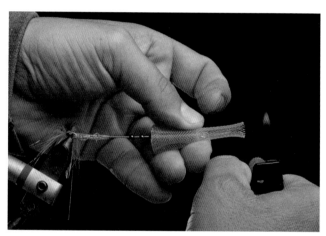

12. Once you reverse the tubing halfway, burn the end of the tubing lightly, being careful not to burn it so much that you close the plastic. Sometimes the end of the tubing where you burned it with the lighter can be hard to push over the Body Tubing. If this happens just pick at the burnt ends until it fits over.

13. Push the remaining Body Tubing back over itself toward the back of the shank. Manipulate the tubing with your fingers to compress it and press on all sides of the body until you get the shape you want.

14. Once you have the right shape, tie it down with tight wraps of thread. Whip-finish and secure with UV resin.

15. The completed underbody should look like this. Massage the tubing with your fingers until you get a nice symmetrical shape.

16. Select a piece of Sili Skin that is 2 inches wide and as long as the entire fly, including some of the monofilament loop. Peel away the Sili Skin's backing a little bit at a time to minimize stretch, starting at the back left corner. Once the backing is removed apply the Sili Skin to the underside of the Body Tubing.

17. Make sure to apply the Sili Skin so that it is centered on the Body Tubing. Rub your fingers along the Sili Skin to firmly press it to the tubing and fold it around the tubing from bottom to top.

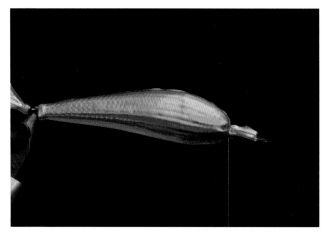

18. Trim the excess on top flush with the back of the fly. Reattach the thread behind the eye of the shank and end of the Body Tubing. Wrap the thread tightly around the Sili Skin and shank keeping the thread wraps directly on top of one another.

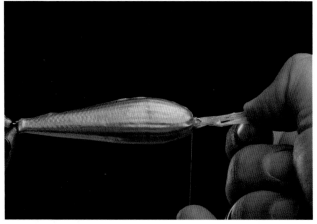

19. After several turns of thread, pull down tight to score the Sili Skin, allowing you to peel it from the mono loop.

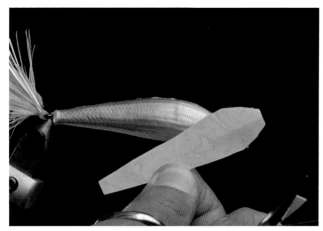

20. Trim a piece of mother of pearl Sili Skin the length of the body. Then cut it in a coffin shape, making sure the width at the front will cover the top third of the back of the fly and taper it toward the tail. Trim the front at an angle to round off the edges.

21. Peel the backing off and start laying the back strap down the middle of the back of the body. Use your finger to help secure it to the body. Trim any excess material hanging over the back and then color the back with marker.

22. Apply flexible UV resin and add eyes.

23. Trim a piece of mother of pearl Sili Skin 1-inch wide by 2-inches long. Peel the backing off and attach the Sili Skin to the top of the mono loop. Make sure to get the skin under the eye of the shank and flush to the front of the head of the fly. Next fold the Sili Skin over and attach it under the monofilament loop. Squeeze the top and bottom together with your thumb and forefinger.

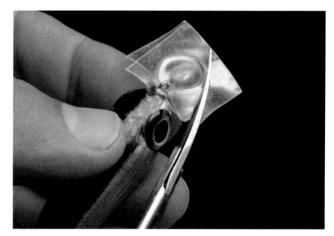

24. Trim the excess Sili Skin from the lip.

25. Apply flexible UV resin to the edges of the lip and to the underside to stiffen the lip.

If you push the Body Tubing forward and pinch it on the sides, you can make a taller slimmer profile much like a shad or bluegill shape.

You can also create smaller diameter pencil poppers with a tighter wobble. I like these when fishing smaller profile baits like silversides or freshwater darters and dace.

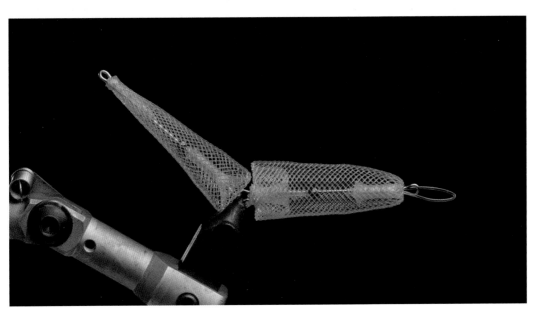

This articulated version of the Flypala draws inspiration from the iconic brokeback Rapala. Though this style of fly takes more work to build, it is worth the effort. I have had many memorable days fishing for trout and bass with it.

6 | T-Bone

The T-Bone gets its name from the way a predator likes to hit its prey—from the side. When you strip and pause a T-Bone, it jackknifes left and right, and it's the side profile that most often draws strikes. Muskies can read, by the way, so all means of persuasion are fair game.

When I was a kid, I loved sleeping over at my grandmother's on Friday nights. I loved her dearly, but my visitation was part of a master plan. We didn't have cable at our house, and she did, so I would wake up early to watch the Saturday morning fishing shows on ESPN. *The Walker's Cay Chronicles* and *The Hunt for Big Fish*—which would come on for five minutes between *Walker's Cay* and Jerry McGinnis's show (*The Fishin' Hole*)—captivated my imagination and showed me that there was a whole world of fish out there beyond the trout and smallmouth that I had been catching. In one episode of *The Hunt for Big Fish,* the exotic sounds of Mongolian throat singing mixed with images of Larry Dahlberg casting large divers to taimen conjured up a sense of excitement, mystery, and awe that I still recall today. At the time I never believed I would make it to Mongolia, but two thoughts occurred to me. One, that I had predators in my own backyard in the form of voracious muskies (I had already had an encounter with one while fishing for smallmouth with my uncle and the fish scared the heck out of me), and two, that I might be able to catch one of them on a fly someday.

My long-time fishing buddy, David Garst, who Harrison Steeves had introduced me to many years ago, introduced me to muskie fishing. Garst had become

Larry Dahlberg, one of my biggest inspirations and heroes, has taught me, and many others, so much about fish behavior and lure and fly design. His knowledge about fishing is second to none.

obsessed with the fish in college and was doing pretty well catching them on conventional tackle. At the time I owned a fly shop and was guiding a lot for smallmouth but I would mark where I saw muskies each day, as they often would chase smallmouth on clients' lines. After a day of guiding for smallmouth, I would meet David at the launch and we'd go out again and try to catch those muskies.

Because I was trying to fly fish for them, Garst would always give me the first shot in the hole. If I was extremely lucky, I could get a fish to move on the fly, but very few fish responded the way they did to his lures. This was back when muskies were unpressured in the river system, and they were abundant and very eager. I'd fish on the bow for an hour and not catch anything; then David would take a turn and move several or catch a couple within an hour—that told me something. I, too, began fishing more conventional tackle to try and learn more about colors, action, and motion in the water that triggered eats from these fish.

As far as fly fishing for them, I knew immediately that I was going to a gunfight with a knife. I didn't have the necessary tools to make it happen. I didn't have the right lines, the right gear, and I certainly didn't have the right flies. I knew that to design an effective fly for muskies, I needed a few things: size, illusion of bulk, disturbance in the water, and enticing movement. Muskies have an amazing detection system through their lateral lines. You can cast a lure 40 feet from them and watch them turn to track it. The most effective lures are the ones that emanate waves under the water, just like the swirl of water caused by someone's legs swimming by you in a pool. An effective muskie fly needed presence—it would have to be noticed from a distance without spooking the fish. The flies we had at the time simply did not push the water in the same way as the large bucktail spinners did, and, for the most part, the fish ignored them.

Around that time there were a lot of exciting things going on in fly tying, especially regarding large saltwater flies. Bob Popovics' approach really opened my eyes and gave me the tools I needed to start creating large flies for my fishery. His first book, *Pop Fleyes,* was hugely influential for me, as were his demonstrations of the Hollow Fleye style of tying that I saw at various fly-fishing shows. The technique of reverse-tying bucktail to give the illusion of mass without adding bulk or weight has, in my opinion, forever changed the pursuit of large predatory fish with a fly. It showed me how I could create the illusion of size in my flies and get them to have more presence in the water.

At the same time, I had been experimenting with foam-disc heads on flies, first in small patterns for smallmouth, but then in much larger sizes for stripers on the Susquehanna Flats. I learned that you could combine sinking lines with floating flies to create interesting actions and that the head design created motion. I combined the large head with a Popovics' inspired profile and then added rooster saddle feathers in the rear for bulk and movement. The rooster saddles tickling in the water have the same effect, I believe, as a curly tail grub, which is kryptonite to a muskie. When all these components came together, the fish seemed to be taking more interest in the flies.

But even though we'd get eats, hooking and landing them was still a problem. I began adding hooks using wire in between them, and noticed that increasing the articulations improved the action. After I lost a few fish when the wire connection failed, I started looking at different ways to connect the hooks. Messing around at my desk one day, I folded over a paperclip and a light bulb came on. I realized I could buy wire and a bender and create my own shanks to connect together. Later, I would meet Martin Bawden at Flymen Fishing Company who helped me refine this idea and design shanks with my specs.

Good friend and fellow guide Jako Lucas holds his personal best muskie taken on a Bucktail T-Bone. All predators—from taimen to muskies—seem to like the T-Bone's profile and action.

Size matters sometimes. John McMinn holds a mid-50s muskie that took a 17½-inch pink T-Bone. Pink is a key color for me.

Now that the articulation was in place, I started refining the flies for different fishing situations. Flies with foam heads weren't right for all fishing applications—even on a fast sinking line they didn't get down in higher or faster water—so I started exploring heads tied with Body Tubing and also using Body Tubing as spreaders in the flies. I had been working a lot with Body Tubing on the Flypalas and knew of Rich Murphy's spreader technique to create lift in a fly, so I began integrating the tubing into the fly. Now I could use the tubing inside of the fly to lift the bucktail and help control taper.

Integrating Body Tubing into the fly does a few things. First, it spreads the material tied directly in front of it and keeps it from compressing in the water while you fish the fly. It also maintains the profile over time, which is a weakness with bucktail flies. Second, the tubing helps you create profile throughout the fly because it affects the material behind it. The farther back you place the tubing over the fibers behind it, the more it will compress them. So by overlapping the preceding fibers less as you move forward

on the shanks, you create increasing height and a tapered profile.

The early flies were super ridiculous in size and had way too much material on them. But that was the only way that I knew how to create bulk. Over time, I have learned to take away as much material as possible to create a fly that still looks big in the water and swims like I need it to. Designing flies that are lighter and easier to cast is an ongoing process in all of my fly designs. Later, the use of synthetic fibers and brushes would greatly simplify the T-Bone, but the original bucktail ones still have a spot in my box. There's always been something magical about the way that bucktail breathes in the water.

The T-Bone Motion

Larry Dahlberg once told me that farm-raised suckers or chubs used as bait for muskies don't work as well as stream borne ones. A lot of times the farm-raised suckers don't get eaten. Why is this? These fish, raised in a relatively peaceful environment where they are fed daily and only have to worry about competing with their brothers and sisters for food, have never met a predator in their lives. When they get in the water, they simply don't act like a resident sucker that has grown up fearful of muskies. When one of these "locals" are on the line, it swims for its life when a muskie comes near, and it gets eaten almost every time. Perhaps this is why I have frequently observed smallmouth bass hanging out with muskies, seemingly content and worry free. As long as they are not acting panicked then they are safe. They haven't done anything to trigger the muskie's predatory instincts. So, what is the lesson? If you want to have your fly get eaten you need to make it swim and jerk like a panicked bait.

The shanks helped me get the length I needed, and they also made the fly move more realistically through the water. By changing the materials in the fly, specifically by altering the head of fly, I discovered that I could get the fly to jackknife in the water. Predatory fish with teeth such as muskies are programmed to attack their prey by grabbing them. The teeth help hold on to the prey item—often, but not exclusively, fish—as well as slice and maim. One of the best ways to grab a large sucker, for instance, is by coming at it from the side. Perhaps the biggest trigger in a muskie fly or lure is a

motion that shows a lot of profile, and the more that you can get your lure to turn like this the better your chances.

The T-Bone is tied to replicate a jerk bait, so whether drifting or anchored, I like a really hard strip with the rod tip in the water and then a pause to allow the fly to turn and show the fish the money shot. Recover a little bit of the slack while you are letting it pause and hang, to maintain contact with the fly, and then make another really long hard strip. The key thing with this fly is showing the fish profile. When they see that profile, they're going to hit it. Gear guys have had the advantage for the longest time, but flies can hover and stay in a fish's face much better than a lure can generally, and sometimes that is what is takes to get a fish to eat.

In the early stages of development, the challenge with the T-Bone was designing the right taper and also matching the head size with the action that I wanted to achieve. The head size dictates how much a fly will jackknife left or right and how much it hovers. The larger and denser the head, the more resistance in the water. And it is this resistance that creates micro eddies behind the fly that help it move in the water. Larger heads tend to hover more, stay higher in the water column, and jackknife more readily. Smaller heads

When the water cools, a slower presentation can be the ticket. On this cold January day, we landed two muskies in short order using a larger-headed T-Bone that suspended better and had more jackknife in the water. This beast ate one of my favorite colors for cold, clear water—chartreuse, gray, and white.

Above: Here is a great example of how wide the turn should be on a proper figure-eight. Keeping the rod down and making long wide turns showing profile longer helps get better reactions from muskies. We often do circles instead of an eight motion.

Right: This photo shows the proper grip and line handling technique while performing a figure-eight maneuver at the boat. It is important to have line in the non-rod hand while figure-eighting in case a fish grabs so that you can strip the line and set the hook. Also holding the butt of the rod with the non casting hand helps to guide the rod through the manipulations but also helps reduce fatigue on your casting arm because the pressure is on the non casting hand guiding the rod around.

sink more quickly. Heads can be created with different materials as well as weighted in various ways. This makes them a critical fly-design element, not just in the T-Bone but for all of my flies.

In muskie fishing you typically get eaten in three spots. The first is within ten strips off the bank or structure. You are fishing straight across current, and your fly is kicking from side to side if you are fishing it properly. Once the current grabs it and starts pulling the fly downstream, you start losing the kick and your chances of a hook up diminish.

The second place is as soon as the fly starts to swing and turns upstream, showing its profile to the fish that may be following. This turn also is accompanied by an increase in speed which is a trigger. This is a short window and once the fly starts to come back

upcurrent and no longer shows profile to the fish I rarely get strikes.

The third place is at the boat, on the figure-eight. Once the fly is at the boat and you make your first turn, you show the fly's profile to the fish for the first time in awhile. Larry Dahlberg pointed out to me that most fish in rivers are going to eat on a downstream turn on a figure-eight. The fish are going to use current to their advantage and can accelerate faster going downstream than they can going upstream.

Tying the T-Bone

Materials

2/0 Gamakatsu B10S (rear) and 5/0 Gamakatsu spinner bait (front) | two 28mm Big Game Shanks for body and 40mm for head | 280-denier olive Flymaster | four pink and olive magnum grizzly saddles for tail | pink and olive bucktail spun around ¼" pink Body Tubing | pearlescent pink Flashabou | ¼" pink Body Tubing covered with mother of pearl Sili Skin and flexible resin | Ice Living Eyes

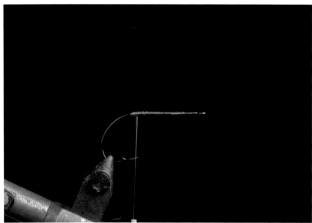

1. Insert the hook in the vise. Attach the thread and wrap a foundation for your materials.

2. Select a clump of bucktail that is approximately twice as long as the hook shank, pull out any underfur, and lay it on top of the hook shank between the barb and hook point. Take two light wraps of thread around the butts and pull straight down, letting go of the bucktail as it spins around the shank. Take a few more tight turns of thread, continuing to flare the bucktail.

3. With your thumbnail and forefinger, squeeze the bucktail to evenly distribute it around the shank.

4. Wrap the thread a few times tightly through the flared butts. This will help secure the bucktail to the hook shank and help keep it from being pulled out by fish or pliers.

5. Select 10 to 12 pieces of pearlescent pink Flashabou. Holding them by the tips, pull out individual strands to create a staggered taper.

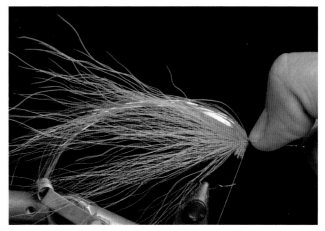

6. Fold the Flashabou around the thread, making sure to have a 75/25 split. This will give a nice taper to the flash. Then tie the folded Flashabou on to the hook just in front of the bucktail, keeping the thread on top of the hook shank. Spread the flash evenly around the top third of the hook shank with your thumbnail.

7. The Flashabou should be evenly distributed around the hook shank and veil the bucktail.

8. Select four long rooster saddle hackles.

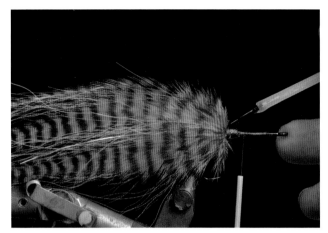

9. Tie them around the bucktail so that they are evenly spaced. Add UV resin to the butts and thread wraps.

10. Select a clump of bucktail about two-thirds the diameter of a pencil and clean out the underfur. You will be adding a lot of material to this fly, so consider that a little goes a long way. The bucktail should be slightly shorter than the first clump of bucktail and extend back over the feathers roughly half way.

11. Just as you did with the first clump of bucktail, flare it around the shank and wrap the thread through the butts to secure it to the shank.

12. Select another 10 to 12 pieces of Flashabou, taper them, and then fold the bunch around the thread with a 75/25 split. Then tie it down and distribute the flash around the top third of the hook shank with your thumbnail.

13. Cut a pencil-width clump of bucktail and pull out the underfur. Reverse-tie it by tying it in so that the tips extend out toward the hook eye. Take a few loose wraps around the butts, leaving a little bit of them exposed, pull tight, and allow the fibers to spin around the shank. The flared butts will be on the inside of the fly after you fold back the fibers.

14. Bring the thread through the bucktail. Push the bucktail back over itself with an old pen casing or your fingers, making sure that the fibers are evenly distributed 360 degrees around the shank.

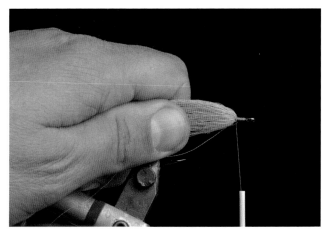

15. While holding the bucktail back, wrap a thread base tight against the base to support the fibers.

16. The fibers should be evenly distributed around the shank and the thread wraps should form a nice, smooth cone to keep the fibers in place.

17. Select two medium long rooster saddle feathers and tie them on each top side of the hook shank. This gives the fly a mottled back color and also helps in its overall movement as it swims. Add UV resin to the thread and feathers.

18. Take the hook out of the vise and slide the hook eye through the back opening of a 12mm Big Game Shank. Insert the shank in the vise. You can wrap the entire shank and close the loop with thread as we will do with some flies in the book, or you can leave the loop open and simply close it with UV resin. If your hook gets dull you can scrape off the resin and reattach a new rear section. Later in the book I will show you how to use a split ring.

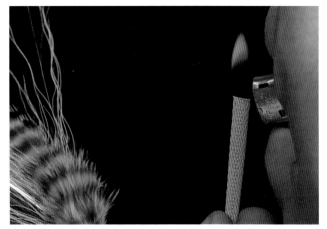

19. Cut a piece of ¼" Body Tubing about 2 inches long. Then singe the end to keep it from unraveling.

20. Tie in the Body Tubing about halfway back on the front shank. Apply a small amount of Loctite to the thread base before sliding the tubing over the shank. This will help secure the tubing to the shank.

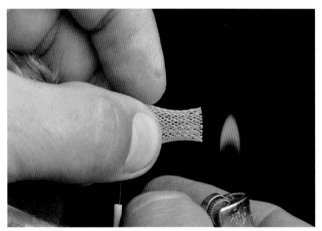

21. Open up the front of the tubing by slightly pushing it backward before you burn the end. Opening it slightly before burning the tips will help keep the tubing open and allow it to slide over itself easier as you reverse it.

22. Reverse the tubing back over itself.

23. Push the tubing forward to the thread tie-in point.

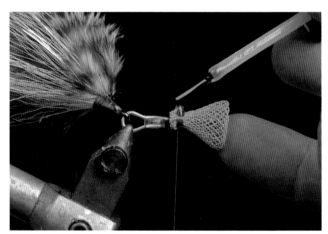

24. Create a trumpet shape and then wrap over the butt ends of the tubing. Add UV resin to the thread wraps and the tubing before or after you clip the thread—it doesn't matter.

25. Fold the tubing back, creating the cone spreader dam. Then reattach the thread in front of the dam approximately one-eighth inch in front of the tubing, forming a slight bump. When you tie in your materials in the valley between the tubing and the bump, the bump prevents your thread from sliding forward and keeps the materials right at the base of the tubing.

26. Cut a clump of bucktail approximately the diameter of a pencil and tie it on top of the shank between the dam and the thread bump. Tie it in as you have done with the other bucktail.

27. Distribute the bucktail around the tubing by simultaneously pushing it with your thumbnail and tightening and loosening the thread tension.

28. Controlling thread tension and tying the bucktail in the valley between the tubing and the thread bump evenly distributes the bucktail around the shank and keeps it in place.

29. Add two wider but shorter rooster saddle feathers or schlappen on each top quarter. This gives more movement to the fly but also imitates the barred back of a fish.

30. Add a 40mm shank, reattach the thread, and wrap a good thread base. This time wrap up over the rear loop to the point shown.

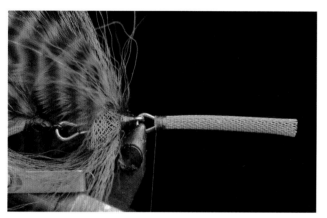

31. Select another piece of ¼" Body Tubing and cut it about 2 inches long. Singe one end and slide it over the shank toward the rear of the shank. Tie it down at the very back of the shank and over the base of the loop, leaving enough room in the loop for the shank behind it to move freely.

32. Singe the other opening to the tubing and reverse it just like before. Tie it off, secure it with resin, and trim the thread. Then reattach the thread in front of the tubing.

33. Select another pencil width of bucktail and flare it around the tubing just as before. This section will be your tallest profile so measure the bucktail so that it is longer than the previous section. Add flash on the top third of the bucktail.

34. Attach another 2-inch section of Body Tubing and reverse it as you have done previously.

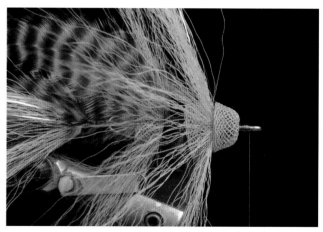

35. Fold the reverse-tied tubing back and reattach the thread. Create a bump of thread about one-eight inch in front of the tubing.

36. Select another pencil width of bucktail and flare it around the tubing. Whip-finish and secure with resin.

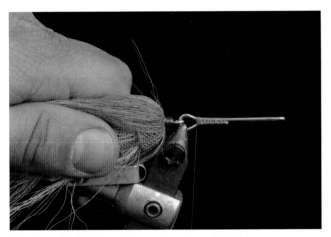

37. Attach the last 40mm shank and tie in your thread, wrapping a good foundation.

38. Tie in two more sections of tubing and bucktail. At this point you can add pectoral fins or not, or add a feather collar.

39. Cut a 3½- to 4-inch piece of ¼" or ½" Body Tubing (if you choose a larger head like the ½" you will have to play around with the length to see what works) and tie it in directly behind the eye of the shank.

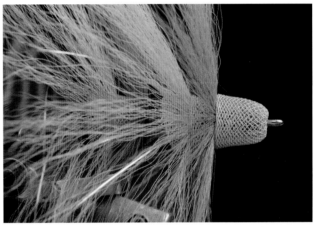

40. Reverse the tubing and tie the thread back in over the top of the previous tie-in point. Then whip-finish and glue the thread and trim. Next fold the tubing back over forming the head of the fly.

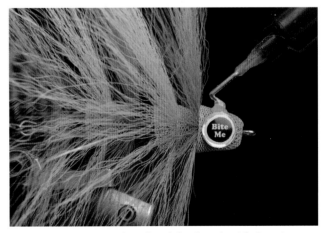

41. Add eyes to each side of the head with Loctite or UV resin, and then cover the entire head with resin.

I hope to make it to all the far-flung places that first captivated my attention as a kid on Saturday morning, but even if I don't, I can take some solace that my flies already have. The T-Bone is now more well-traveled than I am and has accounted for large fish around the world, including this giant Mongolian taimen, caught by Ross Purnell, that appeared on the cover of *Fly Fisherman*.

Marcey Kinkoph (with husband, Rob) shows off her first muskie, which she caught on a gray, chartreuse, and white T-Bone. She made all of five casts before this beauty hit.

T-Bone Variations

Hammerhead. This T-Bone variation, tied with a large foam cylinder head, creates an erratic, big action that can drum up fish. It is tied on a 40mm Big Game Shank and a 5/0 spinnerbait hook.

T-Bone, Single (Fire Tiger). Fire tiger (chartreuse, orange, and black) is one of my favorite color combinations.

Mini T-Bone (Trout). Smaller T-Bones are favorites of mine for brown trout, smallmouth, and largemouth bass, as well as lake stripers when they are on bigger baits. This fly is tied with 20mm and 25mm Fish-Spines and a 1/0 B10S hook. The rooster saddle feathers in the rear, combined with the water-diverting collar, enhance the swimming motion, and the medium Fish-Mask head finishes the fly off nicely.

7 | Synthetic T-Bone

World traveler, guide, and friend Jako Lucas holds a beautiful taimen he caught on a T-Bone style fly tied by our good friend Chris Willen. Jako says that these style flies have changed taimen fishing forever.

The original T-Bone can be tied in very large sizes; however, once you start adding all of that bucktail to shanks, the fly gets very heavy. Additionally, it is difficult to obtain feathers and bucktail long enough, or at least a good enough supply of it. As I searched for a suitable synthetic material that would be lighter than bucktail, I immediately thought of Big Fly Fiber as a possibility. Larry Dahlberg introduced many pike and muskie anglers to Hedron's Big Fly Fiber in the early 1980s when he developed the Dahlberg

Mega-Diver, which is basically an oversized version of his Dahlberg Diver with a long synthetic body. Later, Bob Popovics' Cotton Candy fly, which is a huge fly tied out of Hedron's Big Fly Fiber, was one of the earlier examples for me showing how to create a fly entirely out of synthetics that had more of a three-dimensional look. Whereas Larry's fly had a long tail of Big Fly Fiber to represent general size, Popovics' creation had the overall shape of a large baitfish such as a menhaden or mullet.

Synthetic T-Bone variation tied by Chris Willen. In this example Willen uses EP Fibers Gamechangers Blend, which are long, crinkly, 10-inch synthetic fibers, propped up by Body Tubing spreader dams and an EP Crustaceous Brush head. The EP Fibers have no affiliation with Game Changers or me, but Willen's fly shows that you can use different fibers based on your preferences. Willen often carries scissors in the boat to trim or thin out the fibers if he needs to make some subtle adjustments on the water.

Adapting this material to a platform of shanks and spreaders *a la* the T-Bone was a logical step. Just as with bucktail, I could use the spreader dams to both prop up the material to create height and the illusion of bulk, as well as control the taper for a realistic profile. These flies were much lighter than T-Bones tied with bucktail and had more of a glide in the water. Instead of feathers tickling the currents at the rear of the fly, I swapped Barred Flash, which has the barring but also provides the illusion of motion similar to feathers. Though I probably have a lifetime of feathers, one important benefit of using synthetics is that they are consistent, easy-to-obtain, and affordable.

Flies tied with Big Fly Fiber sink very well and don't hold water, so even giant flies are relatively easy to cast. The translucent fibers pulsate in the water, and the T-Bone design gives this fly great side-to-side movement, similar to a Dahlberg WideGlide lure. Though the flies are giant, the materials collapse easily when the fish eats it. Flies tied in the manner and with this material offer the potential to show fish imitations up to 20 inches, which is sometimes called for when muskie fishing.

One of the things that make Big Fly Fiber so versatile is that it comes in two forms, straight and curled. On the curled fibers, one side has kinky ends and then the fibers smooth out to a taper. This is important because you can use the curled, kinky portion to create bulk and lift in your fly by reverse-tying the fibers. They act very much like the flared butt ends of bucktail do when you are reverse-tying them. Big Fly Fiber also comes in a straight version, which is good for a veiling material as well as in brushes, which I'll cover later.

In this chapter, I show two different styles of fly. The first uses Body Tubing for support and the second one just uses different brushes. The Body Tubing version is slightly heavier than the brush version, however it maintains its shape longer due to the inner structure provided by the tubing dams. I like to have both styles of flies on my boat because they have different actions. The Body Tubing version stalls more in the water than the brush version and has a better jackknifing action, whereas the brush version glides better.

The brush version is not only lighter, but it is also faster to tie once you have prebuilt your brushes. By making your own brushes you can create them with much longer fibers than are commercially available and you can also mix and match materials within the brush to create the effect you desire. For instance you can combine fibers with spring and support with fibers that are longer and softer. The stiffer supporting, or framing, fibers maintain the fly's shape over long periods of use and the softer fibers undulate and flow in the currents. This brush technique will give you a large profile with less mass. The fibers act much like an intertwined pile of branches that take up a lot of space but have relatively little material. In the fly that we tie I use three different styles of brushes to gain volume

Synthetic T-Bones excel in clear water. Along with Hybrid Changers, they have become a staple for me when guiding for muskies in difficult conditions. Eric Stanley gets ready to release his first muskie in a two-muskie day. I knew where the fish would be and Eric sealed the deal on his first cast.

moving forward, increasing the ratio of stiffer SF Fiber to Straight Big Fly Fiber as I move forward, and then integrating Curled Big Fly Fiber in the head for even more lift.

Another design development that transfers to all T-Bones is the split ring. It's frustrating to spend so much time on these flies only to dull the hook on rocks or a few fish. With split rings, you can change out the hook as needed. I prefer a heavy-duty oval-shaped split ring. You can use a circular one, but I feel like the oval-shape helps keep the hook in the right position. Use the heaviest split ring that you can find that will slide through the hook eye easily and not get jammed up. Having a pair of split-ring pliers handy makes this easy.

It's important to mention that while I currently really enjoy tying with Big Fly Fiber, and those are the flies that we feature here, you can adapt a wide range of long synthetic fibers for these flies. Each fiber will have its own characteristics that you will need to evaluate based on the fly-tying and fishing goals you want to achieve, but by using some of the techniques that I show below such as using Body Tubing for spreaders or using UV resin to prop up the fibers, you can achieve great results with a wide range of materials.

This muskie took a Synthetic T-Bone tied with brushes. The brush version is a great jerk bait imitation, and it is an important fly in my box not only for its size (though it can be sized down easily) but for when the fish want a slide and pause retrieve exposing the profile. This fly sheds all water immediately once in the air and is really easy to cast for its size.

Synthetic T-Bone
(Redhorse Sucker)

Synthetic T-Bone
(Fire Tiger)

Materials

Synthetic T-Bone, Body Tubing Version (Redhorse Sucker)
Two 40mm Big Game Shanks | #6/0 Partridge Universal Predator X | oval split ring | brown Flymaster |
¼" white and yellow Body Tubing | white, yellow, and brown Straight and Curled Big Fly Fiber | Hedron
Holographic gold flash and Barred Grizzly in orange | grizzly brown hen pectoral fins | 2" Sculpting Flash
Fiber Brush | Chameleon or Renzetti Molded Moon Eyes (Ghost)

Synthetic T-Bone, Brush Version (Fire Tiger)
Two 40mm Big Game Shanks | #6/0 Trokar Flippen | 6/0 orange Veevus | chartreuse Supreme Hair tail
| sunrise Curled Big Fly Fiber | chartreuse SF Flash Blend, orange Straight Big Fly Fiber, pearl green
Hareline Ripple Ice Fiber brush | Fire Living Eyes

Tying the Synthetic T-Bone with Tubing

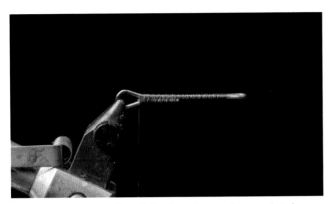

1. Insert a 40mm shank in the vise and completely wrap it with thread, closing up the rear loop to the point shown.

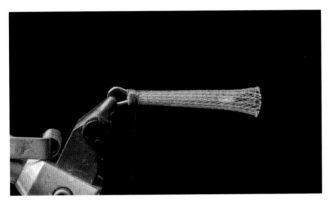

2. Create a rear spreader exactly as you have done with the T-Bone. Cut a 1½-inch-long piece of ¼" Body Tubing and singe the back end. Add a little bit of glue to the very back of the shank, then slide the tubing over the glue and tie it down, keeping the wraps directly over one another. Singe the other end of the tubing.

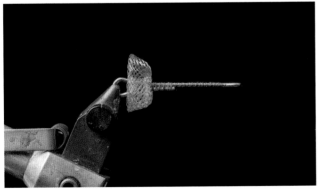

3. Fold the tubing back over itself, secure it with thread wraps, and trim the thread after applying glue or UV resin. Reattach the thread in front of the tubing.

4. Attach a clump of Curled Big Fly Fiber in the middle of the curly part, which will push up against the Body Tubing when you reverse-tie the fibers and create support and the illusion of mass. This also creates a hollow section where we will add a split ring and hook once the fly is complete.

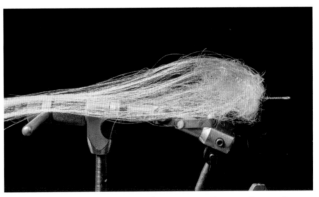

5. Fold back the Big Fly Fiber. You only need to take a few thread wraps in front of the fibers to get them to stay in place.

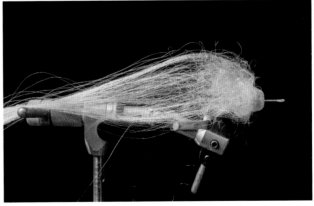

6. Tie in another Body Tubing dam just like you did the first one. Make sure the rear portion of the dam stops just in front of the reversed Big Fly Fiber, helping to hold its shape.

7. Tie in another section of yellow Curled Big Fly Fiber in front of the dam, just as you did with the first hank.

8. Reverse-tie the fibers and comb them back with a dog brush to help distribute them 360 degrees. Look how much profile you have already achieved on the fly. Big Fly Fiber can be a little bit unruly, but once you comb through the fibers and get them going in the right direction, it will start to flow nicely. It is a longer material that tends to hang and droop in the vise, so use a materials clip if you have one.

9. Add some flash (here, Holographic Gold from Hedron) if you like. Wrap it around the thread and pull it to the hook shank. After you tie it in, use your thumb to spread it over the top half of the shank.

10. Tie in another Body Tubing spreader.

11. Finish this section of the fly with a sparse amount of brown Curled Big Fly Fiber and some Hedron Barred Flashabou. The Barred Flash flows well with the Big Fly Fiber and adds dimension and also adds mottling similar to that on the back of a sucker, a prime food source for muskies.

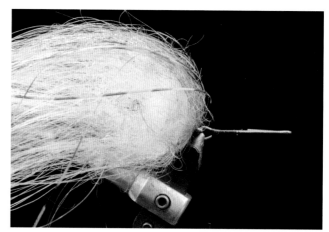

12. Run a 40mm shank through the eye of the previous shank and then attach it to the vise. Attach the thread, and close up the rear loop.

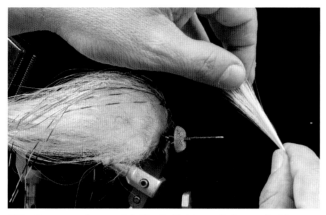

13. Create a dam with Body Tubing. Select a half pencil's diameter of Straight Big Fly Fiber and hand taper it by pinching the fibers in your dominant hand about two inches from the ends. Then with your other hand pull the middle pieces a little at a time to create a taper.

14. The fibers should look similar to this when you are done. Hand-tapering the fibers helps with the final taper when they are tied in and then folded back over.

15. Attach the tapered Straight Big Fly Fiber to the shank right in the middle of the fibers. Before folding it over, manipulate the fibers 360 degrees around the shank with your thumb. Wrap the thread forward, roughly one-eighth inch.

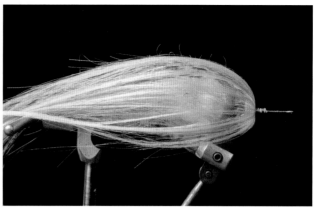

16. Fold the fibers extending over the forward portion of the shank, distribute them 360 degrees around the shank with your fingers, and while holding them in position tie them down. Make sure to press the fibers all the way up against the Body Tubing. If you don't do that, you are not going to create the hollowness that you are seeing in the photo. The thread wraps have to butt up right against the Body Tubing so that the fly holds its shape. Also that material provides a platform for the next section of Body Tubing.

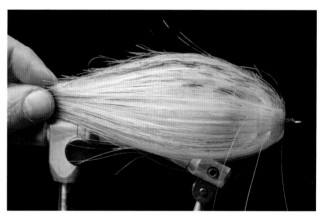

17. Repeat these same steps with yellow and then with brown Straight Big Fly Fiber. Add the barred flash.

18. Front view showing the three-dimensional body. Notice the fuselage shape we have created so far.

19. Attach another 40mm shank, a Body Tubing dam, and then another hank of Straight Big Fly Fiber. At this point we are starting to shorten our tapers. By shortening your tapers, you are also creating height because the fibers are going to want to stand up more as they get shorter instead of fall over and get flat. In the rear of the fly we folded over a 24-inch piece to get 12-inch sections. Here you are using a 12-inch piece, so you have two 6-inch sections once folded.

20. Repeat previous steps with a 12-inch hank of brown fibers. Add pectoral fins, making sure to leave plenty of room for your brush head.

21. Tie in the dubbing brush, and wrap it in tight turns so that you get as dense a head as possible. Comb out the wraps on every full turn. Continue to

wrap until you get to the hook eye and tie off and trim the thread and whip-finish.

22. Trim the dubbing brush to the desired head shape. This can vary depending on the type of bait you are trying to emulate. For this fly I am holding the scissors at a 45-degree angle and trimming 360-degrees around.

23. Mark the trimmed head with different shades of brown Copic markers or whatever waterproof marker you like. A lot of times, I'll match the color schemes of suckers, fall fish, or shad. Notice the head design has an arrow shaped taper. This aids in the swimming action as water will ramp up the head and cause the fly to kick and slide.

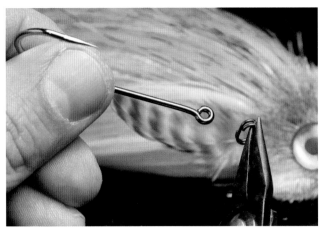

24. For the hook on this fly, I like a longer shank wide-gap hook such as a Partridge Predator X (shown), a spinner bait trailer hook, or a Gamakatsu heavy cover worm hook. Open a split ring with your pliers.

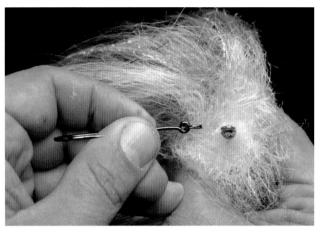

25. Attach your hook with a split ring to the rear of the back loop connection of the shank.

Normally, you wouldn't see the hook at all in this fly, but we dropped it down just to show the interchangeable hook. It is designed for giant muskies, and having a hook in the middle is important for fish that T-Bone this fly.

Tying the Synthetic T-Bone with Brush

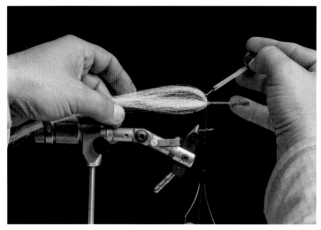

1. Insert the hook into the vise and wrap a thread foundation on the shank. Select a pencil-width diameter of chartreuse Supreme Hair and hand taper it. Tie it in so that 60 percent of it extends off the back of the hook. Fold the shorter fibers pointing toward the eye of the hook back over the longer fibers, and take a few thread wraps in front. Use a little bit of flexible UV resin at the tie-in point to help the fibers maintain their lift.

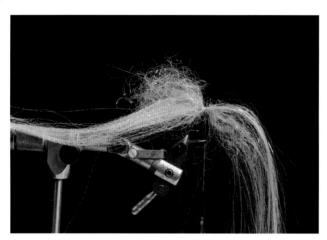

2. Tie in a pencil-width diameter of Curled Big Fly Fiber in the middle of the curly part of the fibers and reverse-tie them. Spread the fibers 360 degrees around the hook and take several thread wraps. Using the natural kink, or curl, of the fibers creates lift and profile.

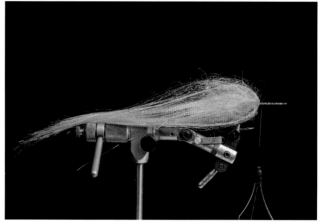

3. Comb the fibers back to help evenly distribute them around the fly. At this point you can also add more flexible resin at the base of the tie-in point of the fibers to help maintain profile over time. The curly fibers provide a good foundation for the brushes to come and starts our taper.

4. Tie in your first brush. This brush consists of Ripple Ice Fiber, SF Flash Blend, and Straight Big Fly Fiber. I like to make this brush wispy and as sparse as possible because when you wrap forward you are going to create a lot of bulk. I want to stair-step the brushes as I move forward, so for this first one I want the back brush fibers to extend two-thirds over the tail section. As I wrap it forward, all the fibers will stand up and provide a lot of body without the need for Body Tubing.

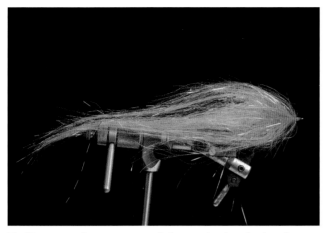

5. Once you have wrapped the entire hook shank with the brush, secure it, and trim the excess with wire cutters. Whip-finish and clip the thread. Pick out the fibers with a bodkin and brush the fibers with a fine-tooth comb to sweep them back and blend them. Add UV resin to the thread wraps.

6. Attach a 40mm shank through the hook eye and insert it into the vise. Wrap a thread foundation on the shank and tie in the next brush at the back of the shank. For this brush I like to add more SF Flash Blend to the mix so that it is bulkier and somewhat stiffer. You want this brush to be 25 to 30 percent shorter than the previous brush to help create taper and prevent trimming.

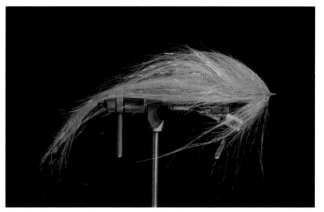

7. Spiral-wrap the brush forward and tie it off at the eye. Trim the wire with cutters, whip-finish, trim thread, and add UV resin. Pick out the fibers with a bodkin or fine-tooth comb as you have done in previous steps. Notice the height and profile created so far.

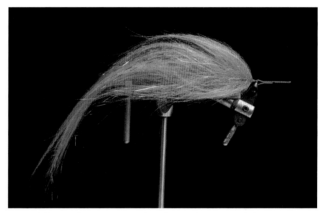

8. Add another 40mm shank to the eye of the previous shank and place it in the vise. Attach your thread and wrap the shank to provide a good foundation for the fibers to grip to.

9. Tie in the third brush that incorporates SF Flash Blend as well as the butt ends of the Curled Big Fly Fiber to aid in the lift and profile of the fly. Wrap this brush two-thirds of the length of the shank, tie it off, and clip with wire cutters.

10. Tie in a pair of short, wide rooster saddles for the pectoral fins on each side of the fly. Make sure to make them long enough to be noticed. Then tie in a 2" Flash Blend Baitfish Brush and wrap it tightly forward to the eye of the shank and tie off and trim the excess brush. Clean up the thread wraps, whip-finish, and add resin.

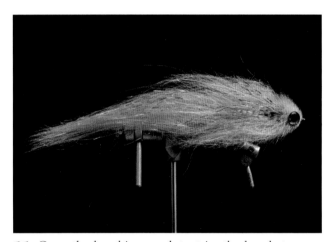

11. Once the head is complete, trim the head at a 45-degree angle, 360 degrees around. Add eyes and secure with UV resin.

Building a Brush

Each brush table is different and should come with detailed instructions that are beyond the scope of this book. In this tutorial, the main things that I want to emphasize are the ratios and blends of different materials to create a brush that works well for these styles of flies.

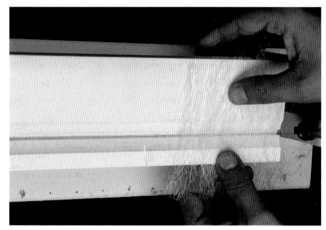

1. Cut the 12-inch hank of SF Flash Blend into three or four equal parts and spread them evenly on the table. This will help keep the brush even and clean when we start the spinning process.

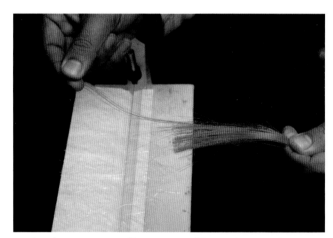

2. Apply a very small amount of Straight Big Fly Fiber, making sure to equally distribute it. The brushes don't have to be super thick, so less is better. Since you are wrapping the brushes on the shanks, you can control the bulk with the number of wraps rather than creating bulky brushes.

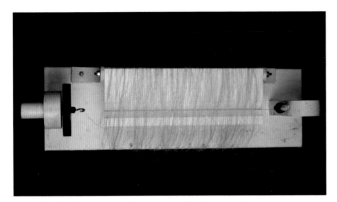

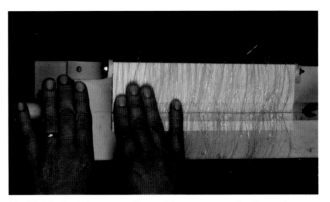

3. A little bit goes a long way. It is very important to evenly distribute the sparse amount of Big Fly Fiber. Adding SF Flash Blend to it gives you a stiffer support fiber that provides height and profile.

5. Hold the fibers on the table as you spin the wire. Once the wire starts to spin consistently, take your hands off the table, drop the tray, and allow the fibers to spin around the ball bearing.

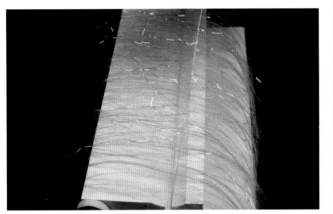

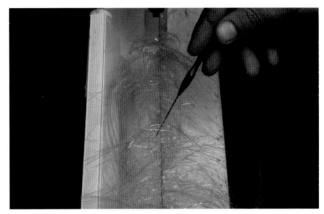

4. Now apply a little bit of Ripple Ice Fiber. This helps to give more life to the fly as light reflects off it in the water. Sometimes flash is not needed or needs to be toned down when dealing with clear water and pressured fish. This is what all three materials should look like. Fold over the wire.

6. As you spin the brush, stop periodically to pick out the fibers with a bodkin to keep them from being trapped under one another. Once the brush is nice and even with no gaps, stroke the fibers with a dog brush to finish freeing the trapped fibers and smooth out the brush.

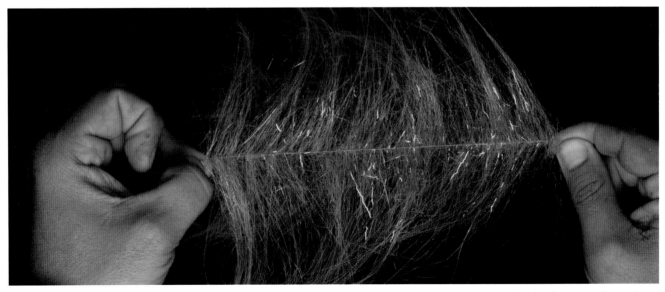

The final brush should be well blended and should have no trapped fibers so that it wraps evenly on the shank. Always comb out the brush at the end to ensure all materials are exposed and clean.

Synthetic T-Bone Patterns

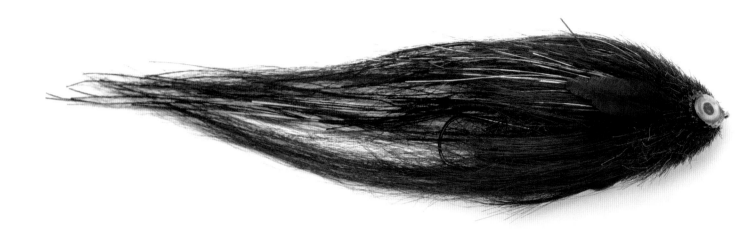

Synthetic T-Bone (Black and Red). This color combination tied with black Curled and Straight Big Fly Fiber and midnight black 2" Flash Blend Baitfish Brush was terrific for northern pike in Saskatchewan. Black is a good color for more educated, highly pressured fish as well, and I seem to get more big fish on this color than any other.

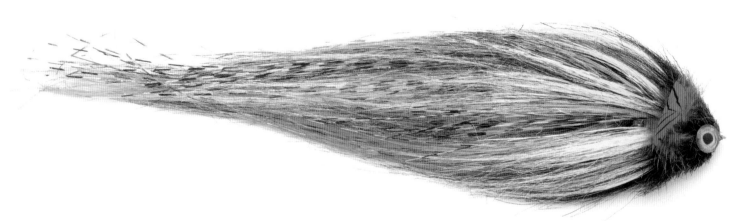

Synthetic T-Bone (Fire Tiger). This variation tied with orange, chartreuse, and black Curled and Straight Big Fly Fiber is one of my go-to colors on bright days or in clear water. I'm not exactly sure why this color combination works so well, but it does, perhaps because it matches sunfish or perch species.

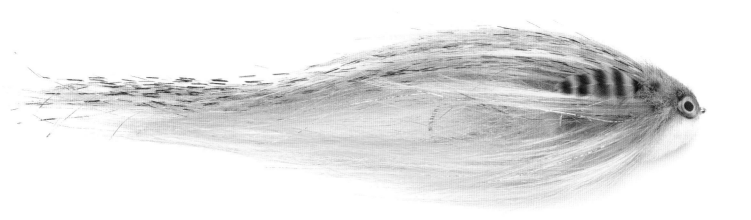

Synthetic T-Bone (Sucker). This natural looking color combination was designed to imitate one of the muskie's favorite foods. This fly is tied with yellow Curled Big Fly Fiber for the tail, olive and yellow Straight Big Fly Fiber, and a white EP Brush head colored with olive marker.

Synthetic T-Bone (Natural). This is another natural, clear water color that can represent anything from suckers to smallmouth bass. Matching the neutral colors in clear water is always a good choice when targeting difficult fish. This tubing version is tied with white Curled Big Fly Fiber and white and olive Straight Big Fly Fiber, and white EP Brush head colored with olive marker.

8 | Finesse Changer (Game Changer Chenille)

I developed the Finesse Changer for pressured smallmouth in clear water but it works for a host of other species that become selective to small baits.

As a full-time guide on the James, New, and Roanoke River systems in Virginia for trout, bass, stripers, and muskies, the success of my business is determined by how well my anglers do on a day-to-day basis. Of course, a number of factors such as weather, water temperature, water clarity, and angler experience can come into play, and I don't have any control over those. However, I can control the fly I put on the end of my client's line.

Over the years I have guided many light-tackle spin anglers, and lures that consistently perform have a swimming action such as the Sebile Magic Swimmer or the movement of soft plastics such as Zoom Flukes, which dart through the water and can also hover, much like a dying or struggling fish. A predator, whether a lion on the African plains or a smallmouth bass in your local river, is programmed to eat or kill something that acts like it is wounded, dying, or easy to get. And when you show a large brown or a muskie something that moves with a start-and-stop motion, has a struggling jerk and twitch, and kicks and falls like a dying bait, you now have that fish's attention.

The movement and success of conventional lures were the starting point and foundation of my obsession to design a fly that would react in the water the way a dying or injured baitfish would. When I was first introduced to the Zoom Super Fluke, I knew I needed to come up with a fly-rod equivalent. From the time that I began guiding for smallmouth, I had in mind a fly that would swim like a conventional lure. I tried using materials behind the fly such as Chuck Kraft's chamois tails and Sili Skin, and I even tried tying them on bead chain and cut tubes strung together on wire or braid, but nothing would achieve the serpentine swimming action that I was looking for.

Lots of water has flowed under the bridge since I started trying to make the fly that I envisioned. I think Thomas Edison said it best: "I haven't failed—I've just found 10,000 [light bulbs] that won't work." After many years of attempts and failures, I, too, found many ways *not* to make a fly that moved the way I wanted, but some good came out of it. For instance, when I

designed the Gummy Minnow I was actually trying to design a realistic imitation of a swimming baitfish-type fly similar to the lures and soft plastics conventional anglers do so well with. While the Gummy looked real, and felt real, and turned out to be a super fly for many game fish, it didn't have the swimming action I was looking for.

Building the Motion

After many failed attempts, I finally had an epiphany. I went back to the roots of what makes a fish swim. First, a fish is powered by its muscles. Second, they move and change direction with their fins aided by their muscles. Third, and most importantly, all of their movement starts with their spine and vertebrae. Stripping line would provide the muscle, and I knew I could place and manipulate material to fill the role of fins. But, I was stumped on the spine. While articulated flies have been tied for years, I was looking for something that would be faster and easier than tying on tubes or broken hook shanks. To really get what I wanted I needed a series of short connections of wire (vertebrae) to form a platform on which I could build a body.

This nice South Holston brown came off a log jam and took an original Game Changer during high water generation. After the cast, I let the 300-grain sinking line sink and retrieved the fly with an erratic strip and pause, making the fly appear to be a wounded and dying baitfish.

Long-time client and friend Gary Swank with a very large smallmouth that took an original Game Changer tied with Body Wrap.

Good buddy, fly tier, and angler Cory Sodikoff holds a great fall lake striper. Not much can beat watching stripers push shad up to the surface in big bait balls. Casting in to the melee takes a steady hand and patience, as most anglers instinctively want to strip fast. A tight-line fall and twitch is most often a much better ploy.

Martin Bawden at Flymen Fishing Company was already making specially designed shanks for Greg Senyo's steelhead and salmon flies. I went to him with my request and together we designed a series of stainless-steel shanks in four lengths (10mm, 15mm, 20mm, and 25mm) that would provide the backbone for Game Changers. This series of shanks—available as a complete system that contains all the sizes (Articulated Fish-Spines) or in packages of individual sizes—can be easily daisy chained to one another to create a backbone for flies with a wide range of swimming motions and sizes.

In addition to the series of interconnected shanks, the other keys to the Game Changer's swimming action are the head shape and body construction. The head of the fly is what starts the serpentine swimming action. From guide, fly designer, and writer Henry Cowen (who interviewed a lure designer at SPRO), I learned that for a lipless fly to swim like a conventional swimbait, it must have a solid or dense arrowhead shape that pushes water out and away from the body. The body and head must be constructed of a material that resists water—the water must have something to push against to start the side-to-side action. The narrower the body, the tighter the wiggle; the broader and denser the body, the wider the wiggle. Now I had the

insight I needed to move forward, which was confirmed through trial and error testing.

The Game Changer has evolved to become a fly-design style, not a specific fly pattern, and I create Game Changers with different materials for different species and situations. So far, the Game Changer in its different iterations has caught many different species of fish all over the world—from trout to roosterfish.

Finesse Fishing

The original Game Changers were first tied with Body Fur, then with Chocklett's Body Wrap. Body Wrap was a huge improvement over the Body Fur, and I was able to create dense flies that swam extremely well. The tradeoff for that excellent swimming motion was that flies were heavier because they trapped more water. Game Changer Chenille was a major breakthrough because it allowed swimming action but shed much more water making the fly easier to cast throughout the day.

Creating a dense head in the front of the fly really helped the fly swim with a serpentine action. On the pause it darts to the left and right. The ability to swim as well as jackknife became the signature movement of the Game Changer. However, the new materials

Sight-fishing to large redfish is as fun as it gets on fly rod. It is a great time feeding them a Game Changer, teasing them into eating. The reactions you get from the fish are priceless.

Game Changer Fishing Tips

The Game Changer design makes fishing the fly easy, and it can be mesmerizing watching it dart and swim back to you. One of the best things about this fly is that normal strips swim and wiggle the fly, but when you pause the fly it hovers, kicks, and falls horizontally. I'm always experimenting with retrieves to find what the fish like best, but I often do a start-and-stop retrieve or short strips with a long strip thrown in. Make sure to pause the fly after several strips as this is where most strikes seem to occur.

Sometimes you want movement without moving the fly too far. This often applies in a situation where you want to keep the fly in prime water for the maximum period of time. If you stripped it out quickly, you never really give the fish a fair chance to see the fly. One trick that I often do with muskies is to jig the Game Changer with the rod tip. Once the fly is in the zone, downstream of the boat, simply twitch the fly with your rod tip and let the current pull line from the guides after each twitch. This way you get movement with the fly while still keeping it in the zone and not bringing it back to the boat too quickly. Strikes can be violent on the Game Changer. It is important to wait when you see the strike before setting the hook with a strip set because the fish tend to rush the fly and overrun it, causing slack. To get a solid hook up, let the fish turn away before you set to avoid pulling the fly out of its mouth and try to strip a lot of line. ∎

provided another unique action. Flies tied with the Game Changer Chenille would fall horizontally like a dying bait, not head or tail first, but simply suspend and drop, which kept them in front of fish for a longer period of time. Their smaller size (under 5 inches) also helped when the fish seemed put off by larger patterns. Even though we tend to think that big fish eat big flies, smaller patterns still have a place.

Finesse Body Chenille, the latest chenille that I developed, takes finesse fishing to an even higher level because the material doesn't have any flash in it. Both Game Changer Chenille and Finesse Body Chenille have applications, depending on the style of fly that you want to tie. Both of the materials take marker extremely well, allowing you to match any naturals in the water you are fishing.

You can also create homemade brushes of Baitfish Emulator, which is very similar to Game Changer

Chenille, or brushes tied with Finesse Fibers, which is the same material in Finesse Body Chenille, but it comes in hanks with longer fibers. I'll use these materials when I want flies that are larger than the 4 to 5 inches that you can get with the chenilles.

When wrapping the Game Changer Chenille a few tips help in the construction of a fly that swims best. First, make sure that each wrap is tight up against the previous wrap. If you leave gaps, you won't be able to create the density that you need. Second, apply a good amount of tension as you wrap so that the fibers flare for more body. It also compresses the core more that allows you to wrap tighter together. The denser the body, the less water can flow through, which gives you better swimming action. Lastly, after every few wraps, pick out the trapped fibers with a bodkin and use a brush or comb to remove any underwrapped fibers and fill in gaps.

Opposite page: 1) During summer's low water, it is possible on my home waters to sight-fish flathead catfish with Game Changers. Once the fly sinks to the bottom in front of the fish let it sit just in front of their face, twitching the fly ever so softly. Not all fish will eat the fly, but enough do to make this technique viable. **2)** Many days in the summer when the water is low and clear, top water is the go-to fishing technique. However, there are times when they are not interested in surface flies and the Finesse Changer is my backup plan when things get tough. **3)** Fall lake stripers can be as finicky as any permit or muskie at times. Finesse Game Changers are the ticket fished slow on intermediate lines. As they fall on a tight line, you only strip enough to take in any slack and feel the take. **4)** Angler and friend Smoot Carter holds a giant false albacore that I caught on an outing off North Carolina's Outer Banks. The translucency of the Finesse Game Changer and realistic swimming motion proved irresistible to the sight-feeding albies. Game Changers outperformed Gummy Minnows that day, which was an interesting experiment in motion versus realism. **5)** This prespawn largemouth fell for a Finesse Changer fished through the edges of weed pockets with quick, short strips followed by long pauses.

Finesse Changer Patterns

Finesse Changer (Black). Black is an excellent color for stained water. This one highlights the Eastern Trophies Game Changer Tail, which is a premade tail made out of suede.

Finesse Changer (Red and White). This is a classic color combo tied with a Baitfish Emulator tail and white and red Game Changer Chenille that I like to use as a searching pattern in stained water. It's also been good for me early in the season chasing spring-run stripers.

Finesse Changer (Bonefish Tan). This clear-water pattern tied with bonefish tan Game Changer Chenille is one of my go-to colors for when fish—everything from snook to smallmouth—are being fussy and they don't want something bright.

Finesse Changer (General Baitfish). This is a favorite color scheme that matches many baits in freshwater rivers. Clear Game Changer Chenille can be marked in a wide variety of colors.

Finesse Changer (Peanut Bunker/Shad). I use this particular color anywhere an area has shad or baby bunker. This fly is tied with homemade brushes of Baitfish Emulator, which look and act very similar to Game Changer Chenille.

Finesse Changer (Sucker). This sucker pattern uses Baitfish Emulator and demonstrates how to make a larger, longer bait with seven longer 15mm spines.

Finesse Changer (Shad). I like to use this fly, tied with Baitfish Emulator, for freshwater stripers in lakes. Grizzly chickabou makes a realistic tail.

Tying the Finesse Changer

Materials

Five 10mm Fish-Spines | #2/0 Gamakatsu SL12 |
6/0 white Veevus | 30-pound Berkley nylon-coated wire
| Baitfish Emulator tail | clear Game Changer Chenille |
gray, olive, and purple markers | Ice Living Eyes

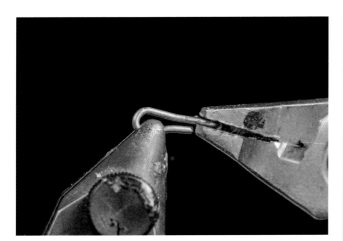

1. Insert a 10mm shank in the vise at the lower bend at the bottom turn of the shank. Grip the shank with pliers and work it back and forth to break it in half at the apex of the bend. You can also use wire cutters. Flymen now has Tail Shanks that come without a rear loop that make this step easier.

2. Reinsert the broken shank into the vise. Start the thread behind the eye, build a thread base back to the end of the shank, and then wrap back toward the eye. These thread wraps are important and provide a good base for the materials.

3. Cut the fibers from the core of the Baitfish Emulator Flash. Baitfish Emulator is translucent, has subtle flash, and wispy fibers that when coated with a flexible UV resin looks, feels, and acts like a real tail in the water.

4. Make sure to use the appropriate amount of material for the tail so that the proportions match the overall baitfish size. Tails on fish are generally thin and translucent not thick and bulky. Tie the Baitfish Emulator to the front of the shank and wrap back to the end toward the vise jaw, making sure to use the entire shank. Fan the fibers to get the general tail shape that you want for the pattern. Then apply flexible UV resin to the material with a brush applicator.

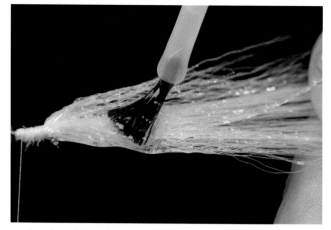

5. Apply a liberal amount to the material starting at the junction of the shank and tailing material and working back to the end.

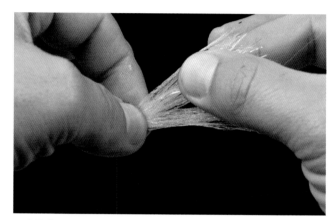

6. With your thumb and forefinger, stroke the resin through the tailing material starting at the junction of the shank and tailing material to ensure the resin is evenly distributed through the tail. With your fingers, shape the fibers into a fan shape as you simultaneously saturate the fibers with resin. When you are happy with the rough shape, cure the resin with the light.

7. At this time, I only trim the tail to even it up and get rid of the excess material.

8. The tail can be done in many ways and in many shapes. I have found that oversizing tails helps with extra swimming action. Experiment—you can make imitative tails or use a wide range of designs and products that add different movements.

9. To finish the tail section, take a 3-inch piece of Game Changer Chenille, trim some of the fibers from the core to expose a tie-in point, and tie it to the back of the shank.

10. Wrap the chenille with a good amount of tension and make sure each wrap is tight against the core. As you wrap, fold the fibers back with your fingers to minimize the amount of trapped fibers. After you have finished wrapping a section, pick out any trapped fibers with a bodkin.

11. Wrap the chenille to the eye, whip-finish, and apply UV resin.

12. Begin trimming the tail. Make your cut at about a 35- to 45-degree angle and trim toward the base of the tail fin. Always trim from front to back on the top and bottom of each section moving forward. Once the top has been trimmed, flip the vise over and trim the bottom.

13. The sides should be cut from back to front at a 20-degree angle (angling out). By adding a slight outward angle you are building taper into your fly and making the fly three dimensional.

14. Once you cut the top, bottom, and sides at this angle, the wrist of fish (the part of the fish before the tail) is done.

15. Connect another 10mm shank through the previous shank eye. Then place it in the vise and attach a thread base, wrapping the thread to the apex of the bend. On all the shanks, if you wrap too far back you will impede the movement of the shanks. If you stop the thread wraps too far forward of the apex you will have undesirable gaps between the sections.

16. Attach the Game Changer Chenille to the middle of the apex of the back opening of the shank. By doing this you are closing the gap between the two shanks allowing the chenille to veil over the previous section. The end result makes the two sections look as one.

17. Wrap the chenille tightly forward to the eye, tie it off, and clip the excess. Whip-finish and then coat the thread wraps with UV resin.

18. Trim the top and bottom from front to back at roughly a 35- to 45-degree angle. It's very important to trim each section as you go to get the cleanest and seamless looking flies. This allows you to eliminate any gaps between the sections, and you can stair step the shape of the fly as you go from the tail to the head.

19. Trim the sides as you did the back section—at a slight 20 or so degree angling outward. Remember to cut from back to front on the sides. You can change the angle based on the overall profile you want to achieve. Sharper profiles will produce broader flies.

20. Slip another 10mm spine through the eye of the previous shank and insert it into the vise. Attach the thread and Game Changer Chenille and wrap it forward to the eye.

21. Whip-finish and add resin or glue to secure the thread wraps. Take note that we are still stair-stepping our way forward creating profile, trimming top and bottom and sides at the same angles.

22. Repeat the previous steps. Insert another shank, and attach and wrap the chenille. Trim a little less as you move forward to gain height and maintain the taper you have established.

23. Look at the overall taper of the fly at this point. There's a nice profile and taper and the body of the fly looks as if it is one piece instead of four.

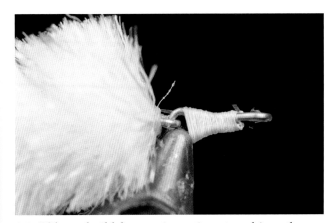

24. I like to build five or six sections to achieve the minimum amount of movement that I prefer. Starting the chenille at the apex of the rear connection loop on each shank helps achieve that seamless look.

25. The last section of this fly is tied and trimmed the same as the previous with very little trim work. It is important to add UV resin to the thread wraps after you whip-finish each section for maximum durability. These flies are time consuming to tie but I expect to be able to use them for many outings.

26. Thread position on the shanks is very important. If you wrap too far back you close the rear loop and impede the movement of the shanks. If you stop the thread wraps too far forward of the apex you will have undesirable gaps in the sections.

27. Insert the hook into the vise. Select a 3-inch section of 30-pound nylon-coated wire. Tie in the wire just behind the eye on the top of the hook shank on the side nearest you. Then wrap your thread back slightly down the bend. When you tighten up the wire, the spines from the back sections will be in line with the hook shank, which makes the fly swim true. Thread the wire through the eye of the shank and fold it over.

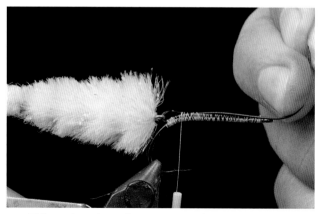

28. Take a few thread wraps over the wire and pull it to form a loop that is the same size as the gaps on the

previous shanks. You want it to be as small as possible while still allowing movement and preventing a gap between the tail section and head.

29. Trim the excess wire with wire cutters. Cover the wire liberally with thread wraps to secure the wire to the hook shank. Once the wire has been secured, apply UV resin to the thread to help lock the wire onto the hook shank. This step also adds bulk, a little more height, and will give more mass to the head section of the fly.

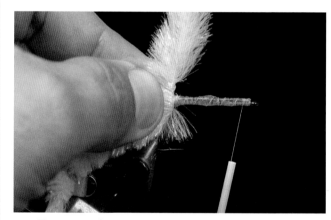

30. Tie in another section of Game Changer Chenille and wrap it forward to the hook eye. Wrap the material tightly, pulling on the core to stretch it and fold the fibers back as you wrap forward on the shank. Comb or pick out the fibers after every few wraps as you move forward. This helps to free any trapped fibers and results in a better looking fly.

31. After wrapping the chenille to the eye, secure it, and trim the excess. Whip-finish the thread and apply UV resin. Check the fly over one more time and comb or pick out any trapped fibers.

32. To trim the head of the fly, start by resting the scissors against the hook eye at about a 45-degree angle. Cut the fibers at this angle and then turn the fly over and repeat the same cut on the bottom.

33. Cutting the angles on top and bottom starts the nose/face of the fly and forms the 360-degree ramp that water pushes and flows against, which is critical for the serpentine swimming action.

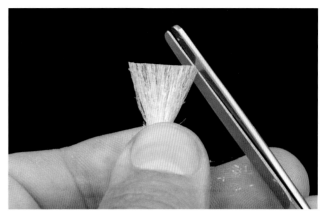

34. I like to trim the tail once the body of the fly is finished so that I can ensure it is in proportion to the rest of the fly. First cut the length to match the size of the fly. Then trim the sharp points off the edges.

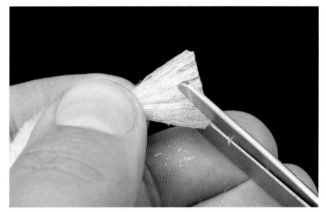

35. Different baits have different tails, but I'll often trim a V shape out of the center. Be careful not to cut too deep or too steep of an angle. I like to do more of a shallow angle to start and if I'm not satisfied with it I can then cut more out.

36. The final tail helps as a rudder in the swimming action of the fly and its profile matches most prey species.

37. Once I have the shape, I will trim any straggling fibers on the tail and also on the body of the fly to clean it up, if necessary.

38. The finished fly shows the clean profile of a general baitfish imitation. This style can be modified to suit any baitfish profile by just changing the angles of the cuts.

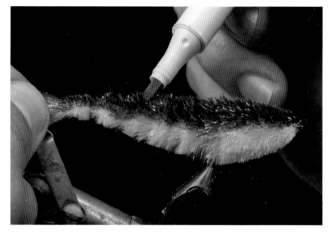

40. The second layer is olive topped off with a dark purple to show transitions more clearly.

41. Cut out a small pocket for the eyes to sit in for more durability and to make the pattern look more natural. Add flexible UV resin for the eye.

42. Attach two eyes on top of the resin and cure them to finish off the fly. Some variations follow this fly. They are all tied in a similar manner, with six 10mm spines and a short-shank wide-gap hook.

39. Coloring the fly can be as simple or complex as you desire. This particular one demonstrates multiple colors to show depth and transition points more clearly. I don't always color the flies—one of my favorite colors is all white. On this one, I'm starting a base layer with gray.

9 | Bucktail and Deer Body Game Changers

The original Bucktail Changer design with a Craft Fur head, which helps divert water and makes the fly swim well.

I knew the Game Changer design would be extremely effective for muskies, but the larger flies that I was tying from Body Wrap were very heavy and hard to cast. I didn't want my clients to have to work harder than necessary and wear themselves out. It was time to start exploring other materials to work into the Game Changer platform that would allow me to be able to have a fly that I could fish in sizes more appropriate for muskies, stripers, and giant trout. I needed a fly that swam well, but was also easier to cast.

I had made some progress figuring out movement with the T-Bone. Experiments with tying T-Bones tied on multiple shanks proved very successful for fish, so it was an easy next step to tie a Game Changer from bucktail, using reverse-tying methods taught to us by Bob Popovics and his Hollow Fleye and Bulkhead

Deceiver. The best hair for Lefty's Deceivers and Clouser Deep Minnows is from the middle to top portion of the tail because it doesn't flare that much. Bob Popovics showed many of us that the lower portion of the tail could be used for its hollow fibers that flared when you spun them on the shank, so that when you pull hair back in a reverse-tie, the butts provide support for them.

I struggled a bit getting the profile that I wanted by simply reverse-tying the hair, until it occurred to me to stack the tips in a hair stacker first. This allowed me to even up the tips, trim the uneven butts, and then use the butts to support the fibers and add density to the fly. This creates more of a barrier so that the water pushes up and out instead of through the material. This method also results in a clean even look to the finished fly.

These flies are a more impressionistic version of the Game Changer, but they still retain the three-dimensionality and movement typical of that style of tying. Equally as important, they were a critical first step in solving my weight problem for flies in the 10- to 14-inch range for stripers and muskies. With that said, bucktail is semi-buoyant, so if you need this style of fly to get down you'll need to fish it on a fast sinking line.

One important design feature of this fly, and many of flies in this book, are the prominent pectoral fins. When I can, and when it makes sense in the design of the fly, I like to include them for a few reasons. First, I think that they help push water and also enhance the swimming action a little bit. Water grabs the cupped shape and creates more vortices. Second, they also provide a natural silhouette, especially when viewed from below. This extra layer of realism doesn't take much time to add to a fly and gives me more confidence when fishing.

The Deer Body Changer

Once I began refining the design of the Bucktail Changers, my clients were doing very well with them for muskies that first winter, which was the winter of

Guide and fly tier Justin Pribanic holds a beautiful brown trout taken on a Bucktail Changer. This fly's versatility is one reason why I always have them with me in my travels and on my home water. The heads can be modified to fish in different water columns and current speeds.

Adding a deer-hair Muddler-style head really helps the fly hover and also aids in the swimming action. The larger head will also allow the fly to kick more on the pause showing profile.

Bucktail Changer, Galloup head

Bucktail Changer, Buford head

Bucktail Changers for trout and smallmouth such as these tied by Justin Pribanic can easily be scaled up for other species such as muskie. The heads that Kelly Galloup uses on his Zoo Cougar designs create a great glide-and-dart action that smallmouth and trout find irresistible. The Buford head design suspends a little higher for fishing with an intermediate or sinking line over wood and pushes more water.

2013. Later that season, just after Super Bowl weekend, Steve Dally, of Dally's Ozark Fly Fishers in Cotter, Arkansas, invited me down to tie at Streamer Love Fest, a fly-tying gathering hosted by him and his shop. We'd also be able to spend a day fishing on the White River, which is one of the country's premiere trophy brown-trout fisheries.

I got down there the day before the festival and we spent the night tying flies together and talking about the White's fishery. Dally shared some of the flies that worked well on the river and it was clear that a common material ingredient in many of them, such as Double Deceivers, was bucktail. I had thought about tying up some smaller versions of the bucktail patterns we were using so successfully for muskies on my home waters that year. Instead of using bucktail, however, we tried deer body hair because Dally had some in the colors that tended to work well on the river. Like many things, I had wanted to experiment with deer body hair, but I just hadn't had the time due to a busy guiding season—plus, up until that time, I didn't really have

a need for a downsized version since muskies wanted them big. I love natural materials and bucktail and deer hair are proven fish catchers that are also extremely durable. Both are light while at the same time both can be tied to achieve a big profile in a fly. That night I tied one from olive and yellow deer body hair that was about 7 inches long, and I couldn't wait to try it on the water the next day.

Even though we had bright sun, wind, and low, clear water—terrible streamer fishing conditions—Chris Willen, Gabe Blevins, and I hit the water for a quick float before the evening's festivities. We moved only a few fish that followed the fly but were ultimately noncommittal with the traditional strip-and-stop retrieve. Since fishing was slow, and it was cold and windy and we had places to be, we decided to push downstream so that we could budget the rest of the float better and not be late for the festival. As the takeout approached, I fished the last good bank.

Perhaps the most important aspect of hunting big trout in big water is the mental game. You simply do

Above: Chris Willen and I admire a beautiful 27½-inch White River brown trout that took a Deer Body Game Changer. I was able to fool this fish in low water with a two-hand retrieve. Playing on the predator's instincts to make a quick decision can make a bad day into a day to remember.

Left: The first Deer Body Game Changer was born at Steve Dally's kitchen table. Phone cameras weren't as good as they are now.

Here good friend and fellow guide Chris Willen (Chris Willen Guide Service) who guides northern Wisconsin, southeastern Michigan for Schultz Outfitters, and the southernmost range of muskies in Tennessee holds a monster muskie and his personal best on fly. The fish took a 14-inch fire tiger Bucktail Changer on a bright winter day. Big fish like big meals and this girl was no exception.

not have the luxury of keeping entertained with 12-inch trout, and you must be focused on the prize. Because what we were doing wasn't working, I decided to revert back to what I would do when muskie fishing in clear water and started burning the fly back with a two-handed retrieve. Sometimes in low, clear water, a fast retrieve forces a quick decision. Within sight of the takeout, I made a long cast to the bank, stripped six to eight times, and a 27½-inch brown boiled up on my fly. This not only solidified my belief in the pattern, but gave me confidence from that day forward in the fast-strip technique for catching trout in less than desirable conditions.

In the Bucktail Game Changer, I use a combination of different things to lift the fibers. In some cases, I will use Body Tubing; other times, I use UV resin. You can also get lift by incorporating Filler Flash or using the butts of the fibers themselves. You really have a lot of flexibility depending on the size fly you are tying and what materials you have on hand. In the Deer Body Changer, I rely primarily on the hollow butts to prop up the fibers when tied reverse-style. Because of this, and the relatively smaller size, this fly is pretty fast to tie.

This fly is fairly buoyant, so it will ride higher in the water column and keeps you from getting hung up. If you need these flies to sink, you can overcome the buoyancy with different lines or internal weight such as coneheads or dumbbell eyes. Even though the fly worked a miracle for me that day, I could see that it would not be the best choice for faster flows, because the fly wouldn't get down in the zone fast enough and it would come back to the boat too high in the water column, possibly having the boat spook the fish. These situational deficiencies would eventually lead to the Feather Game Changer, but the Deer Body Hair Changer certainly did its job that day.

First I'll show you how to tie a muskie version of the Bucktail Game Changer in a color combination that has produced well for me over the years. Then I show tying steps for a Deer Body Hair Changer very similar to the pattern I fished on the White many years ago. I am going to move through the steps on this pattern fairly quickly because they are the same exact steps as with the Bucktail Game Changer except that you are using body hair. I do want to emphasize how we construct the tail on this fly because the splayed feathers supported by hair is a different variation that you can incorporate in many flies. Also, instead of a deer hair head, I show how to use a Fish-Mask, which is faster, more consistent, and also helps the buoyant fly get down a little faster. You can use these Fish-Masks on many of your patterns and the steps are the same.

Tying the Bucktail Game Changer

Materials

Three 28mm Big Game Shanks, 40mm Big Game Shank | Gamakatsu #2 B10S (trailer) and #5/0 Gamakatsu Heavy Cover Worm hook | 6/0 chartreuse Veevus | 60-pound Berkley nylon-coated wire | Baitfish Emulator | Grizzly and chartreuse saddle tied in the round with chartreuse and gold Flashabou | white, chartreuse, and gray bucktail | clear Body Tubing | grizzly schlappen | grizzly saddle pectoral fins | white 2" Flash Blend Baitfish Brush marked chartreuse and gray | Ice Living Eyes

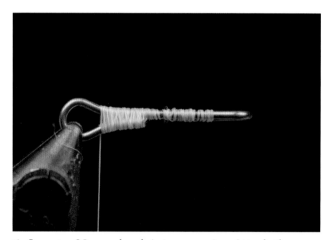

1. Insert a 28mm shank into your vise. Attach the thread, wrap a base, and wrap back over the rear loop, stopping at the point shown.

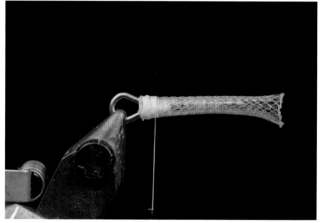

2. Cut a 1½-inch piece of ⅛" Body Tubing and singe the end. Apply some Loctite to the rear wraps, slide the Body Tubing over the shank, and tie it down.

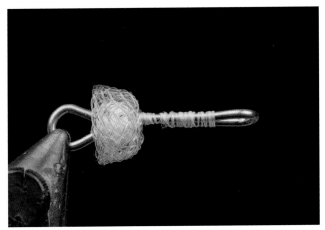

3. Singe the other end and reverse it. Tie it down and add glue. Trim the thread. Reverse the Body Tubing, creating the dam.

4. Tie in Baitfish Emulator and take only two to three wraps to add support for the feathers. On smaller size flies the dam is optional. Here it works because it is a large fly and we want it to maintain profile in the rear.

5. Tie in two chartreuse feathers on top, two grizzly on the sides, and two white underneath.

6. Add another Body Tubing spreader, just as you did previously. Slide on the Body Tubing, adding glue before you secure it with thread. When you slide the Body Tubing over the shank, you want the tip of the Body Tubing to cover the butts of the feathers. This will help the feathers hold their shape.

7. The finished spreader just covers the feathers. I want to maintain some height with the feathers so that they have a fan shape. Also, over time, repeated fishing is going to compress the feathers so the dam will help them hold their shape.

8. Tie in two chartreuse feathers on top, two grizzly on the sides, and two white underneath. Palmer a grizzly chartreuse saddle in front, whip-finish, and add resin to complete the tail.

9. Connect another 28mm shank to the tail assembly and insert it into your vise. Then wrap it with thread, stopping at the point where the bottom leg of the rear loop ends.

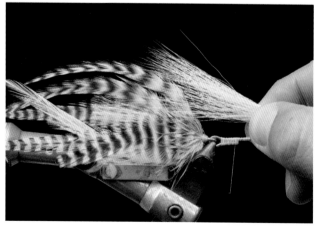

10. Measure the bucktail so that the tips extend back far enough to cover the thread wraps on the tail shank.

11. Switch hands, being careful not to shift the fibers, and trim the butts even.

12. Switch hands again and take a few loose wraps around the bucktail, gradually wrapping with more pressure so that the fibers spin evenly around the shank.

13. The bucktail should look like this. I leave the butt sections in the back to help support the bucktail moving forward. In some versions I will use Filler Flash for this purpose, but I want to show you the technique that incorporates the butts.

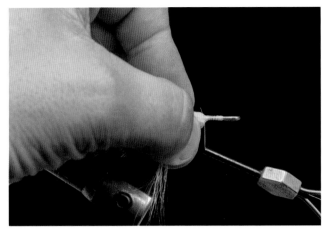

14. Wrap the thread through the fibers, stroke them back with fingers or a tool, and wrap your thread to prop them up.

15. Fold the flash around the tying thread and position it on top of the shank.

16. Once the flash is in place, manipulate it around the top half of the shank with your thumbnail.

17. Select another small clump of bucktail and measure it so that it is the same length as the previous bunch of bucktail that you tied in.

18. Trim the butt sections and manipulate the bucktail around the shank. Flare and spin the hair around the shank with thread tension and manipulate it until it is evenly distributed around the shank.

19. Reverse-tie the bucktail. For a little more height, don't wrap over the base of the hair as much as you did in previous sections. Sometimes I will use flexible UV resins to also gain the height, which can be faster. Be careful that the bucktail isn't propped up too high. This is the wrist of the fish, where the profile is lower before the tail. Add flash if you desire.

20. Measure and cut a bundle of gray bucktail and tie it in like the two previous colors.

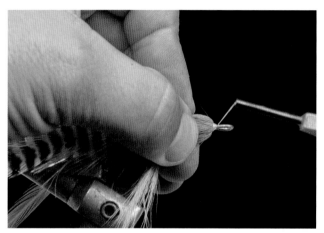

21. After you reverse-tie the hair, wrap back over the base to get the height you desire, whip-finish, and clip the thread. Again, you can also tie off the thread and use flexible UV resin.

22. This front view shows the height and even distribution of the hair. With each one of these steps, take your time to get the hair right.

23. Slide a 28mm shank through the eye of the previous shank, insert it in the vise, and attach your thread.

24. Tie in the next clump of white bucktail one-eighth inch behind the shank junction so that the butts cover the thread wraps. Pre-measure the bucktail so that it covers approximately one-half inch over the previous section. Tie in chartreuse bucktail the same way, so that it overlaps the previous section a little bit.

25. Add one more bundle of gray bucktail a little longer or the same length as the chartreuse.

26. Reverse-tie the bucktail and add a little bit of flash for accent.

27. I like to add a few turns of schlappen to help divert water, which helps the overall swimming action of the fly. The less water that can flow through the fibers, the better the swim.

28. After you wrap the feather to the head of the shank, secure it with thread, whip-finish, and apply UV resin.

29. Insert a short-shank, wide-gap hook into the vise, wrap a thread base, and then tie in a 4-inch piece of 60-pound coated wire. Wrap over the wire slightly down the hook bend, slide the tip of the wire through the eye of the shank, and fold it back over, taking a few threads wraps over it to secure it to the hook shank. Pull the wire to roughly match the size of the connection behind it, or slightly bigger. Continue binding down the wire with tight thread wraps, and then apply glue or UV resin.

30. Once the glue has cured, wrap your thread so that it is between the point and the barb of the hook. Clip another clump of white bucktail, making sure that it is the same amount as the previous clump, or slightly more—however, a little goes a long way because we will be adding three clumps of bucktail per shank. Measure it so that it goes at least two-thirds up the previous shank.

31. When you reverse-tie the bucktail through this section, you want more height with the fibers, so don't wrap as far over the base of the fibers. Add a little bit of flash.

32. Add chartreuse and then gray bucktail, gaining height as you move forward on the shank. Leave a little room to add another schlappen feather and take a few turns with it.

33. Add a 40mm shank and wrap the thread so that it is about one-eighth inch behind the shank junction connection. Cut a 1½-inch-long piece of ¼" Body Tubing. Singe the end and apply a small amount of Loctite to the thread base before sliding the tubing over the shank.

34. Create the Body Tubing spreader. Select and measure a longer section of white bucktail. For this section I look for a slightly stiffer hair, which helps the overall profile of the fly in the long run. I am not looking for a lot of movement from the bucktail. The articulations provide the movement and the bucktail fibers are there to create three-dimensional body and mass.

35. A thread bump about one-eighth inch in front of the Body Tubing creates a valley for the bucktail when you tie it in. This way the bucktail stays in plays when you spin it and doesn't slide forward.

36. Tighten and loosen the thread as you manipulate the bucktail around the shank, evenly distributing it.

37. Moving forward a bit, I have tied off the white bucktail and added another Body Tubing dam that should slightly overlap the previous bucktail, but barely touch it. This is my way of setting the bucktail to match the flow and profile of the fly moving forward. Tie another thread bump ahead of the Body Tubing, creating a valley. Select a clump of chartreuse bucktail, trim the butts, and tie it in so that the butts face the hook eye. Spin the chartreuse bucktail around the shank.

38. Manipulating the bucktail with your thread and your thumb evenly distributes the bucktail around the shank.

39. Tie in and form another Body Tubing dam. Cut a bundle of gray bucktail and measure it so that it is approximately the same length, or just a little longer, as the white and chartreuse bucktail.

40. Distribute the gray bucktail around the hook shank. Add some barred flash. In the remaining space, tie in a schlappen feather and wrap it forward on the shank to the eye.

41. Insert the hook, connect the rear portion with 80-pound nylon coated wire as you have done before, and tie in a Body Tubing dam. After that, create a thread bump ahead of the tubing before tying in the bucktail.

42. Measure a clump of chartreuse bucktail so that the height is three-quarters the previous section and tie it in. Add some flash if you like and tie in another Body Tubing dam.

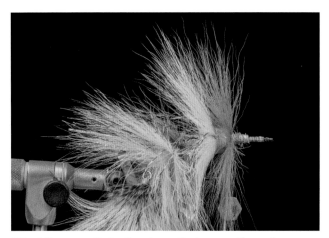

43. After you tie in the dam, tie in a section of gray bucktail.

44. Add flash. Select four rooster saddle feathers for pectoral fins and tie two in one each side.

45. Tie in a white 2" Flash Blend Baitfish Brush and wrap it to the eye, with turns as close together as possible to create a dense head for maximum movement.

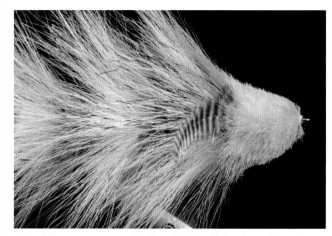

46. After you wrap the head, tie off the brush, and clip it. Trim it to a 45-degree angle, 360 degrees around, creating a ramp for the water to push up against.

47. Color the head gray over white with a little chartreuse on the side. Add flexible UV resin on each side of the head where the eyes will be, place the eyes on the resin, and cure them with the light. This is one of my favorite clear water colors for big muskies.

Bucktail Changer Variations

Bucktail Changer (Sucker). One of my favorite flies for chasing toothy critters such as muskies. In this fly, the butts of the white, tan, and olive bucktail support the fibers; I have since started using more filler to support the fibers. The saddle hackle in front of each section helps divert water and add contrast. The head is 2" mullet Flash Blend Baitfish Brush.

Bucktail Changer (Original). The black, yellow, and white color combination is a favorite of mine and other guide friends, especially for tannic water; it has worked extremely well on the James and New in the winter in clear water as well. Each section of white and yellow bucktail is capped off with a few turns of a black schlappen feather to add contrast/barring and improve flow of water through materials. The head is 2" yellow Flash Blend Baitfish Brush.

Three versions of Deer Body Hair Changers. The olive over white version (top) uses pearl Filler Flash to blend everything together. The middle fly has foam discs in the front to provide more of a pronounced diving action behind a sinking line and also has internal pearl Filler Flash. Bottom fly has a red Craft Fur head that helps it sink a little faster. It is a terrific fly for medium to shallow depths.

Tying the Deer Body Hair Changer

Materials

Six 15mm Fish-Spines | #2 Gamakatsu SL12 Short and #2/0 B10S | 6/0 olive-brown Veevus | 30-pound Berkley nylon-coated wire | mallard feathers separated by olive bucktail | mallard pectoral fins | golden olive and yellow deer body hair | gold Polarflash | grizzly hen saddle | medium Fish-Mask | Ice Living Eyes

1. Insert a short-shank, wide-gap hook in the vise. Attach the thread and wrap a solid base. Trim a small clump of deer body hair from the hide, clean out the fluff, stack the fibers, and measure them so that they extend a little beyond the hook bend.

2. Spin the deer body hair around the hook shank.

3. Select and marry two mallard feathers, peel off the fluff at the base of the feather, and tie them in so that the tips are even with the bucktail you just tied in.

4. Tie in the mallard fibers on each side of the shank and wrap forward approximately two eye lengths. When the water hits these splayed feathers, it is going to really help accentuate the movement of the fly and the tail.

5. Add a little more deer body hair to just slightly cover the tail. Here we are using all hair, but Filler Flash, Finesse Body Chenille, or other materials can be substituted easily, depending on how you want the finished fly to look.

6. Trim the butts and wrap over them, creating a smooth base on which to wrap your feather. Tie in a hen saddle feather and wrap it to the eye of the shank. Tie it off, trim the excess, and whip-finish. Add UV resin.

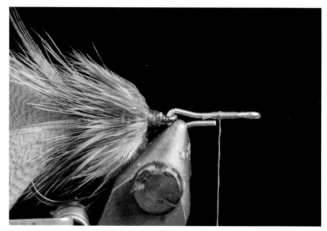

7. Slip a 15mm shank through the eye of the previous one and insert it into the vise. Attach the thread in front of the loop return. You can coat this shut with UV resin as we showed previously so that you can easily swap out your stinger hook if it gets dull.

8. Each bundle of deer body hair that you tie in moving forward is prepared the same way. Remove the fluff from the base of the hair with a comb, stack the fibers in a hair stacker, and trim the butts even. Tie the fibers in so that the tips are pointing toward the eye, take two loose wraps of thread, and pull down, flaring and spinning the hair around the hook evenly.

9. Getting an even distribution may take some practice if this technique is new to you, but it is the exact same method that you use to distribute bucktail around the shank except that deer body hair will flare more.

10. Bring the thread between and in front of the fibers as you sweep them back with an empty pen casing or your fingers, or a combination of the two. Wrap back over the base of the fibers to get the angle that you desire, starting with a fairly low angle in the rear of the fly and increasing height as you move forward.

11. Tie in the flash by wrapping it around your thread and pulling it tight to the top of the hook shank. This method allows you to place the flash precisely where you want it.

12. Distribute the flash around the shank with your thumb and pointer finger.

13. Repeat these steps with another bunch of olive deer body hair.

14. Attach a total of six sections of deer body hair, alternating between yellow and olive to complete the rear section of the fly. Insert a B10S hook and attach the rear section with wire.

15. Tie in one section of yellow deer body hair making sure the tips are a little longer than the previous section and cover the transition. Add flash if you desire.

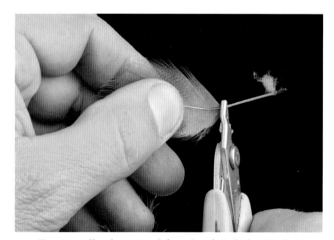

16. Tie in mallard pectoral fins. It often helps to flatten the stems with pliers to prevent them from rolling on the hook shank. You may need to do this for the mallard feathers that you attach to the tail as well, though the deer body hair provides a platform in that case.

17. Moving forward, the body of this fly is tied exactly the same as the Bucktail Game Changer. However, the stiffer body hair creates a slightly different effect.

18. Tie in one or perhaps two more clumps of deer body hair, wrapping a feather in between them if you desire. Use fluff from the mallard feather dubbed on the thread, or dubbing or chenille, and create a base for the Fish-Mask.

19. Wrap a base for the Fish-Mask.

20. Mark the inside of the head to match the color of the overall fly, in this case golden yellow.

21. Add a generous amount of flexible UV resin.

22. Slide the Fish-Mask over it and cure it with a UV light.

23. Apply UV glue to the socket on the Fish-Mask, stick your translucent eye to it, and cure with UV light.

The head design dictates how a fly swims. A larger head creates more wobble wobble and increases the jackknifing action. A smaller head usually results in a tighter wiggle. A flatter profile turns more in the water whereas a broader head stalls out and hovers more in the water column.

Deer Body Hair Game Changer Variations

Deer Body Hair Changer (Brown/Yellow). These two photos illustrate how Finesse Body Chenille (yellow, here) will lift the fibers. The cone head built into the head itself adds weight, which not only helps the fly sink but also makes it easier to cast.

Drunken Changer (Deer Body Hair). Tommy Lynch's Drunk and Disorderly wedge-shape head is trimmed and then coated with flexible resin for more support and to hold shape. The 60-degree jig hook adds to the erratic swimming action that also pitches left and right. This clear-water fly lacks Filler Flash for a more drab, subdued appearance.

10 | Feather Game Changer and Variations

The Feather Game Changer swims with little movement, pulses while still, and hovers in the water column, staying in the fish's face while at rest. The combination of these attributes has proven time and again to be deadly not just on bass but on a variety of gamefish around the world.

In Arkansas, giant trout, fish over ten pounds, were following the Deer Hair Changer, only to peel off right at the boat. I think they were doing this because the fly didn't get in the zone until it was too close to the boat, and by that time the fish detected us. It simply took too long to sink. Fortunately, we did land that one monster brown, but it was far away from the boat and the fly was traveling very fast, perhaps triggering a reaction strike.

You can add weight to any fly to get it to sink, but in many cases I have found that adding weight inhibits the fly's swimming action. All the way back from Dally's in Arkansas I was pondering the puzzle of how to get an unweighted Game Changer to sink faster, especially in faster water, and stay there. On a Monday morning, right after Super Bowl Sunday, I explained all of this to Bob Popovics on the phone, and he asked:

"Did you ever try feathers?" This question sparked my imagination like a lightning bolt.

Immediately after getting off the phone with him, I began experimenting with hen saddle and schlappen feathers wrapped around shanks on a sculpin pattern. By increasing the size of the feathers as I moved forward on the shanks, I could create a tapered body. I immediately tied up a sculpin feather Game Changer and did the bathtub test—it swam just like a real fish. The soft webby fibers were dense enough to push water out and away from the body, creating an enticing action. The pectoral fins not only looked unbelievable, with a great profile and silhouette, but they pulsed when the fly came to rest. You had movement, without having to move the fly.

When you wrap hen saddle on the shank, it creates the illusion of mass. By tying the feathers in by the tips, you increase this effect as the fibers stand up and block water. In the same way I created a ramp with Game Changer Chenille or deer hair, I could achieve the same effect with tapered feathers. Granted, the size of these flies are limited by the size of the feathers at your disposal, so even with the best of feathers, hen saddles and schlappen combined, you can't get a fly much longer than 7½ to 8 inches.

The first versions were tied completely with feathers. After a while I started using filler material, which had numerous advantages. Marcos Vergara at Hareline first sent me Cactus Hackle, which sped up the fly and saved precious feathers. I would use Cactus Hackle for half of the shank and then feathers for the other half, which reduced the number of feathers used by half. Using the filler material in this way supported the feathers and added lift, an enticing underglow, and made the fly lighter to cast. I eventually worked with Hareline to develop Filler Flash, which was easier to work with for Feather Changers.

One of the things that I love about this fly is the integration of synthetics with natural materials that complement one another, not only enhancing the aesthetics of the fly, in my opinion, but also the ease of tying, durability, and action. When I tie this fly it gives me an enormous amount of satisfaction, perhaps because it takes me back to the roots of my fly tying. There is no cutting involved; you are selecting feathers from different parts of the saddle and using them to create the taper. This style of Game Changer would soon become my favorite, not only for the swimming action, but because it sunk quickly, was super durable, and flat out caught fish.

The choices of filler material are also almost endless. While versions tied only with feathers are still a viable option, especially for those looking to go all natural, you can easily incorporate various premade and

On this trip to Louisiana, jig-style Feather Game Changers were the ticket for bottom-crawling reds. A twitch-and-pause motion hovers the fly in front of the the fish making it hard for them to refuse. GREG DINI PHOTO

I've learned more about fish behavior from smallmouth bass than any other fish. The fact that they eat everything from bugs to baitfish and hold in many different water types makes them a great study fish.

Good buddy Peter Vandergrift with a nice hybrid bass we caught on an exploratory outing. Carp, stripers, smallmouth bass, largemouth, and hybrids fell for Feather Game Changers that memorable day.

Big stripers in the spring are my favorite fish to target in my local rivers, and the Feather Game Changer, fished on a strip and fall back retrieve (while on anchor, strip in line and then let it slip out through your fingers) can be the ticket.

When the water becomes stained in high water, I really like black with a dense, wide head that has more presence in the water. Fishing current breaks with sinking tips can be a deadly combo.

homemade brushes, or even other natural materials. You can also add any other feathers, tied in the round or as a topping to provide color contrast, which leads to the Mallard Changers.

And so too are head designs, which we will show some different examples of in the spread on page XX and in the tying steps to come. You can tie these on jig hooks, with Sculpin Helmets or dumbbell eyes, or tie them with floating heads made out of everything from deer hair to foam. The possibilities really are limitless.

Veiling and Taper

Filler and feathers are the basic component of the standard Feather Game Changer, but there are several important nuances regarding the interaction of the fill and the feather that are important. To achieve a fly that not only looks nice in hand and in the water, but also fishes well, you need to consider veiling and taper.

Veiling means using fibers in your fly, whether bucktail, feathers, or synthetics such as Craft Fur, in such a way that they overlap a material under them. This not only creates the brushpile effect that I talk a lot about, that internal supporting framework that creates bulk without mass, but the length of the fibers creates your taper and also closes off any gaps from the previous section.

My goal, and what I teach tiers to do, is to make sure that the material overlaps the previous material by at least half, and in some cases up to three-quarters of the length. The less that you overlap the fibers, the slimmer your overall imitation will be. In the back sections of the fly, bring the fibers half way up the previous section. As you move forward toward the middle of the fly and head, you want more bulk so you select longer feather that overlap the previous section by three quarters.

Thread wraps also helps control the height of the feathers throughout the fly. Because you want a narrow tail section, in general, wrap back over the feathers slightly to compress them to make them flatter and keep the taper. By the time you are in the middle section of the fly you don't compress the feathers at all

The top fly is an original, early model Feather Game Changer tied only with hen and schlappen, and without any Filler Flash. The bottom fly showcases Filler Flash and really illustrates how you can use it to not only provide an inner sparkle to the fly but also support the feathers.

Fall on the South Holston is not only one of the most beautiful times to be on the water but also some of the best fishing for brown trout.

with thread wraps. Tying the feathers in by the tips also helps them stand up and not compress.

One of the great things about hen saddle feathers, or any chicken feather for that matter, is that they are presized for you on the cape. By choosing the feathers at the base of the cape and working up toward the top of the skin you can create a natural fish taper without having to cut any of the feathers. With each section, move up the cape a few rows to get feathers with longer fibers and achieve the proper amount of overlap. The natural evolution/design of the hen saddle help with the taper by naturally increasing size roughly 20 percent every two rows. Increasing feather size increase

the height, build taper, and it is also going to veil over the previous section more, which will hide any gaps between the shanks. I also increase the amount of Filler Flash to the point where, on the forward portions of the fly, I often use two pieces of Filler Flash and twist them together for maximum bulk.

By the time you reach the middle of the fly (just past the two-thirds point, generally) you want to stop trying to build height and then begin tapering back down by adjusting the length of the fibers and also the thread wraps over the base of the feathers. At the head of the fly, schlappen often becomes necessary for the fiber length, at least for larger flies.

Tying the Feather Game Changer

Materials

One 10mm, six 15mm Fish-Spines | #2/0 B10S | white 6/0
Veevus | 30-pound Berkley nylon-coated wire | pearl Filler
Flash | white and red hen saddle and schlappen | jungle cock
eyes coated with flexible UV resin

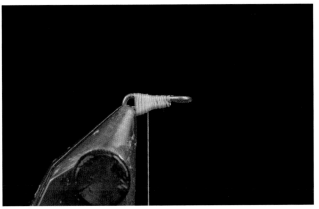

1. Insert a 10mm shank in the vise and attach the
thread. Wrap the thread up and down the shank to
provide a good base for the tailing materials.

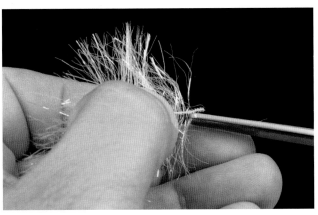

2. Cut a section of Filler Flash and trim the first
quarter inch, exposing the core.

3. Tie in the Filler Flash starting at the very back of
the shank.

4. Stroke back the fibers as you begin your forward
wraps. Make two wraps and then tie it off and trim
the excess. If you trapped any fibers as you wrapped
them, you can pick them out with a bodkin. Do this
throughout the fly.

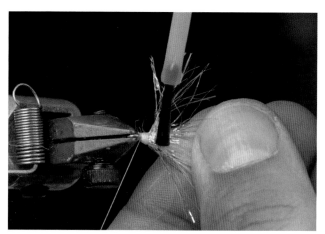

5. This creates a natural fan shape that closely imitates many naturals' tails.

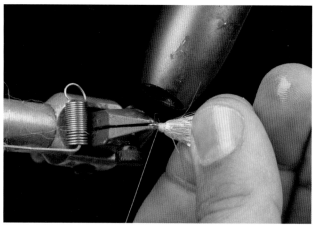

6. Apply a small amount of flexible UV resin at the base of the Filler Flash fibers.

8. Select a large, webby feather from a magnum hen saddle. The fibers, when wrapped, should cover the length of the Filler Flash extending off the shank.

9. Peel off the webby fluff at the base of the stem.

7. Once the flexible resin is in place, squeeze the fibers together flattening the tail. Then shoot it with the light to cure the resin. Once the resin has cured, the fibers should be flat and fan shaped to replicate a fish tail.

10. Grab the tip of the feather and stroke the sides down. This will help the fibers fold around the stem as you wrap the feather.

11. Tie in the feather by the tip just in front of the Filler Flash and trim the excess.

12. Pull the fibers back as you wrap the feather to help them lie back over the Filler Flash.

13. Wrap the feathers forward to the eye of the shank. Tie off the stem, trim the excess, and whip-finish the thread. Clip the thread, coat with UV resin, and cure with light.

14. Slide a 15mm shank through the eye of the tail shank and insert it in the vise. Attach the thread and wrap a foundation on the shank, making sure to wrap back over the rear connection loop. The back connection loop only needs to be as open as the eye of the shank that it connects to for good movement. Leave the thread hanging one-eighth inch behind the junction point, where the top and bottom of the shank come together.

15. Since the wrist of the fish (the part before the tail) is the narrowest, you need to trim the Filler Flash before tying it in. We do not want to add lift at this point. The Filler Flash should only extend over the previous eye and slightly up the tail. Once you have your measurements, pre trim the Filler Flash before wrapping it in. I have trimmed the fibers about one-half inch for this particular fly.

16. Take two to three wraps forward to a point just forward of the rear loop, stroking back the fibers as you wrap them. Tie the Filler Flash down with a couple thread wraps and cut the tag end. If you need to, pick out any trapped fibers with a bodkin.

17. Select two feathers from the base of a hen saddle. Make sure the feathers will overlap, but are not longer than, the Filler Flash. We still are not trying to build any height into the fly at this point.

18. Marry the two feathers and peel off the fluff at the base of the stems. Then grab the two feathers by the tips and stroke the fibers down the stem so that they stand out.

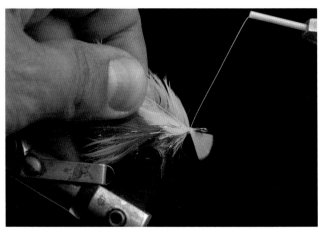

19. Tie the feathers in by the tips and secure them with several tight wraps of thread. Then trim the remaining tips.

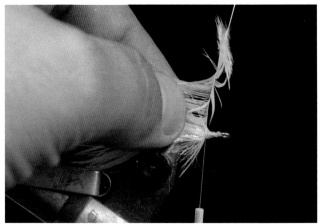

20. You can wrap the feathers at once or one at a time—it is totally up to you. When wrapping them together take care to make sure the feathers don't wrap over one another. If they do, use a bodkin to pick the fibers out. Fold the feather fibers back as you wrap them forward. This will train the fibers back just like tying a soft-hackle wet fly. Make sure you fold the feathers back during each wrap until you get to the eye of the shank.

21. When you've reached the eye of the shank, tie off the feather (or feathers) and trim the tag. Take a few wraps to smooth over the butts and whip-finish. Coat the wraps with UV resin. Notice that the feathers extend back even with the Filler Flash and cover the connection between the two shanks. The lower profile of this portion sets you up to build taper and profile moving forward.

22. Connect another 15mm shank to the previous shank and insert it in the vise. Secure the shank and rear loop with thread wraps, leaving only enough room for the shank behind it to move freely. Stop the thread wraps one-eighth inch behind the junction point. You want to tie in the Filler Flash here and not higher up on the rear connection loop because separating the tie-in points allows you to gradually build profile.

23. Tie in the Filler Flash and wrap three turns forward before you tie it off and trim the excess. Trim the Filler Flash so that it extends halfway over the previous section.

24. Move up the hen saddle about two rows and select two more saddle feathers. Check the length of the fibers by wrapping them around the shank *before* pulling them off the skin, much like you would do with a dry fly hackle. The fibers of the feathers should be even with or be slightly longer than the Filler Flash. Once you've picked the feathers, tie them in, wrap them forward, and tie them off. Coat the wraps with UV resin and cure with the light.

25. Repeat the previous steps with another section tied on a 15mm shank. Trim the Filler Flash in this section only a little. Since we are starting to gain more height, the Filler Flash should come back over the previous section between ½ and ¾, leaning more toward the ¾ length. Move up another two rows on your saddle, checking the measurement of the feather before plucking it from the skin. Take note that the feathers are getting longer and wider as we move up the skin.

26. Attach another 15mm shank, but this time tie the Filler Flash closer to the connection loop to bulk things up more and give more height when tying in the Filler Flash and hen saddles. Moving forward you will no longer have to trim the Filler Flash. It should naturally extend back ¾ over the previous section because you moved back the tie-in point. Move up a few rows on the saddle and select two more feathers after checking the fiber length before plucking them from the skin.

27. On the next shank, tie in the Filler Flash back farther on the connection loop as you did before. Here you can also twist the Filler Flash to help gain more bulk and stiffness to help support the overall height and profile. Spinning the flash tightens the core and condenses the fibers as well as makes the fibers stand out much like stacking deer hair. Select two more feathers moving up the skin two more rows.

28. There comes a point on the larger flies when hen feathers aren't going to be wide enough to match the taper any more. At that point you can switch to schlappen for feathers with longer fibers. Also I start to use three feathers at a time for the remaining sections to gain more bulk.

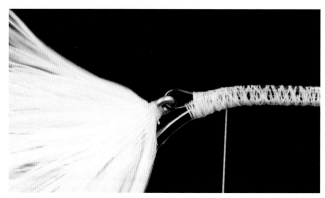

29. Insert a short-shank, wide-gap hook in the vise and wrap a thread base. Cut a 4-inch piece of wire for the connection from the back body to the hook. Tie down the wire on the top side of the shank closest to you, taking a few wraps slightly down the bend. Slide the wire through the shank, and pull it to form a loop the same size as the shank eye. Lash the wire down on the far side of the top of the hook shank and coat everything with UV resin.

30. Tie in Filler Flash just in front of the wire loop connection. This will help fill the gap between the two sections and add more mass. On larger profile flies I will make a dubbing brush from Baitfish Emulator to gain enough height and length to overlap the previous section by three quarters.

31. Wrap the Filler Flash forward to a point between the barb and hook point. Then select three schlappen feathers.

32. Once you select the feathers make sure they extend back ¾ of the way over the previous section. Tie them in by the tips and wrap them singularly or all together, folding back the fibers as you wrap them forward.

33. Tie off the feathers, trim the excess, and wrap over the butts. Whip-finish and then apply UV resin.

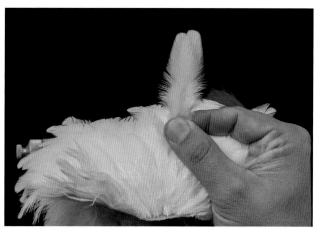

34. Select two narrow hen saddle feathers from the base of the skin for the pectoral fins. Pectoral fins provide an accurate silhouette which I think converts to more fish, but I feel like they also help with the swimming action as well—diverting water and creating more turbulence.

35. Peel away all excess fluff to expose the stems. Tie them in on each side of the hook shank extending back to the bend of the hook shank. Once satisfied with the length, trim the excess off the front and clean up the fibers and any remaining stem with thread wraps.

36. Tie in and take four to six turns of Filler Flash or Baitfish Emulator Flash in a dubbing brush. If using Filler Flash, spin it tightly before wrapping to achieve a higher profile.

37. Add three more schlappen feathers to finish off the head of the fly. Select and measure feathers that will extend three quarters of the way up the previous section.

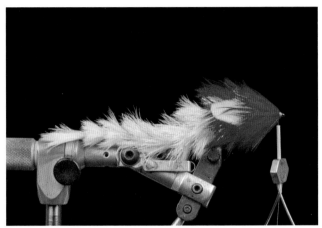

38. Wrap the feathers forward, trim the excess, and wrap a neat head in preparation for the eye. Coat the thread wraps with UV resin.

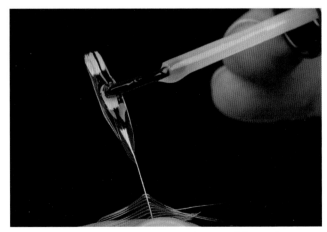

39. This step is optional, but I like to add jungle cock eyes. You can substitute with tab eyes, imitation jungle cock, or whatever you wish. If you choose to use jungle cock, add a flexible resin to the feather and then cure with a light to add durability.

40. Tie in the jungle cock on each side of the head. Trim the stems off the feathers, whip-finish, and trim the thread.

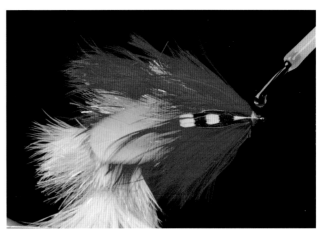

41. Add UV resin to complete the head on the fly.

This all-natural version of the Game Changer is my current favorite, and the fish respond well to it. I owe a lot to Bob Popovics for the inspiration.

Feather Game Changer Variations

The Feather Game Changer, like all Game Changers, is more of a style of tying. Not only can you tie it in a range of shapes and color schemes, but you can change the head designs very easily to achieve different actions in the water. Adding deer hair, foam (group shot in materials chapter), Fish-Masks, Fish-Skulls (shown in following steps), dubbing, and dubbing brushes are all options that produce well under different conditions. They can be tied drab and without Filler Flash for more subtle approaches. ■

Feather Game Changer (Original).
Sometimes I still like to fish original Feather Game Changers without flash, especially for spooky fish.

Feather Game Changer (Deer Hair Head).
The trimmed deer hair head not only adds diversion of water but also adds buoyancy that makes the fly rise a little bit as you stop stripping it.

Feather Game Changer (Fish-Mask Head).
Tied with only feathers and the heavier Fish-Mask, this fly sinks faster than ones tied with Filler Flash.

Feather Game Changer (Blended).
This shad-type pattern showcases blended feathers and a 1" Sculpting Fiber Brush for the head.

Feather Game Changer (Fire Tiger). You can marry different feathers to achieve a mottled appearance. I love this for clear water and bright days. The head is 1" chartreuse Sculpting Flash Fiber Brush.

Feather Game Changer (Jig Style). Tan is one of my favorite colors. Dumbbell eyes allow the fly to sink quicker in the water column and add a jigging action to the swimming motion.

Feather Game Changer (Brush Head). This variation with the 1" olive SF Flash Blend brush head keeps the fly a little higher in the water column then the all-feather version.

Drunken Feather Game Changer (Fire Tiger). The wedge head combines a Rapala-like wobble with the swimming action of a Game Changer. I like to fish this fly with an erratic strip and pause motion, which allows the head to dig and wobble while the rest of the body wiggles and swims.

Sculpin Feather Game Changer. A realistic, non-flashy version of a sculpin for trout and smallmouth.

Tying the Feather Game Changer Jig

This fly shows another weighting option to imitate baits that dive for cover. File the sides of a regular dumbbell eye to scuff the edges and provide a better surface for glue to adhere to. This step, which is optional, provides a more realistic look when using dumbbell eyes. Wrapping two different color feathers together creates layers in the fly, enhancing its realism. I like this technique for pressured fish or clear water. Color schemes are endless with this technique.

Materials

Six 15mm Fish-Spines | #1 Ahrex 26 Degree Bent Streamer Hook | 6/0 lavender Veevus | 30-pound Berkley nylon-coated wire | barred ginger rooster saddle feathers | tan Finesse Body Chenille | light tan hen saddle followed by ginger schlappen | tan or camel 2" Sculpting Flash Fiber Brush | dumbbell eyes covered with Ice Living Eyes

1. Insert a 10mm shank in the vise. Attach the tying thread and wrap a foundation on the shank. Tie in large Finesse Body Chenille in the middle of the shank and advance your thread. Take only two wraps of chenille, tie it off, and trim the excess.

2. Select six ginger grizzly hen or rooster saddles for the tail. I usually like them to be roughly 1 to 1½ inches long for this particular size fly. Tie them in spaced evenly around the shank, clipping the excess as you go or after you've tied them all in. Wrap over the butts, whip-finish, and coat the thread wraps with UV resin.

3. Slide a 10mm shank through the eye of the previous shank and insert it into the vise. Attach the tying thread and tie in medium Finesse Body Chenille in the middle of the shank. Take two wraps of chenille, tie it down, and trim the excess.

4. Select one light tan hen saddle and one dark ginger hen saddle from the bottom of the base of the skin. Marry them and tie in tips first. Wrap your thread to the tie-off point. Wrap them together to the eye of the shank and secure them with thread. Clip the excess fibers, whip-finish, and apply UV resin to your thread wraps.

5. Slide a 15mm shank through the eye of the previous shank and insert it in the vise. Wrap a thread base on the shank and up the rear loop, closing it off so that it matches the size of the previous shank eye. Trim and tie down a section of tan medium Finesse Body Chenille approximately two-thirds of the way back on the shank. Take two to three wraps forward to where the lower leg of the rear loop ends and tie it off. Select two more hen saddles, moving up the skin approximately two rows, and premeasure them so that they extend over half the previous section. Marry the feathers and tie them in by the tips. Wrap them together to the shank eye, tie off, and trim the excess. Add UV resin and cure with light.

6. Slide another 15mm shank through the eye of the previous shank and insert it in the vise. Attach the thread and wrap a foundation. Trim and tie in large Finesse Body Chenille two thirds of the way back on the shank and then wrap it forward to the shank junction point.

7. Front view of the Finesse Body Chenille and how full and three-dimensional it becomes. It is a perfect base for the feathers to rest against.

8. Select one light tan and two dark ginger hen saddle feathers from approximately two rows higher on the skin. Measure them before plucking them from skin. Marry the feathers, tie them in by the tips, and wrap them forward at the same time to the eye. Tie them down, trim the excess, whip-finish, and apply UV resin to the thread wraps.

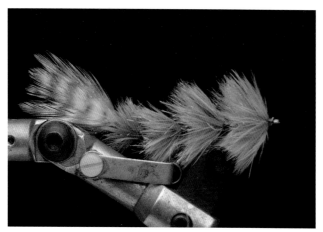

9. Slide another 15mm shank through the eye of the previous shank and insert it into the vise. Trim and

tie in large tan Finesse Body Chenille on the shank two thirds of the way back and wrap it to where the rear loop comes together, approximately three to four wraps. Select two larger light tan and two dark ginger hen saddles by moving two rows up the skin, tie them down, and wrap them forward. Trim thread and apply UV resin.

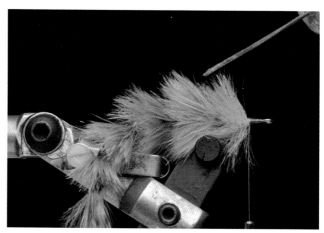

10. Slide another 15mm shank through the eye of the previous one and insert it into the vise. Trim and tie in a section of large tan chenille at the rear of the shank, as far up the loop as possible. Tying it in farther back adds mass and helps with the overall profile. Notice that the wraps cover the preceding shank halfway. Wrap the chenille to the rear loop junction and tie it off. When you add the hen feathers you want to overlap three quarters. This shoulder section should have the most mass and height.

11. Select two more light tan and then two dark ginger hen feathers from the hen skin, two rows up the saddle. Tie them in and wrap them together to the eye of the shank, tie them down, and trim thread. Whip-finish and coat the thread wraps with UV resin.

12. Insert a short-shank 60-degree jig hook in the vise, eye turned down. Attach the thread to the hook shank and wrap a thread base. Attach nylon-coated wire to the hook shank at the point shown and wrap the thread over the wire, coming a little bit down the hook bend. Slide the wire through the rear assembly and tie it down, adding UV resin over your thread wraps. Trim and tie in large chenille to the back of the shank and wrap forward three to four turns.

13. Select two light tan and two dark tan hen saddle feathers from the skin, moving up another two rows to get larger feathers. Tie in the feathers by their tips and wrap them forward. As always, make sure to pick out any trapped fibers as you go to keep the fly looking its best.

14. Add another two wraps of Finesse Body Chenille and four more feathers. Tie in pectoral fins on each side of the fly and then tie in four more feathers and wrap them forward. Tie them down, trim, and whip-finish. Add UV resin.

15. Attach a dumbbell eye right where the shank begins to bend with tight figure-eight wraps and add UV resin to the thread wraps. Be sure to take several wraps around the base of the eyes, above the shank but under the eyes, to tighten the figure-eight wraps.

16. For this fly we are going to show a head-style variation tied with Senyo's Laser Dub, using light tan fibers for the bottom and dark tan fibers for the top.

17. Rotate your vise and tie in a clump of light tan on the bottom of the shank in approximately the middle of the clump. Turn your vise upright and tie in a clump of dark tan fibers over the same thread wraps. Pull the top clump back and take a few thread wraps over the base of the fibers, then pull the bottom clump back and wrap over the base of the fibers. Pull both clumps back and take a few more thread wraps.

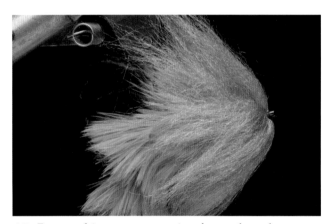

18. Repeat this process, moving forward on the shank, until you get to the eye. You can also use a brush to achieve the same look, or use spun deer hair.

19. Once you get to the eye, whip-finish the thread and trim the head to the desired shape starting on top

and bottom. Then trim the sides, exposing the lead eye. Add UV resin to the thread wraps. Next take a file and rough up both sides of the lead eye so that when you add UV resin to it the eye will adhere to the surface better.

20. Add UV resin to each dumbbell eye, place the translucent eyes, and then cure them with the light.

21. When the eyes are glued into place you can't tell there's a dumbbell eye on the fly. As I said this is an optional step, but I think it's a nice touch and doesn't take much time.

I caught my largest peacock bass on the Feather Game Changer while in the Brazilian Amazon. These fish are amazing fighters—I broke a fly line on one and a few times broke 40-pound fluorocarbon on them. I can't wait to get back and tangle with these beautiful fish again.

A brown trout version of the Feather Game Changer fooled this aggressive, fat pickerel while fishing for trout. TUCKER HORNE PHOTO

Tying the Feather Game Changer Sculpin (Brush Head)

This bottom-darting pattern is an important variation that illustrates another head option for Game Changers and T-Bones. Brushes make it simple to create a fast, great-looking head that pushes water. To keep the fly deep, and also to ensure that the hook point rides up, you can coat the underside of the head with a mixture of UV resin and tungsten powder. This flashier variation is designed for dingier or higher water. A drabber version is shown in the spread on page 165. In these steps, I move rather quickly through the rear portion of the fly because it is the same as with other Feather Game Changers.

Materials

Four 15mm shanks | #1 SL12 Short and a #2/0 60 Degree Gamakatsu jig hook | 6/0 rusty brown Veevus | 30-pound Berkley nylon-coated wire | chickabou grizzly | rootbeer Filler Flash | grizzly olive and grizzly brown hen saddles | mullet brown Flash Blend Baitfish Brush head (2") | Ice Living Eyes

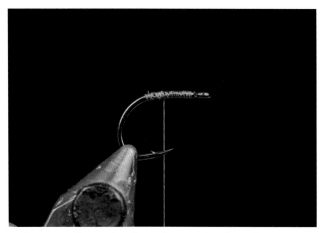

1. Insert a short-shank, wide-gap hook in the vise. Instead of a rear stinger hook, you can use a shank if you like.

2. Select two chickabou feathers, marry them, and tie them both on top of the shank at the same time with a pinch wrap. These feathers match the barred, rounded tail of a sculpin nicely.

3. Trim the excess and wrap a smooth thread base. To maintain a very narrow profile at the rear of the fly, skip the Filler Flash and tie in a mottled hen feather by the tip.

4. Take three or four wraps, tie off the feathers, and trim the excess. Whip-finish the thread and apply UV resin to finish the tail.

5. Slip a 15mm shank through the eye of the stinger hook, tie in Filler Flash, followed by hen saddle. Repeat this three more times for a total of one stinger hook and four shanks in the rear.

6. Attach the rear assembly to a 60-degree jig hook. This is a bottom bouncing fly and we want the hook to ride up.

7. To get the fly to ride properly, attach weight to the top of the hook shank as it appears in your vise, which will be the bottom of the hook when the fly is in the water since it is inverted. Dumbbell eyes also work, but this method is useful and worth knowing.

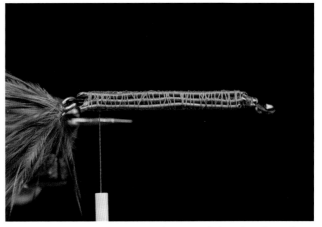

8. Lash the folded wire to the top of the shank and then coat it with UV resin.

9. Tie the body with Filler Flash and hen saddle, just as with previous versions of the Feather Game Changers. Tie in hen saddle pectoral fins.

10. Tie in Flash Blend Baitfish Brush. You can also use Sculpting Flash Fiber, which is a little heavier as it would absorb water a little more. Wrap it forward, stroking the fibers to the rear as you go.

11. Pick out any trapped fibers with a bodkin.

12. Make the first cut flat to imitate the natural's flat belly. A flat belly also helps the fly ride and glide in the water naturally.

13. Then cut the head all the way up and around at a 45-degree angle, creating the shape of a natural sculpin's head.

14. The profile should look like this.

15. You can modify the tapers to suit your taste and preferences, but this is a good shape to start out with, whether using brushes or a spun deer-hair head.

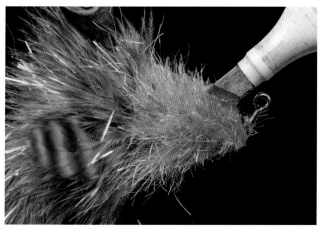

16. Mark the fly up to match naturals in your area. I like to do this in layers, first applying a base of olive and then different shades of brown to create depth.

17. The darker color over the lighter color creates a nice mottling effect.

18. Apply flexible UV resin to the belly and cure it with the light. To prevent the fly from turning over I have sometimes glued a washer or coin to the belly as well.

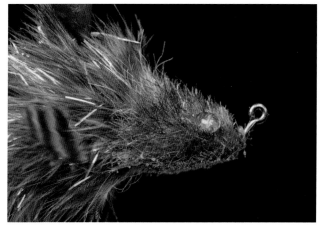

19. Trim out the eye sockets with scissors and apply UV resin.

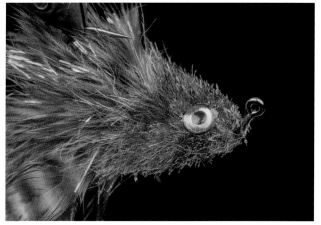

20. Place the eyes in the sockets and cure the glue through the eyes with the UV light.

Tying the Feather Game Changer Sculpin (Sculpin Helmet)

Flymen Sculpin Helmets are another great way to finish off flies designed to be fished right on the bottom. They accept eyes well and you can color them if you like. Sometimes I have found that the Sculpin Helmet is not enough weight to flip the fly over. Adding weight to the underside of the shank or the bottom of the Sculpin Helmet can keep it oriented properly.

Materials

15, 20, and 25mm shanks | short-shank wide-gap stinger and #2/0 Gamakatsu 60 Degree Jig | 6/0 olive Veevus | 45-pound Berkley nylon-coated wire | chickabou tail | natural brown and olive hen saddles | olive Filler Flash | large Flymen Sculpin Helmet (black) | Ice Living Eyes

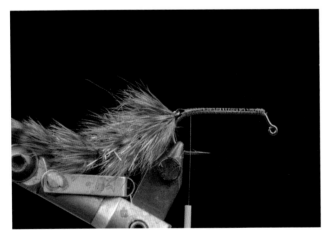

1. Attach the tail assembly to the 60-degree jig hook. All the steps up to this point are the same as with the other Feather Game Changers we have tied in the book.

2. Add Filler Flash to support the hen saddle and also provide a seamless transition from the junction wire to the front portion of the fly.

3. Tie in and wrap the hen saddle feathers as you have for other Game Changers. Though you still need to add the pectoral fins, I like to first measure with the Sculpin Helmet to make sure that the front portion of the fly is full and without any gaps between the hen saddles and the Sculpin Helmet.

4. Sculpins have prominent pectoral fins, so I like to choose wider hen feathers. I also tie them in at a downward angle to match the overall profile and shape of a true sculpin.

5. Add another few turns of Filler Flash and then two more hen saddles. After pre-measuring the Sculpin Helmet, you may need to tie in more than two hen saddles. The goal is to get the front of the fly nice and full so that it transitions into the rear portion of the weighted head.

6. Slide the Sculpin Helmet over the hook eye to check the fit one last time.

7. Apply UV resin underneath the Sculpin Helmet.

8. Use the syringe that came with your resin to shoot more resin into the head of the fly. Cure the resin with the UV light.

9. Add resin to the eye sockets in the head and attach the eyes. Cure the UV resin. Sometimes I add resin over the eyes as well for maximum durability.

This sculpin pattern dives and glides through the water down on the bottom where the naturals live.

Smallmouth bass were responsible for the creation of the Game Changer series. They love an imitation to swim, kick and dart in the water erratically. Adding different heads to the flies, such as the deer-hair head in the middle image (Cory Hasslehahn photo) changes the action. When fishing for prespawn bass in cooler water temperatures (right) the hovering undulating action is perfect for the mood of these fish during this time of year since the water is usually high and still cold.

11 | Crafty Changer

This leaper sucked in a Crafty Game Changer fished with a fast, two-handed retrieve. Few flies I've tied swim like Crafty Changers.
BRIAN GROSSENBACHER PHOTO

I loved everything about the Feather Game Changer, but with feathers I was limited to flies under 7 to 8 inches—and that was the best-case scenario with exceptional feathers. I was on the lookout for a material that would provide the same level of swim but that would have fibers long enough for larger profile flies. I found it in Craft Fur, a synthetic hair that comes on a "skin." It is widely available in fly shops, but also craft stores, which is a major benefit of the material.

Craft Fur gave me the same, if not better, swimming action the feathers did. By using Filler Flash in the rear to support the fibers and then building out the forward portion of the fly with Body Tubing like the T-Bone, I could create giant flies that swim extraordinary well.

Granted, the larger flies do get heavier, but that is one of the trade-offs that I was willing to accept for a fly with this kind of action. Because flies tied with Craft Fur hold water, they sink very quickly, which can be a benefit when fishing in higher flows.

Though the material is very easy to work with, presizing the fibers makes the tying process more efficient. Any given clump of Craft Fur typically has roughly four different lengths of fibers to work with. After trimming the fibers from the skin, pick out all the longer fibers from the bunch and set them aside. Then repeat this process a few times to get several bunches of approximately the same lengths of hair. Doing this with every bunch you cut, and then hand-stacking the new

I caught my largest male brown trout to date on a Crafty Changer, in bright sun, on the South Holston River, while fishing with good friends Bob Cheers and Jay Nichols, who snapped this shot that appeared on the cover of *Fly Fisherman*. Because of that one alpha male's willingness to eat this fly in absolutely terrible conditions for hunting large browns, the Crafty Changer will forever be one of my favorite patterns for targeting large browns.

A shad that passed through a tailwater dam and a Crafty Changer lookalike. Many tailwaters across the country have shad kills in the lake systems every fall, winter, and spring, which creates a buffet line for the big predators below.

bunches of same size fibers that you sorted, ensures that you have different fiber lengths to create the taper that you need in each fly.

As with the Bucktail Game Changer, I reverse-tie the stacked fibers (hand-stacked, not stacked with a tool). Filler Flash props up the fibers in the rear, and then as I need more height I use a variety of different methods ranging from Body Tubing spreaders to UV resin. Sometimes I use a brush made from Baitfish Emulator. All of these techniques have already been covered in previous flies and they all serve a purpose in Craft Fur Changers. Body Tubing, though a little heavier, allows the fly to hold its shape longer than the Filler Flash or brush, and that is the technique we illustrate in this chapter. All of the Craft Fur is reverse-tied for height and bulk and Filler Flash to support. If you want to tie larger flies, you can make your own brushes with Baitfish Emulator or similar fibers for internal support.

One technique that I like to use to create more bulk on larger flies is to spin Filler Flash, which twists the fibers and makes them fuller, adding density and rigidity. As you wrap the Filler Flash forward, the flash will stand out more and fill up the space faster, creating more body without added weight.

A benefit of tying with Craft Fur is that once you tie in the fibers, you can pick at them with your fingers to trim them, unlike with bucktail. You still want to premeasure the fibers so that they come roughly half to three-quarters up the previous section, but if you tie

them in a little long it's no big deal to pick at them and get them the length you like.

Tying in clumps of Craft Fur, rather than winding a chenille or brush, makes it very easy to tie two-tone flies to imitate local baitfish. To achieve a seamless look between the two different colors, flatten and distribute the fibers with your thumbnail after you tie them in to close the gaps between the top and the bottom and envelop all of the fibers around the shank, covering the Filler Flash. Comb out the fibers after you do this.

You can use feathers for pectoral fins, but I often use rubber legs on these patterns as well, which provides a different look and action. You can vary the tail and head configurations easily. The version below has a rooster-saddle tail tied in the round. I really like the way it wags in the water when it's swimming. I also find that it is a little more durable. There are plenty of feathers in there to work in the current even if aggressive trout nip away a few of them.

The fly below incorporates two hooks. I like to use two hooks for toothy fish that have a tendency to grab flies like trout or pike. For bucket-mouth fish such as tarpon, striped bass, or largemouth bass or peacock bass where the fish will inhale the whole fly without grabbing at it, the back hook is not necessary. However, even though smallmouth bass will inhale a fly and often attack it from the side, I like to add a second hook because they can't always suck the entire fly in like a largemouth.

Need for Speed

Good friend Rob Kinkoph casts a big Crafty Changer to likely spots on the South Holston River in eastern Tennessee for trophy brown trout on a cold fall morning. Two-handed strips can cause wary browns to make a hasty and poor decision in clear water.

In clear water or on bright days, I have often found that to get a fish to eat the fly you have to retrieve the fly quickly. A lot of times, burning it back to you with a two-handed retrieve triggers a fight or flight response in a predatory fish that works to your advantage. A fast retrieve from the start forces a quick decision from a fish before it gets too close to the boat, which could spook it.

Other times, you may need to speed up your fly during a normal retrieve where the fish is following but noncommittal. When you retrieve any fly for apex predators, you want to have several gears to work with, and this means controlling your retrieve so that you can speed it up if necessary. When a big predator moves on the fly, it can be a cat-and-mouse game and sometimes the fish needs a little more coaxing to finally commit to the fly. The natural predator-prey response is for the prey to flee when the predator starts its attack. I know I am mixing metaphors here, but I have found that my clients understand the swim speeds best in terms of running. Many times you want to walk the fly back to the boat to start the retrieve (first gear) and if a fish moves on the fly and starts following but doesn't eat, you then want to start to jog the fly back (second gear). If the fish speeds up on it and shows more interest but still doesn't eat, I then run the fly away from the fish (third gear). This is

usually when the fish makes its final assault and clobbers the fly. We all want something that we can't get.

Sometimes you will need fourth gear to get the fish to commit, and you won't have it if you begin your initial retrieve too fast. Everything is happening fast at this point and the eat is usually at or near the boat. When you run out of space at the boat, it is time for the figure-eight. This is popular for muskies, but I have also caught large browns with it. When the fly gets within two feet of your rod tip, stick the rod tip deeper into the water and move the fly in figure-eight patterns or at least a wide oval with a change of direction. Once you go from the retrieve to the eight you should not slow down or stop the fly—you should increase the speed, especially on the turn. Make as wide a turn as possible. Tight turns make it hard for larger fish to change direction.

There are several ways of doing a two-handed strip. The one I like is to place the rod under your casting arm with the rod tip pointing at or into the water. This angle, which I maintain even when doing a standard retrieve, allows you to have good contact with the fly at all times, reducing unwanted slack in the line and minimizing the chance of missing a strike. You strip in a continuous manner by pulling the line in an upward angle with your casting hand while at the same time pulling straight back with your other hand. ∎

Tying the Crafty Changer

Materials

Two 15mm and two 25mm Fish-Spines | #2 Gamakatsu SL12 short and #2/0 B10S | 6/0 silver doctor blue Veevus | 60-pound Berkley nylon-coated wire | pearl Filler Flash and blue grizzly rooster saddle | blue and white Hareline Craft Fur | Baitfish Emulator | white ¼" Body Tubing | white Sculpting Flash Fiber (2") | Hareline Rainbow Shimmer Legs | Chameleon or Renzetti Molded Moon Eyes (Ghost)

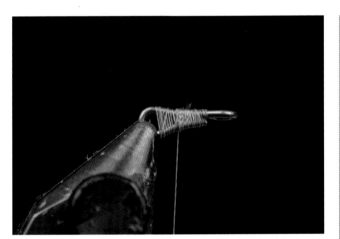

1. Insert a 10mm shank in the vise, attach the thread, wrap the entire shank with thread, and stop halfway on the shank, right where the bottom of the rear loop becomes almost parallel with the shanks.

2. Trim some of the fibers from a section of pearl Filler Flash, exposing the core. Tie it in just behind the opening of the connection loops, which will eventually create a ramp for the tail feathers and enhance the fan shape.

Opposite page: All of the flies are tied with Flash Blend Baitfish Brush heads, except for the second fly from the top, which has a reverse-tied Craft Fur head. Different types of silicone legs from Hareline replace pectoral fins. Top two flies are tied with Magnum Predator Legs, third fly Barred Crazy Legs, and bottom fly chartreuse black flake Crazy Legs. The second and last fly have color schemes that have performed well for me. The top fly imitates a redhorse sucker and the third fly a brown trout.

3. Wrap the Filler Flash forward, simultaneously stroking the fibers rearward. Take two full wraps, tie down the flash, and trim the excess. Make sure to leave enough room for two sets of feathers plus one more application of Filler Flash.

4. Select four rooster feathers and measure them so that they extend 1½ times the length of the Filler Flash, past the Filler Flash.

5. Tie in three dark feathers on the top and one light feather on the bottom, making sure that they are all evenly spaced.

6. Tie in and take two more wraps of Filler Flash to gain a little bit more height and support for two more dark feathers and one more light feather on the bottom. After the feathers are tied in, whip-finish and add UV resin. The finished tail should look something like this.

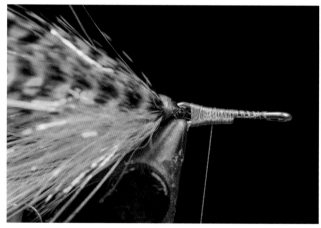

7. Slip a 15mm shank through the eye of the previous shank and then place it in the vise. Attach the thread and wrap the entire length of the shank, coming slightly up the back connecting loop to close it off. Leave enough space to equal the opening of the previous shank eye. Advance the thread to a point one-eighth inch behind the junction of the shanks.

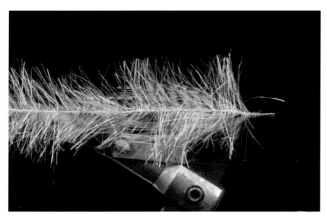

8. Select some more Filler Flash, trim the fibers to expose a little bit of tag, and tie that in. Since we're not trying to create bulk at this time, moving forward to this point before tying in the fibers allows them to lie down more.

9. Take two wraps forward, making sure to fold the fibers back as you wrap. On some flies you may have to trim the Filler Flash a bit so that it doesn't extend over the tail too much, but here the fibers are a perfect height after wrapping back over the base of them with thread. From the very beginning of the fly it is important to be thinking about taper.

10. Color the flash with a permanent marker to match the color scheme of the fly, if you desire.

11. Craft Fur comes in a wide variety of colors and is available in lots of big-box craft stores. However, fly-tying material distributors such as Hareline offer premium hair with long fibers.

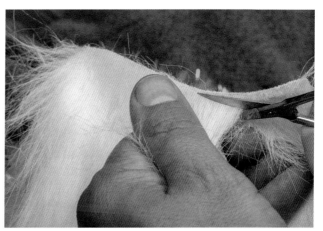

12. Select a clump of Craft Fur, holding one end by the tips and cut it as tight as possible to the skin for maximum length.

13. Pull out the shorter fibers at the base just as you would clean up deer hair or bucktail that you are stacking.

14. Pick out the longest fibers and set them aside for later.

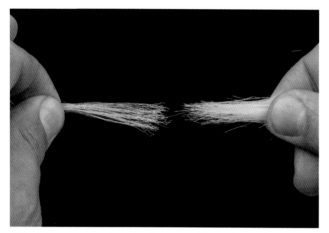

15. After separating the longest fibers from the bunch, you should still have a generous amount of mid-length Craft Fur.

16. Take the remaining Craft Fur and hand stack it so you have one bunch with equal lengths.

17. Measure the Craft Fur so that it is slightly longer than the Filler Flash, then trim the butts even.

18. Flip the vise upside down. Tie down the fibers on the bottom of the shank and then take two secure wraps to keep the fibers in place.

19. Flatten the fibers with your thumbnail and distribute them around the bottom half of the shank. This hides the Filler Flash and also prevents gaps between the two different colors of Craft Fur.

20. Rotate the vise upright and repeat this process for the top blue fibers. Craft Fur can get heavy in the water, so remember that a little bit goes a long way. For Game Changers you want less in back and more up front. After you have massaged the top section with your fingers, brush out the two sections to blend the fibers together so there are no gaps.

21. Pick out the fibers to the perfect length. One of the huge benefits of using Craft Fur is that you can fix mistakes and not be overly concerned with exact length while you are tying the fibers in.

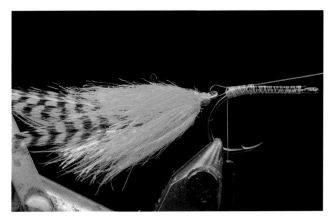

22. Chose a rear hook that is a little longer than your last shank, in this case a 15mm shank, to keep the overall flow of the fly. Tie in the 30-pound coated wire

as you have done with previous flies. Take only a few wraps over the doubled over wire and pull it to the proper length before finishing your wraps over the two strands. Trim the wire and wrap over the edges. Coat the wire with UV resin and cure it.

23. Trim and tie in Filler Flash between the hook point and the hook barb, advance the thread, and wrap the Filler Flash three or four times toward the hook eye. Tie off and trim the excess. Color the top half with marker to imitate the back of the baitfish you are trying to imitate.

24. From here on out you are going to repeat the Craft Fur tying steps, first tying in the white belly and then the blue top. However, select slightly larger clumps to add more mass moving forward. You still do not need the longest fibers, so set those aside before you hand-stack the clump. Before reverse-tying both clumps of Craft Fur, measure them so that they reach approximately half to three quarters over the previous section. Use your thumb and forefinger to press down on and distribute the fibers when you first tie them in and also before you wrap the thread in front of the fibers to begin the reverse tie. The goal is to make sure that the top and bottom blend into one another. The reverse-tying process is the same as with other materials.

25. The completed top and bottom of the hook part. You can control the height of the Craft Fur with flexible resin for a precise taper. Add a little bit to the base of the Craft Fur making sure to not go too far up the fibers, manipulate the fibers to the height that you want, and then hit it with the light to keep the fibers in that position. Pick out the fibers to fine tune your taper.

26. Slip a 20mm shank through the eye of the hook and clamp the shank in the vise. Attach the thread and wrap the entire shank, closing the rear loop and only leaving enough room to allow the hook free play.

27. Tie in the Filler Flash on the upward sloping part of the rear connection loop to create more height and bulk. Spin the Filler Flash with a dubbing loop tool

and clip attachment to help it gain rigidity and height. Wrap the Filler Flash to a point roughly halfway up to two-thirds up the shank.

28. Select a clump of Craft Fur that is equal to or a little larger than the previous clump. You do not want to ever go lighter now; you always want to increase the amount of fibers. Hand-stack it and measure it so that it overlaps the previous section by three quarters of the way. As before, use your fingers to press down on the fibers to distribute them after you tie them in.

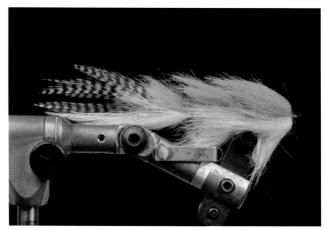

29. Bring the thread forward, reverse the Craft Fur, and tie the thread off. Add flexible UV resin over the thread and a little bit onto the base of the Craft Fur, top and bottom. Work the fibers into position and once you have the height that you desire, cure the resin with the light. Once you have set the position, you can add another coating for more durability.

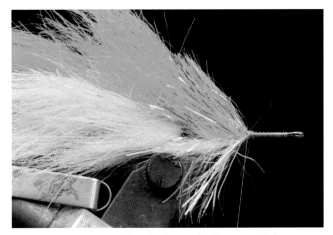

30. Insert a 25mm shank through the eye of the previous one and tie in Filler Flash directly in front of the loop connection. Spin the filler and take up to eight wraps, depending on how tightly you wrap the fibers together as you move forward. You want it to be as dense as possible while still leaving between one half and one third of the shank free for the Craft Fur.

31. This is a larger fly, so I am going to show how to use Body Tubing to gain added height at the shoulders, which is the point at which the fly needs to be broadest. Create a spreader exactly as illustrated in the T-Bone steps. You want the Filler Flash to be as full as possible so there is no need for the rear of the spreader to compress the fibers, just make sure it touches them slightly.

32. At this point, the longer fibers that you've been setting aside come into play. Tie in the white bunch on the bottom, followed by the blue bunch on the top. Measure them so that when they are folded back they cover three quarters of the previous section. Keeping a good amount of the butt sections in this part of the fly adds bulk and height once you reverse-tie the Craft Fur back over the Body Tubing.

33. Reverse-tie the fibers and then whip-finish the thread. Add flexible UV resin to help support the Craft Fur and achieve height.

34. Insert the forward hook into the vise and attach the rear portion of the fly with wire and coat that with UV resin. Tie in and create a ¼" Body Tubing dam making sure that the rear of the tubing reaches the middle of the loop formed with the wire. Tie in another section of Filler Flash or, if you have it, Baitfish Emulator Flash (shown above) with longer fibers. Take only two or three wraps forward because you need space to add several more pieces of Body Tubing.

35. After you have tied off the filler material, color it to match the top of the fly. Tie in another section of ¼" Body Tubing and form your spreader. Tie in a clump of long white fibers (the longest that you have saved) and a clump of blue by the butts with the fibers extending to the rear. We are not reverse-tying at this point because you don't need as much height as before and you want to start reversing the taper. Tie in another section of Body Tubing, the same size as before, and tie in another section of Craft Fur the same way, making sure it overlaps the previous section by three quarters.

36. Tie in six to eight silicone legs on each side of the fly for pectoral fins. You can use feathers if you wish; I just want to show options that add movement to the fly.

37. To finish the head, you can reverse-tie more Craft Fur. Tie off the thread behind the fibers before you stroke them back and finish setting their position with flexible UV resin. In this version, however, I'd like to show you how to add a dubbing-brush head, in this case 2" Sculpting Flash Fiber. Tie it in and wrap it side by side, combing it out at you wrap forward.

38. The number of wraps required is determined by how much room you've left on the hook shank. The more wraps, the denser it becomes, the more it diverts the water, and the better the fly swims. Pick out any overwrapped fibers with a bodkin and comb the body.

39. Tie off and trim the excess brush with wire cutters and whip-finish. Trim the dubbing-brush head at a 45-degree angle, all the way around.

40. Mark the top of the head to match the rest of the fly. Add flexible UV resin and then your eyes, and then cure the resin. The eyes here are Chameleon from CCG; however, Renzetti's Molded Moon Eyes are a great substitute.

I think the Crafty Changers swim as good as any fly I have seen. The fibers breathe and move in the water unlike anything else. The variations on the following page showcase different color combinations of this same pattern. Note that the brown trout has a reverse-tied Craft Fur head.

Crafty Changer Variations

Crafty Changer (Fire Tiger)

Crafty Changer (Shad)

Crafty Changer (Brown Trout)

Crafty Changer (Rainbow Trout)

This brown came off a midriver ledge system and hammered a 10-inch Crafty Changer. When streamer fishing, make sure to cover all types of water and not just the banks.

12 | Polar Express Changer

This large muskie inhaled a Polar Express Changer on a winter trip. This is a fairly new pattern born from the need for a speedier version of the Crafty Changer that still had plenty of movement in the water.

Polar Fibre is similar in many ways to Craft Fur, and like Craft Fur is available on a synthetic skin. The fibers tend to be wispier and smoother, however, and provide a slightly different appearance to the finished fly, as well as a different action. You can tie smaller Game Changers with Polar Fibre in exactly the same manner as with Craft Fur—hand-stacking clipped fibers and tying them in. But the real benefit of using Polar Fibre is that you can buy different size Polar Fibre brushes (¾", 1½", and 3") and wrap them on the shanks, saving a lot of time. All you do is follow the steps outlined in the previous chapter for the Crafty Changer, but substitute different size Polar Fibre brushes. Increase the size of the brush as you move up the fly to create your profile, making sure that the fibers veil over the previous sections according to the

This large tarpon sucked in a Polar Changer. Game Changers tied with Polar Fibre—standard and also the express versions with the Deceiver-style tails—have worked well for everything from pike in Saskatchewan to big reds and jacks in Louisiana. GREG DINI PHOTO

tapers that we have been following with all of the previous flies.

Brushes alone make tying these flies quick; however, in the Polar Express Changer I take another shortcut to speed up the pattern even more. The longer Deceiver-style tail provides a time-tested swimming action and gives movement to the fly without the need for so many shanks. Tying the tail in this manner results in a great action and only requires three shanks and a hook. You can use this style of tail on Crafty Changers as well if you want a different action and also want to speed up the tying time. It is just another variation to explore. I should also note that if time is a concern and you have a brush maker, you can make your own homemade brushes from Craft Fur and replicate this express pattern with that material.

The action of the Polar Express Changer is different than the serpentine swimming action of a regular Game Changer and reminds me a lot of a fluke or Larry Dahlberg's plastic bait, Mr. Wiggly. The flatter sides allow you to use this fly as a jerkbait on the hard strip and pause as well as a swimbait style with a steadier retrieve. This flexibility makes it a good choice when you want options—a hard strip kicks it side to side and an even two-handed strip makes it swim.

The underbody on these flies can be a variety of materials, including Finesse Body Chenille if you are tying them in the 3- to 4-inch range, and Filler Flash up to the 5-inch version. As I tie larger flies, I like to use stiffer materials to help the fly maintain its shape. In the one shown here, I use Filler Flash in the back and then a homemade Baitfish Emulator brush to help achieve height in the shoulders. You can trim the sides of the filler materials to maintain the flatter profile that helps the water flow over the fly faster and create a tighter wiggle.

Tying the Polar Express Changer

Materials

Two 15mm Fish Spines and one 35mm Fish-Skull Articulated Shank | #1/0 Partridge Attitude Extra and #2/0 B10S | tan Flymaster | 60-pound Berkley nylon-coated wire | Grizzly ginger rooster saddle hackles for tail and pectoral fins | rootbeer Filler Flash and Baitfish Emulator | mullet brown (or tan) Polar Fibre Streamer Brush (¾", 1½", and 3") | Ice Living Eyes

1. Insert a 15mm shank in the vise. Tie on the thread and wrap a solid foundation on the shank, stopping the thread at the highest point of the rear connection loop. Select four grizzly ginger saddle hackles and tie them in Deceiver-style (two pairs, each cupped in) at this point. You can flatten the stems with pliers or wrap a small pillow of dubbing before tying in the feathers to keep them from rolling on the shank.

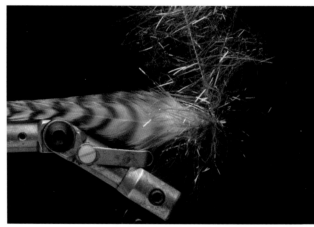

2. Secure the thread wrap with UV resin. Trim and tie in Filler Flash, take two wraps forward, and tie it down. Trim the excess.

3. Tie in a ¾" Polar Fibre Streamer Brush in front of the Filler Flash and take two wraps forward. As you wrap forward, stroke the fibers back and also use a bodkin to pick out any trapped fibers. Tie down the brush, clip the excess, and apply UV resin to the thread wraps.

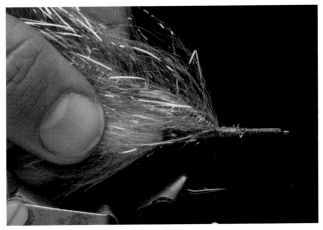

4. Insert a SL12 or equivalent hook in the vise and attach the back shank to it with coated wire. Tie in Filler Flash just over the barb and take four to five wraps forward, leaving about three eye lengths behind the hook eye bare.

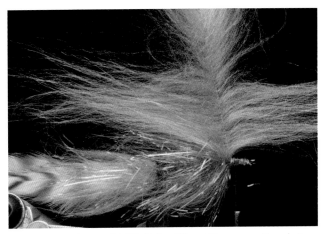

5. Tie in a piece of 1½" Polar Fibre Streamer Brush in front of the Filler Flash and take two complete wraps, picking out the fibers with a bodkin as you go. Tie the brush off and trim the extra. Whip-finish, add UV resin to the thread, and cure it.

6. Comb all the fibers back to help smooth everything out and distribute them around the hook completely.

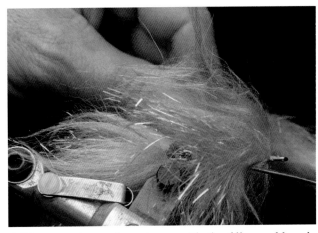

7. We are trying to form taper with the filler and brush so shoot for a half-inch overlap over the previous section. To fine tune your length, pinch the ends of the Polar Fibre and pick out the tips. This will make it look natural as you get uneven ends verses cutting the fiber with scissors.

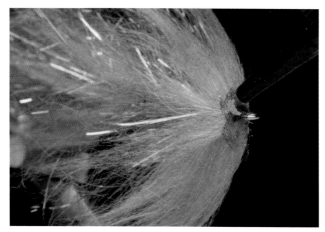

8. Once you are satisfied with the length, add flexible UV resin at the base of the fibers, moving up approximately ¼ of an inch into the fibers. This will help maintain the profile over time as this material is soft and tends to want to collapse, especially after time in the water.

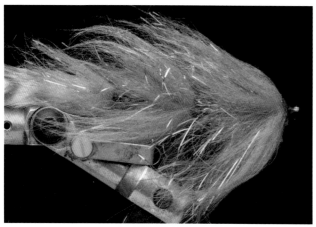

9. Slide a 35mm shank through the eye of the stinger hook and insert it in the vise. Wrap the entire shank with thread and select some Filler Flash, or in this case Baitfish Emulator. Tie it in two-thirds of the way back on the shank and wrap it forward to a point one-third behind the shank eye. Tie in a section of 1½" Polar Fibre Streamer Brush and take two wraps forward, picking out the fibers with a bodkin as you wrap. After you tie it off, use flexible UV resin to set the shape as you did previously.

10. Insert a #2/0 B10S or equivalent hook in the vise and attach the back section with 60-pound nylon wire. Tie in your homemade Emulator brush on the shank before the hook bend and wrap it forward to near the hook point. Tie in a 3" Polar Fibre Streamer Brush and take two wraps, adding flexible UV resin at the best of the fibers for support when you are finished.

11. Add two pectoral fins to each side and repeat previous steps with Baitfish Emulator brush and anywhere from three to four wraps of 3" Polar Fibre Streamer Brush—whatever you need to fill out the hook. Fix the front of the brush head with flexible UV resin after you pick the fibers to length and position them. You want the fibers to cover ¾ of the portion behind it.

12. Add flexible UV resin for the eyes, place the eyes, and cure with UV light.

The Polar Express Changer has a distinct action in the water and is one of the fastest Game Changer variations to tie.

Anglers Clayton Shick and Rob Kinkoph admire a beast of a northern pike caught at Wollaston Lake, Saskatchewan, on a Game Changer.

13 | Mallard Changer

The butterfly peacocks climbed all over the Mallard Changer in the Brazilian Amazon. To enhance this fly's swimming jerkbait-style action, I added a foam slider head hidden under the mallard feathers. This created a cool darting and hover swimming action that really got the peacocks going.

The Mallard Changer evolved naturally from my love of mallard feathers and its distinct barring since first learning to tie trout flies. Flies such as Kelly Galloup's Zoo Cougar and Tommy Lynch's Drunken Disorderly use these feathers on the back of the fly, and I had seen firsthand, with Tommy's fly especially, the seductive action in the water. Water flows easily and freely over the smooth feathers, and I thought that the smooth feathers combined with the articulations would create a tighter, more pronounced swimming movement that is unique in the Game Changer family.

I think this fly showcases the concept of framing at its finest. The Filler Flash or Finesse Body Chenille provides the bones and muscle; the feathers, the skin. The challenge with this fly is obtaining the right size of mallard feathers, which can be mitigated by using a full skin instead of having to sort through loose feathers. Just as with hen saddle, you can work up the skin to get larger feathers. Wider, shorter feathers with fairly even tips are ideal—more or less the same feathers that you would select for dry-fly wings—but you sometimes have to work with what you are given. In the example below we show how to use feathers from the regular packs available in fly shops. It takes longer to sort through the feathers and select the best ones, but you can definitely make them work.

I am a little torn about this fly just because of the time that it takes to tie and also how hard it is to get the right feathers, but I enjoy tying it and watching it come alive with every step. I guess to me it is like a full dress version of a Game Changer that might bring as much satisfaction in properly tying it as it does fishing it. And it does fish well. I took this fly with me to the Amazon for peacocks and it was the top-producing pattern of the trip. It was more durable than I thought it would be, and I caught well over 100 peacock bass on one fly.

You can create different profiles with this fly to imitate different baits, as shown in the shad example at the end of this chapter. You can also add weight or more buoyant materials under the feathers to create different actions. The example at the end of this chapter has a foam slider head disguised by the feathers, which makes the fly kick up and down, dart and hover, and rise after a strip.

In the steps for the fly featured in this chapter, we are going to move fairly quickly through the process, as there is really nothing different about tying this fly from other Game Changers, other than reverse-tying the mallard flank feathers and setting them. Instead of mallard, you can use a lot of different feathers from teal to pheasant. By varying the colors or the type of bird feather, you can create a lot of dimension and depth to this fly.

The basic concepts behind the Mallard Changer can be replicated with other feathers, such as this Game Changer tied with pheasant. Outer feathers not only help shape the fly but their smoothness improves laminar flow.

Tying the Mallard Changer

Materials

Three 15mm and one 25mm Fish-Spines | #1 Ahrex Gammerus and #2/0 B10S | 6/0 olive Veevus | 30-pound Berkley nylon-coated wire | furnace brown rooster saddle | olive Filler Flash | olive and gold mallard flank feathers | Wind Living Eyes

1. Insert a 10mm shank into the vise, attach your thread, and trim and tie in Filler Flash in the middle of the shank. Select eight Indian rooster neck hackles from the base of the skin and tie them in, one feather at a time, around the shank. Trim the butts, whip-finish, and add UV resin.

2. Slide a 15mm shank through the eye of the 10mm shank and insert it in the vise. Attach the thread and wrap a foundation on the entire shank, wrapping back to the opening of the rear loop and stopping in the middle of the shank where the main shank and the back opening meet. Trim some fibers from the Filler Flash, exposing the core, and tie it to the shank. Then trim the Filler Flash so it is only long enough to cover the head of the tail section. You don't want long fibers here to maintain a low profile.

3. Wrap the Filler Flash forward to the eye of the shank. Trim the butts and wrap a clean thread base for the mallard feathers. Select four smaller, wider mallard feathers with flat tips—three gold and one olive—for the top feather. Marry them and pull away the base fibers, exposing only the length of feather that you need. As with other Game Changer style flies you want the feather tips to veil over the previous section just enough to cover the connection and the thread head.

5. After the four feathers are tied in, with the olive one on the top, trim the stem butts and add some thin UV resin to the thread wraps.

4. Flatten the stems with pliers and then starting at the side closest to you, tie in one at a time with the tips pointing toward the eye and the cup side facing out.

6. Bring your thread forward to just in front of the feathers and fold the feathers back. While holding them in place, wrap back over the base of the feathers until they lie at a low angle. Add UV resin.

7. Insert a 15mm shank through the eye of the previous one and tie in another piece of Filler Flash in the middle of it. Wrap the flash to the eye of the shank, picking out any trapped fibers with a bodkin. Trim the flash so that it veils over the previous section by ¼ and then wrap a nice even base for the feathers to come.

8. Select four more mallard feathers, size them so that they veil over the previous section by ½, and strip away the bottom fibers. Flatten the stems and tie them in, one at a time, cupped side out. Apply UV resin to the thread wraps and then bring the thread forward and fold the feathers back. Wrap back over the feathers to get the angle shown. Whip-finish the thread and add some flexible resin to the thread and base of the feathers for added reinforcement.

9. Insert another 15mm shank and repeat. Note that when you fold the feathers back at this point you do not wrap the thread onto the base of the feathers because you want them to be higher. Just butt the thread against the feathers or use flexible UV resin, which I prefer because it saves time by not having to wrap a bunch of thread. Once that section is done, attach the rear section to the hook. This is done the same way all the other Game Changers.

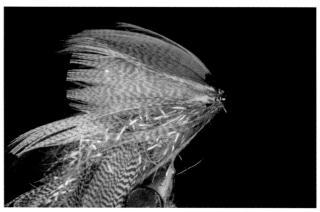

10. Add more Filler Flash, but at this time use a dubbing spinner to twist it so that it stands up. Wrap it forward a little more than two-thirds of the shank. You only need enough room for the feathers. Tie in the feathers so that they cover two-thirds of the wing on the previous shank. Use a generous amount of flexible UV resin in the front to set and secure the feathers at the desired angle and height.

11. Repeat this step two more times with two more 15mm shanks.

12. Insert a hook and attach the back section to the hook with wire. Tie in and wrap Filler Flash, spinning it for maximum height and volume. Add pectoral fins, which are the same feathers that you used for the tail. Then add more Filler Flash, wrapping it to the eye.

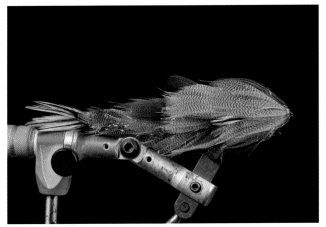

13. Select your last four feathers and tie them in just like the previous sections. You want to tie them in just behind the hook eye for a nice head. I like to whip-finish the thread at the tie-in point of the feathers before they are reversed tied. After you trim the thread, apply thin resin over the wraps and cure it. Then fold back the feathers and apply flexible resin at the base while holding them in place. Once you have the desired angle, hit the resin with the light to fix everything in place.

14. Add eyes with flexible UV resin and cure with the light. The Mallard Changer reclaims some of the realism of the original Game Changer but with natural materials that provide a scale effect.

Mallard Changer Variations

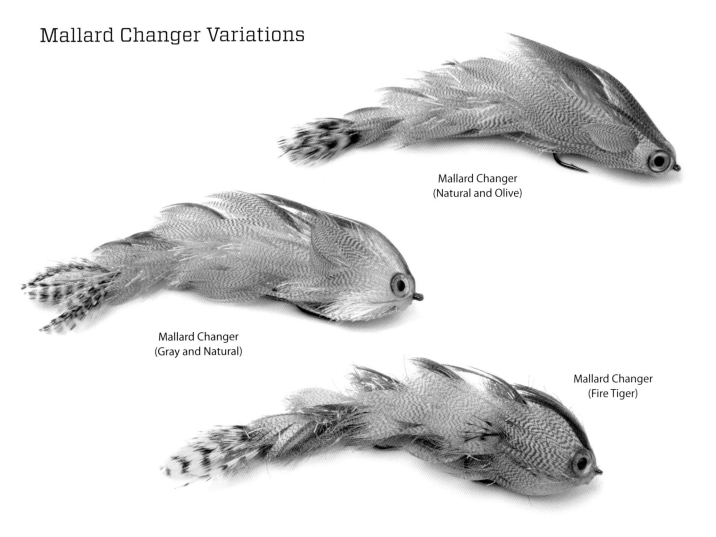

Mallard Changer
(Natural and Olive)

Mallard Changer
(Gray and Natural)

Mallard Changer
(Fire Tiger)

Casting Large Flies

One of the biggest challenges when fishing for predators is casting large flies throughout the day. While there will always be some work involved to reap these giant rewards, improvements in rod, line, and fly design have all made casting large flies for a sustained period of time manageable. JAMES JOYNER PHOTO

Though I have continually tried to create large flies that are easier and easier to cast, the fact of the matter is that you must use proper equipment and technique in order to cast them efficiently, especially for any length of time. It's one thing to be able to huff and puff and get the fly out there at the beginning of the day, and entirely another to be able to fish hard all day, which is what these predators sometime require. I'm not going to lie. Throwing large flies for a fish such as muskie takes some practice. I teach a lot of anglers how to do it, but some practice ahead of time will pay big dividends on a guided trip.

When muskie fishing, there are so many other things that can go wrong. You can't plan for such things as poor conditions, fish that are acting like jerks, or eats with poor hookups. Having the right equipment and a strong foundation of rigging and casting—what Larry Dahlberg calls "mechanics" in the Foreword—is essential. At least that way you are leaving more bandwidth to deal with these unknowns and

you'll be able to stay in the game longer, which can make all the difference in the world.

First, a little bit about the rods. We're lucky that today so many rod manufacturers have rods designed for predator fishing, which means being able to cast heavy flies, work them back to the boat effectively, and fight large fish. I have been fortunate enough to have had a hand in helping to develop a few of them such as Sage's muskie and pike rods and Temple Fork Outfitter's ESOX series.

Fast-action rods are great casting tools if you are casting light flies or making relatively few casts, but when casting all day with heavy flies I much prefer a rod that has more flex in the butt section, which helps absorb a lot of the shock and makes casting a lot easier on your arm and shoulder after a long day. Reducing shock also reduces the amount of slack generated at the end of the line from the recoil. If the rod bends deeper it tends to limit the amount of slack in the cast, which results in a better cast. All of this casting creates stress on the rods as well, which is why most manufacturers are now using composite grips instead of the traditional cork that is easily damaged from the daily grind of predator hunting.

Another key design for a good predator rod is an elongated butt handle and foregrip. Extending the butt handle a few inches allows for several things. First, you can use the butt during the cast to support your wrist on the back and forward stroke. Your forearm becomes an extension of the rod. Breaking your wrist excessively while casting is inefficient even on a trout stream, but with heavier rods, lines, and flies it can ruin your cast and your arm. Pinning the butt of the rod against your forearm as you come back on your backcast supports the wrist and hand. I can't tell you how much this can save you during a long day of casting. Not only does it reduce the stress but also makes you twice as strong—it is much easier to pull something than push it, and anchoring the rod butt against your arm throughout the cast allows you to pull the rod throughout the casting stroke.

Second, an extended butt helps you out in a number of ways when you are fishing. While stripping the fly through the water, you can anchor the butt against your arm, which reduces stress and fatigue when fishing large flies all day. It is also almost essential for figure-eighting fish where you need to place your line hand on the butt of the rod.

An extended foregrip is also important. When fishing and casting larger flies my hand tends to migrate up the rod to the top of the grip. I also noticed my clients would do the same. First by gripping up on the rod it shortens the rod making it feel lighter in hand and helps the extended butt rest on your forearm. Second it shortens the rod, making it a little stronger and quicker as well as reducing how much weight you are carrying through the air.

Switch and Spey rods have become important tools for me, especially when guiding. Using them my more inexperienced clients have been able to cast larger flies farther, getting them into the zone, whereas with a single-handed rod, they may have been unable to consistently cast far enough throughout the day. With a little coaching, being able to use two hands to cast the rod has been a big help. By matching the line with the fly and the rod, which is always critical, especially when casting larger flies, the longer rods are much more effective for larger flies. You can use two hands to overcome the weight of the rig and you eliminate the double haul, which is often a problem area for anglers. Even my more experienced casters now like to use two-handed rods simply because they are a lot less work.

The rod you choose is also directly related to the other piece of equipment that is critical for success—your fly line. You can fight very large fish with lightweight fly rods, but you need lines with mass or weight in them to be able to cast large flies efficiently. I do not like rating rods according to "weights." I don't really know what that means. But I do understand that the line and fly will dictate how the rod is going to react. When I designed a rod for TFO, we decided to label it with a grain weight range: 300 to 400 grain and 400 to 500 grain. They both will handle big flies and big lines, but the larger the fly the heavier the line that you want to fish so that it makes casting these large flies as easy as possible throughout the day.

Floating and intermediate lines definitely have a place, especially for smallmouth fishing, but when casting large flies for muskies, I most frequently use sinking lines. Because a lot of the styles of flies in the book don't sink quickly by themselves, full-sinking lines (250- to 450-grain heads, type 3 to type 6) are necessary to get them to swim at the right depth. Additionally, once you learn how to cast them, they are the best tool for delivering larger flies to fish. Matched with the right line and rod, casting large muskie flies can be fairly effortless. Lines like the new Sonar Titan Sink 3/Sink 5/Sink 7 and the Int/Sink 3/Sink 5 from Scientific Anglers are a good example of how manufacturers are designing lines specifically for predator fishing. The triple density lines also allow for a constant straight-line connection to your fly while fishing. These lines are specifically designed to cast larger flies with a shorter head for quicker turnover and a larger diameter running line that makes stripping the flies back easier. Smaller running lines slip in your hands easier making for missed opportunities when strip-striking and fighting fish.

REFINING THE BACKCAST

Being able to present the fly on the backcast is an essential skill, especially when fishing from a boat. It allows you to present the fly to either side of the river and prevent casting over the inside of the boat, which are two critical things, especially when there are two anglers in the boat. Presenting a large fly on the backcast in my opinion is a whole lot easier than doing it on a forward cast, especially with big flies, because it is easier to pin the rod butt against your arm as you are pulling back during the backcast and you are much stronger pulling than you are pushing.

To make this cast, you do not turn your hand and try to flip the fly at the target with a backhand motion. Instead, simply make a regular cast and release the fly on your backcast. Turn your back to your target, so that your hip is pointed at or slightly in front of the target, and make sure you stop abruptly on your backcast. If you want a higher trajectory on your backcast, you need to make sure that you have a lower forward cast so that you can stop the fly with the rod in an upward trajectory, but do not follow through. Stop on the backcast as you would stop on the forward cast. ■

Whenever I can, I prefer to present a large fly on a backcast rather than a forward cast. You are much stronger pulling than you are pushing, and you can lock the rod butt against your forearm for extra power and less fatigue. Casting large flies requires different casting styles and strokes. When making a backcast with big flies, I pin the rod butt against my forearm for support and leverage. This allows me to pull the fly through the air with less stress on my arm and with more power.

On the forward stroke, either when false casting (which you should do as little as possible) or presenting the fly, pinning the rod butt against your forearm also reduces fatigue and provides power.

14 | Giant Changers

The Mega Changer has been one of my go-to flies for chasing any species of big fish, though the need to consistently catch muskies during tough conditions has played a large part in its development. This fly is my best effort at realism to date.

With a traditional Game Changer you are limited to sizes around 6 inches, and even though I had made improvements by using newer materials that shed water, larger flies were heavy. Additionally, even though the Bucktail Game Changers and T-Bones were solid muskie flies, I had thought for a long time that having a giant Game Changer that was ultra-realistic—basically a muskie sized counterpart to the original Game Changers that were so effective for picky fish—would be money, especially during clear water. As is often the case, the innovation here is not so much in the design, but the material, which allowed me to achieve something that I had been thinking about for a long time.

The two flies in this chapter illustrate how a pattern can evolve fairly quickly once the right materials are in hand. The first fly that we will tie is the Mega Changer, which uses a single brush, and then we will finish with the Hybrid Changer, which is a giant Game Changer tied with several brushes, one for support and the other for flow. Both of the flies have proven themselves as go-to options for muskies, as well as any time I need a large imitative baitfish imitation for discriminating fish, whether that is tarpon busting mullet in clear water or giant reds. Both of these flies shed a lot of water, which makes them surprisingly easy to cast for their size, are relatively quick to tie, and are infinitely adaptable.

211

Mega Changer

Because the Mega Changer is tied entirely with brushes, it is extremely fast to tie. Not only are you simply tying in each brush and wrapping it on the shanks, but by using pre-sized brushes in incremental sizes you don't have a lot of trimming to get the taper that you desire. Flash Blend Baitfish Brushes come in several sizes, and for most of the flies that I tie I use three, 1", 2", and 3" brushes. Then it is a simple matter of trimming at each step, as you would normally trim a Game Changer.

Flash Blend Baitfish Brushes are made of fairly stiff, kinky fibers. Once wound on the shank they hold their shape very well and create the illusion of bulk, with minimum amount of material and without the need for internal support. Since the bodies do not have to be as dense to still show the right profile, they are lighter, not just because they require less material but water literally pours out of it as the fibers don't trap any water. When you pull this fly out of the water, within seconds, 90% of the water is out and in one shake it is completely dry. That is a big advantage when you are throwing a 12-inch-long fly. These flies are a little lighter to cast, for this reason, than the Hybrid Changers, though because

they lack the outer, smooth surface, you give up some of the swimming action that you gain with the Hybrid. Like everything, there are tradeoffs, which is why both of these flies have a place on my boat.

I designed this fly for tough situations where fish may want something more imitative, such as the sucker or shad shown in the variations. Solid colors work very well but to really leverage this pattern, markers can take whatever base color you choose and bring it to life. Water clarity and volume as well as ambient light and time of year can play big roles in the colors that work best, and that is one of the advantages of the Mega Changer. The Flash Blend Baitfish Brush takes marker very well and you can dress them in any color of the rainbow to match the hatch.

To speed up the fly, pre-formed tails made out of Ultra Suede, showcased below in the patterns tied by Justin Pribanic, are an excellent option. Ultra Suede adds weight and absorption of water which helps you get a little wiggle in the back. Not only do you have a much more durable tail, but you also keeping the profile of the real baitfish throughout.

One of the things that excites me the most about this new generation of large Game Changers is how easy they are to cast.

Oliver White holds a fish of a lifetime. Not only was this his first muskie on fly but it was a giant, coming in at 53½ inches long. This fish took a Mega Game Changer 20 feet from the boat.

Hybrid Changer

It's fitting to end the book with the Hybrid Changer because in many ways it represents the culmination of many years of trial and error. For the longest time I was challenged with coming up with a fly that swims for smallmouth, and once I achieved that goal (for now, at least—things keep evolving) it was always important for me to be able to scale that up, while at the same time always try to improve the flies for casting and general performance on the water.

The Hybrid Changer blends together techniques and materials to create what I feel is my best design to date, at least for fish that eat large baits. Through the use of different brushes, it combines the realism of the Finesse Changers with the core-and-veil construction concepts of the Feather Changer to create flies that are between 6 and 12 inches (though you can go larger). In my opinion, previous to these flies, a large fly that moved in the water like a Game Changer that was also *easy to cast* simply didn't exist. These flies move and breathe even better in the water than the Mega Game

Changers, and it is almost as easy to tie if you have the right brushes prepped.

The concepts of the core and veil cannot be understated. They are everything in this fly and are what make a swim signature in the water that has really proven deadly over the past couple seasons while I have been testing them on the water. The general concepts are the same that I first discovered and fine-tuned with the Feather Game Changer, though they are scaled up for larger flies. The basic idea is that a stiffer support system provides a backbone for a smooth outer veiling, or skin, which enhances the swimming motion.

First, the support system. As flies become larger, it is important to use a stiffer support under the veiling fibers. However, in a large fly, you want to minimize the amount of materials so that the fly sheds water and is easy to cast. You also want fibers that are stiff enough to stand the test of time in the water—they must hold their shape for an entire season of fishing. To explain this, I always return to the metaphor of a brush pile

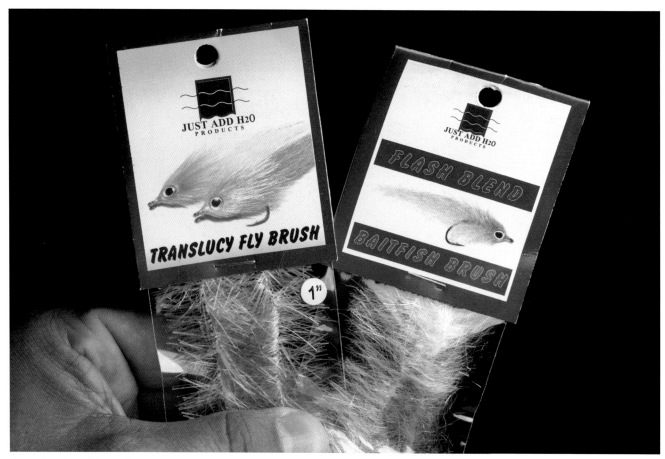

Flash Blend Baitfish Brush is the support system for the Hybrid Changer and acts very similar to branches of a bush or a tree that holds the leaves of a tree. Translucy Fly Brush has straighter fibers which provide more of a laminar flow—think of a sports car where the water flows off of the smooth surfaces and provides a better swim with less effort.

that looks large and takes up spaces, but is actually made up of relatively little material. If you jump on the pile and try to smash it down, it rebounds back. Flash Blend Baitfish Brush has the proper kinkiness and stiffness for an excellent core/support material and comes in a wide range of colors and three sizes.

For any flies larger than 12 to 14 inches, you will need to build your own dubbing brushes with stiffer fibers such as Kinky Fiber, Slinky Fiber, Ultra Hair, or Supreme Hair. These are a crimped nylon fiber with a good deal of rigidity. They tend to stand up and not droop if you held them upright by butts. Incorporating these very stiff fibers into larger flies (larger gives you a much lighter fly because you don't need as much material to support the veiling material. I should mention that it is not necessary to buy a brush table. Since you only need a few turns of filler material on each shank before your veiling material, you can make do with inserting your stiffer fibers into a dubbing loop, as we illustrate with Baitfish Emulator in the Mega Changer tying steps.

The Feather Game Changer first taught me the importance of smoother veiling fibers, and on smaller flies, feathers, Craft Fur, and Polar Fibre worked well. Larger flies present challenges, but on the Synthetic T-Bone, for instance, I overcame them with Straight Big Fly Fiber. I could see that the straighter and flatter the veiling fibers were, the better the swim. Water flows over the fly with less resistance and that provides a very smooth swimming action. With the Hybrid Changer, Translucy Fly Brush solved this problem. It is made up of softer flat fibers that come in different sizes to make the tapering process much easier. These fibers shed

water extremely well and, as their name implies, have a translucent quality when wrapped on a shank, creating a very realistic "skin" appearance in the water.

Not only can you make these highly imitative but you can also modify them to match fishing conditions in other ways. For instance, in low, clear water this past season we needed a fly that would hang in the fish's field of awareness for a long time—they just weren't willing to chase it. This required me to switch to a much slower sinking line paired with a fly with deer belly hair as the support/core (Translucy Fibers veiling) to keep the fly a little more buoyant and not hang up. These two adaptations (line and fly design) produced time and time again in these conditions.

Only time will tell how these designs evolve from here, but at this point the Hybrid Changer has been the ultimate balance for me between ease of tying, ease of fishing, and effectiveness. I have never fished something so effective for pressured or lethargic muskies—even in bright light or clear water.

I've been using this design for the past couple seasons and have had some remarkable results. One example is that muskies are known as fish that follow lures and flies. Also very difficult to get to eat a fly or lure for that matter. What I have observed is that we don't get the follows that I used to get using other style flies. Instead the fish that are interested just eat it when in countered. It has been an eye opener for me and my clients, not only because of the trophy muskies we are catching with it but also its effectiveness on tarpon, redfish, and cobia, just to name a few species that have fallen for this pattern.

1/2) These giants ate a black Hybrid Game Changer tied with deer hair. This fly was my winning ticket that season for low, clear water. 3) John Chinuntdet admires a fish of a lifetime. 4) Eric Stanley caught two big muskies this day—one on his first cast of the day and one on his last. This is his last. 5) I've had my clients get doubles before, but never before with fish of this magnitude. 6) Jared Renner and I admire a true giant before release on a January guide trip.

Tying the Mega Changer

Materials

Four 20mm Fish-Skull Articulated Shanks and 55mm Fish-Skull
Articulated Shank | #3/0 and #5/0 Gamakatsu Heavy Cover
Worm | 6/0 yellow Veevus | 50-pound Berkley nylon-coated
wire | yellow dyed grizzly rooster saddle supported by Baitfish
Emulator | rooster saddle pectoral fins | yellow 1", 2", 3" Flash
Blend Baitfish Brush | Ice Living Eyes

1. Insert a 20mm shank in the vise. These are lighter
than Big Game Shanks, which makes the fly a lot
lighter to cast and to fish.

2. Attach the thread to the shank and wrap a base,
stopping at the point where the rear loop begins.

3. Create a dubbing loop with your thread. Fold a
12-inch piece of Baitfish Emulator in half and insert it
into the loop. Trim the core holding the flash and spin
the loop to form a tight brush.

4. Take two to three wraps on the shank, picking out the fibers as you wrap. Save the dubbing loop you created for the second set of feathers.

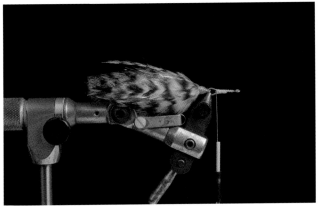

5. Select four rooster saddle or cape feathers from the very bottom of the skin. Tie them in the round, encompassing the Baitfish Emulator. Reattach the leftover loop of Baitfish Emulator and wrap it two turns on the shank. Add four more feathers to finish off the tail. Run another 20mm shank through the previous shank, insert it in the vise, and attach your thread.

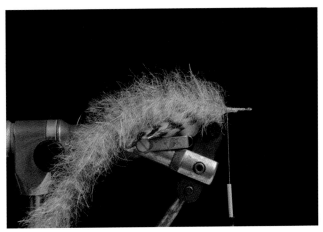

6. Attach a 1" Flash Blend Baitfish Brush to the shank, at the beginning of the rear connection loop.

7. Bring the thread forward to the eye of the shank and wrap the brush forward. It doesn't have to be super tight. Tie it down and trim the excess. Pick out the body with a bodkin to release any trapped fibers.

8. On the top and bottom, cut a 30-degree angle toward the tail (from front to back). Then cut a 20-degree angle on the sides from back to front, so that the angle is sloping out. These are just guidelines. Feel free to adjust depending on the baitfish you may be trying to imitate.

9. Tie in and wrap another section of 1" Flash Blend Baitfish Brush.

10. Trim the taper of the third section to match the previous section, only leave slightly longer fibers, as shown.

11. Insert a 20mm shank. Tie in a 2" Flash Blend Baitfish Brush this time to start to increase the taper, and wrap it forward. Trim it to the shape shown. Connect this assembly to a wide-gap hook with 60-pound-test wire.

12. Tie in another piece of 2" Flash Blend Baitfish Brush and wrap it forward to the eye. Tie it off, clip the excess, and add UV resin to your thread wraps after you whip-finish. Trim the fibers on top and bottom and then on each side so that you follow the taper you've established.

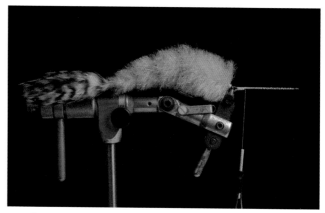

13. Insert a 55mm shank through the eye of the hook and insert it in the vise. We are using a long shank here to match the length of the hook in the previous section to help maintain the proper taper for the fly. Attach the thread and wrap a base over the shank, stopping at the point where the rear loop connection begins.

14. Tie in a section of 2" Flash Blend Baitfish Brush and take approximately three wraps. Then, tie in a section of ¼" Body Tubing and create a spreader dam to add lift and create broader shoulders.

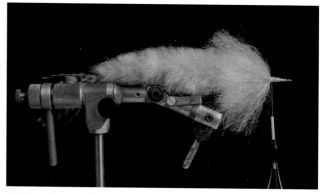

15. Tie in another section of 3" Flash Blend Baitfish Brush and take two or three turns. The goal is to cover approximately two-thirds of the shank before the next Body Tubing dam. There is no need to create the thread bump in front of the spreader when working with a brush.

16. Tie in another section of ¼" Body Tubing and create a dam. Reattach the thread in front of the tubing.

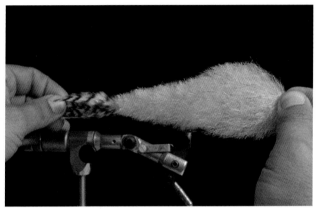

17. Tie in another piece of 3" Flash Blend Baitfish Brush and wrap it to the eye of the shank. Tie it off, trim the excess, and whip-finish. Coat the thread wraps with UV resin. Notice the gradual taper moving forward, creating a nice baitfish shape.

18. Insert a 5/0 hook in the vise and connect the previous section with 80-pound wire, making sure to coat the wraps with UV resin. Create a Body Tubing dam, tie in 3" brush, and wrap forward. The goal here is to create shoulders in the thickest part of the fly. You want to bulk this area up because over time things are going to get compressed.

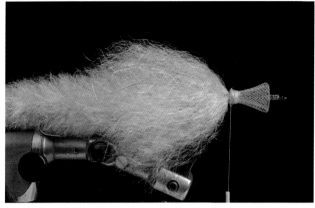

19. Create another Body Tubing dam. Instead of showing the finished one here, this photo illustrates the trumpet profile right before we finish the thread off and glue it and then fold the Body Tubing back.

20. Tie in another 3" brush and take three to four more wraps and then add pectoral fins and then another Body Tubing dam. We haven't trimmed our brush yet, but you can see the bulk and the height that we are gaining here moving forward.

21. Add another section of 3" Flash Blend Baitfish Brush and take two or three wraps. You need to budget your wraps, anticipating needing to have enough space to finish off the head with a few wraps of 2" brush.

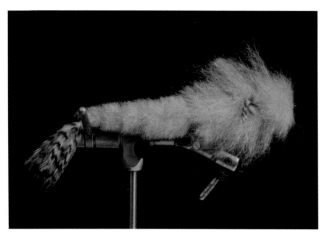

22. Tie in a section of 2" brush (you should have some left over) and finish off the head. Notice how dense the brush head is before being trimmed.

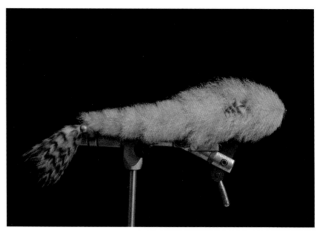

23. Trim the head at a 45-degree angle for the top, bottom and sides, to create the baitfish shape.

24. Attach the eyes with a flexible UV resin. Mark up the finished fly to the desired color. In this case we want to create bars to match a perch or a hog sucker, which is a top muskie bait in the waters that I guide on. The variations below show different color combinations that have been effective for me. All are tied with three incremental sized Flash Blend Baitfish Brushes, 1", 2", and 3". The olive and yellow is tied with bleeding yellow, the sucker is tied with mullet brown, and the sexy shad is with white Flash Blend Baitfish Brush colored with marker.

Mega Changer Variations

Mega Changer (Sucker)

Mega Changer (Perch)

Mega Changer (Sexy Shad)

Tying the Hybrid Changer

Materials

Five 15mm Fish-Spines | #2/0 Kona BGH and #3/0 Kona BGC |
140-denier pink Veevus | 30-pound Berkley nylon-coated wire |
Keough saltwater rooster saddle feathers | 1" and 2" white Flash
Blend Baitfish Brush | 1" and 2" steelhead gray Translucy Fly Brush |
2" Sculpting Fiber Brush | Ice Living Eyes

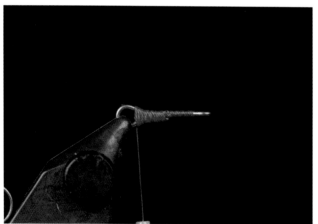

1. Insert a 15mm shank in the vise. Attach the thread
and wrap it up the rear connection loop to the point
shown. By tying in the brush high on the shank you
create more of a ramp that will help prop up the
feathers once you tie them in.

2. Tie in a section of 2" Translucy Fly Brush. You do not
have to trim off any fibers. Wrap the thread to a point
between where the rear connection loop starts and
your tie-in point.

3. Wrap the brush forward, stroking back the fibers with your left hand. Tie off the brush and trim the excess. Wrap up and down the shank to create a nice thread base on which to seat your feathers.

4. You are going to tie in two sets of four saddle feathers for the tail. Select the first four saddle feathers and measure them so that they are approximately 20 percent of the total fly length.

5. Trim the base fluff from the feathers and tie them evenly around the shank. Wrap the thread forward to the point shown to begin tying in the next set of tail feathers.

6. Select four more feathers and measure them so that they are slightly shorter than the first set and tie them in the same way. This second set of feathers creates a diversion of water before the first set of feathers, in much the same way as the head of a Game Changer creates disturbance for the rear of the fly. I like to think of this as being similar to what happens in a paddle tail design in a soft plastic bait.

7. Once you have finished tying in the second set of feathers, attach a 1" Translucy Fly Brush and wrap it forward. Trim the fibers to create the wrist of the fish, which is the transition from the tail to the body of the fly. You want to keep this part small, so aim for around a quarter of inch height all around. Tie off the thread and add resin.

8. Slip another 15mm shank through the eye of the previous one, insert it into the vise, and attach the thread. Wrap a nice base on the shank and stop the thread halfway between the back opening of the loop and the point at which the shank comes together. By tying in the brush at this point, you don't have to trim the fibers as much and you also alleviate bulk, which allows the fibers to compress under pressure and provide the desired taper. In this part of the fly you don't want unnecessary bulk that would keep the veiling fibers up—instead you want them to be able to lie down. In the back third of the fly you want to veil over the previous section by half.

9. Tie in a section of 1" Flash Blend Baitfish Brush and wrap it to the point shown.

10. Trim the fibers to approximately half their height so that once you wrap back over them a little bit they will lie approximately halfway over the previous section.

11. Tie in the 1" Translucy Fly Brush and wrap back over the fibers halfway to help create taper. Wrap a neat thread base, whip-finish, and apply UV resin.

12. Insert another 15mm and repeat this process. Your goal is for the fibers, when compressed, to extend halfway over the previous section. The prominent pink thread here is intentional. I think it adds an attractive inner hue that I have found effective at times.

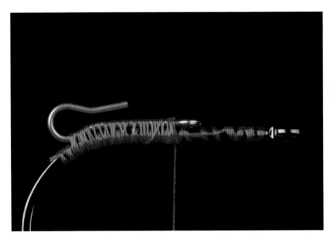

13. Insert a 2/0 Kona BGH, wrap a thread base, and then tie a 15mm shank upside down on the hook shank. The contour of the smaller shank fits the hook bend and the flat eye of the shank keeps it stabilized on top of the hook shank when you wrap over it.

14. Connect the rear third of the fly to the 15mm shank. Wrap back over the shank to close off the opening.

15. Tie in a section of Flash Blend Baitfish Brush and wrap it three to four times. Tie it off and trim the excess. Here, it should cover the previous section by two-thirds.

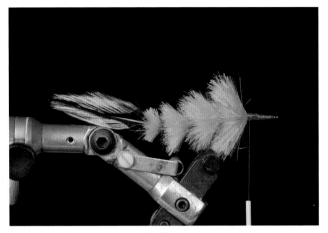

16. Tie in 2" Translucy Fly Brush and take two wraps. Trim it to achieve a two-thirds coverage.

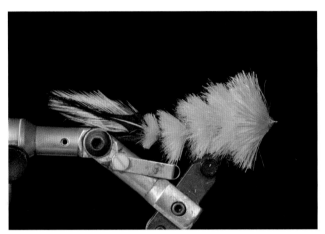

17. Repeat one more section of core and veil on the hook shank to build up the forward portion of the fly. Tie it off and add resin.

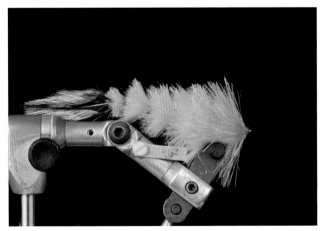

18. Insert a 15mm shank through the eye of the hook and insert into the vise. Repeat the steps with a Flash Blend Baitfish Brush core and a Translucy Fly Brush veil, maintain a two-thirds coverage.

19. Insert a final 15mm shank through the eye of the hook and insert it into the vise. Tie in two sets of core (Flash Blend Baitfish Brush) and veil (Translucy Fly Brush). As you move into the front third of the fly you try for ¾ to full coverage over the previous section depending on how much shoulder you want the fly to have. We are going for a full-shouldered shad profile on this fly.

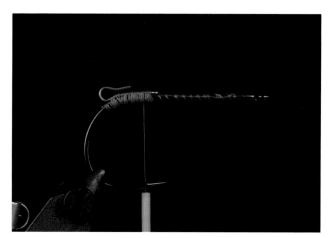

20. Insert a 4/0 Kona Big Game Carnivore in the vise and tie in another 15mm shank on top of the hook shank, making sure to match the curvature in the spine with the profile of the hook shank.

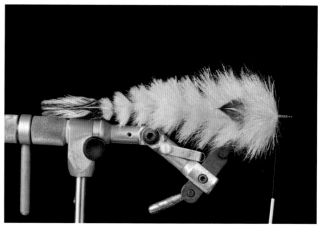

21. Tie in core, veil, pectoral fins, then another set of core and veil. Leave enough room on the hook shank for the Sculpting Flash Fiber head. You can also use a variety of other head styles, from deer hair to foam depending on the type of action you desire.

22. Wrap the brush for the head and trim.

23. Color the back with a gray Chartpak marker to imitate a shad, and add eyes.

Aquamarine Translucy Fly Brush over white Flash Blend Baitfish Brush

Brown Translucy Fly Brush over tan Flash Blend Baitfish Brush and brown Sculpting Flash Fibers head

Electric yellow and gray Translucy Fly Brush over white Flash Blend Baitfish Brush and white Sculpting Flash Fibers head marked with cool gray Copic

Index

Fly Pattern Index

About the Author

"The most innovative fly tier out there, Blane Chocklett and his approach to creating lifelike flies has truly changed the game and opened the door to catching more—and bigger—apex predators on fly."

—OLIVER WHITE, WRITER, FOUNDER OF INDIFLY, AND CO-OWNER OF ABACO LODGE

Blane Chocklett (blanechocklett.com) is a full-time muskie, smallmouth, striper, and trout (among other species) guide on the many rivers and lakes near his home state of Virginia. From 1996 to 2008 he owned and operated Blue Ridge Fly Fishers, a full-service fly shop in Roanoke, Virginia. He was been a signature fly designer for Umpqua Feather Merchants from 2001 until 2018 and his best-selling fly, the Gummy Minnow, has been responsible for many world-record catches. Blane has served on the board of the American Fly Tackle Trade Association (AFFTA) and has worked as a consultant and brand ambassador for many fly-fishing companies, including Yeti Coolers, Patagonia, Temple Fork Outfitters, Costa Del Mar Sunglasses, Adipose Boatworks, Scientific Anglers, and Renzetti. He works closely with industry leaders such as Hareline Dubbin' and Flymen Fishing Company to develop cutting-edge fly-tying products for Game Changer flies. In 2019, Chocklett partnered with Flymen Fishing Company to bring commercially tied Game Changers to anglers around the world, and they are available through Flymen Fishing Company's website (flymenfishingcompany.com) as well as local fly shops.

Chocklett is Southeastern Field Editor for *Fly Fisherman* magazine, popular presenter at fly fishing shows and clubs, and he has been featured on several television shows and commercials, including Larry Dahlberg's *The Hunt for Big Fish*, Yeti Stories: *Mega Grande*, *The Obsession of Carter Andrews*, and *Fin Chasers*. In 2018 he was recognized by *Fly Fisherman* magazine as one of the fifty most influential fly fishers in the last fifty years. He lives just outside of Roanoke, in Troutville, Virginia.

MARTIN BAWDEN PHOTO

LANDON MAYER PHOTO

Photographer Jay Nichols has been a full-time editor, publisher, writer, videographer, and media specialist in the fly-fishing industry since 2001. He is the Northeast Field Editor and Contributing Photographer for *Fly Fisherman* magazine and the fly-fishing editor for Stackpole Books. Nichols is also the publisher and owner of Headwater Books (headwaterbooks.com), a boutique book publishing company specializing in fly-fishing and fly-tying titles written by experts and the principal of Headwater Media Group, an integrated media company specializing in instructional video.

Nichols has written several books, including Tying Dry Flies and the best-selling *1001 Fly Fishing Tips*, and has coauthored or been the lead photographer on a number of fly-fishing books with the sport's legends, including *Casting with Lefty Kreh* (Kreh and Nichols), *Fundamentals of Fly Casting* (Kreh and Nichols), *Clouser's Flies* and *Fly Fishing for Smallmouth* (Bob Clouser and Nichols), and *Fleye Design* (Bob Popovics and Nichols).

In 2018, Nichols was awarded the Charles K. Fox "Rising Trout Award" from the Cumberland Valley Chapter of Trout Unlimited, and in that same year was named one of the fifty most influential fly fishers in the last fifty years by *Fly Fisherman* magazine. He lives in Carlisle, Pennsylvania.